Frommer's®

SO-AXN-683

Stockholm
day BY day™

2nd Edition

by Mary Anne Evans

WILEY

John Wiley & Sons, Inc.

Contents

Editorial Director: Kelly Regan
Production Manager: Daniel Mersey
Commissioning Editor: Fiona Quinn
Development Editor: Fiona Quinn
Project Editor: Hannah Clement
Photo Research: Cherie Cincilla, Richard H. Fox, Jill Emeny
Cartography: Simonetta Giori

Wiley also publishes its books in a variety of electronic formats and by print-on-demand. Some content that appears in standard print versions of this book may not be available in other formats. For more information about Wiley products, visit us at www.wiley.com.

British Library Cataloguing in Publication Data

A catalogue record for this book is available from the British Library

ISBN 978-1-119-97002-6 (pbk), ISBN 978-1-119-97260-0 (ebk),
ISBN 978-1-119-97037-8 (ebk), ISBN 978-1-119-97036-1 (ebk)

Typeset by Wiley Indianapolis Composition Services
Printed and bound in China by RR Donnelley
5 4 3 2 1

A Note from the Editorial Director

Organizing your time. That's what this guide is all about.

Other guides give you long lists of things to see and do and then expect you to fit the pieces together. The Day by Day guides are different. These guides tell you the best of everything, and then they show you how to see it *in the smartest, most time-efficient way*. Our authors have designed detailed itineraries organized by time, neighborhood, or special interest. And each tour comes with a bulleted map that takes you from stop to stop.

Stockholm is a city of surprises. Take a boat trip around the 14 islands or out to the archipelago, wander through the past in the winding medieval streets of Gamla Stan then shop for the best contemporary Scandinavian design. And don't forget to savor the new Nordic cooking and drink an *acquavit* at midnight looking out over the Baltic. Whatever your interest or schedule, the Day by Days give you the smartest routes to follow. Not only do we take you to the top attractions, hotels, and restaurants, but we also help you access those special moments that locals get to experience—those "finds" that turn tourists into travelers.

The Day by Days are also your top choice if you're looking for one complete guide for all your travel needs. The best hotels and restaurants for every budget, the greatest shopping values, the wildest nightlife—it's all here.

Why should you trust our judgment? Because our authors personally visit each place they write about. They're an independent lot who say what they think and would never include places they wouldn't recommend to their best friends. They're also open to suggestions from readers. If you'd like to contact them, please send your comments our way at feedback@frommers.com, and we'll pass them on.

Enjoy your Day by Day guide—the most helpful travel companion you can buy. And have the trip of a lifetime.

Warm regards,

Kelly Regan

Kelly Regan, Editorial Director
Frommer's Travel Guides

About the Author

After co-writing learned volumes on Japanese prints and guitars, **Mary Anne Evans** turned to her more immediate surroundings and became one of the leading travel writers on London and Britain, particularly on restaurants. Several guide books and many magazine articles later, Europe beckoned. Stockholm has always been close to her heart as she is married to a Finn and has spent many happy holidays in Stockholm and Finland.

Acknowledgments

My special thanks to photographer Ossi Laurila for his wonderful pictures, and to Sylvie Kjellin and Johan Tegel at the Stockholm Visitors Board and Philippa Sutton at Visit Sweden for all their sound advice and help.

Star Ratings, Icons & Abbreviations

Every hotel, restaurant, and attraction listing in this guide has been ranked for quality, value, service, amenities, and special features using a **star-rating system.** Hotels, restaurants, attractions, shopping, and nightlife are rated on a scale of zero stars (recommended) to three stars (exceptional). In addition to the star-rating system, we also use a **kids icon** to point out the best bets for families. Within each tour, we recommend cafes, bars, or restaurants where you can take a break. Each of these stops appears in a shaded box marked with a coffee-cup-shaped bullet ☕ .

The following **abbreviations** are used for credit cards:

AE	American Express	DISC	Discover	V	Visa
DC	Diners Club	MC	MasterCard		

Travel Resources at Frommers.com

Frommer's travel resources don't end with this guide. Frommer's website, **www.frommers.com**, has travel information on more than 4,000 destinations. We update features regularly, giving you access to the most current trip-planning information and the best airfare, lodging, and car-rental bargains. You can also listen to podcasts, connect with other Frommers.com members through our active-reader forums, share your travel photos, read blogs from guidebook editors and fellow travelers, and much more.

Advisory & Disclaimer

Travel information can change quickly and unexpectedly, and we strongly advise you to confirm important details locally before traveling, including information on visas, health and safety, traffic and transport, accommodation, shopping and eating out. We also encourage you to stay alert while traveling and to remain aware of your surroundings. Avoid civil disturbances, and keep a close eye on cameras, purses, wallets and other valuables.

While we have endeavored to ensure that the information contained within this guide is accurate and up-to-date at the time of publication, we make no representations or warranties with respect to the accuracy or completeness of the contents of this work and specifically disclaim all warranties, including without limitation warranties of fitness for a particular purpose. We accept no responsibility or liability for any inaccuracy or errors or omissions, or for any inconvenience, loss, damage, costs or expenses of any nature whatsoever incurred or suffered by anyone as a result of any advice or information contained in this guide.

The inclusion of a company, organization or Website In this guide as a service provider and/or potential source of further information does not mean that we endorse them or the information they provide. Be aware that information provided through some Websites may be unreliable and can change without notice. Neither the publisher or author shall be liable for any damages arising herefrom.

How to Contact Us

In researching this book, we discovered many wonderful places—hotels, restaurants, shops, and more. We're sure you'll find others. Please tell us about them, so we can share the information with your fellow travelers in upcoming editions. If you were disappointed with a recommendation, we'd love to know that, too. Please e-mail: frommers@wiley.com or write to:

Frommer's Stockholm Day by Day, 2nd Edition
John Wiley & Sons, Inc., 111 River St., Hoboken, NJ 07030-5774

12 Favorite
Moments

12 Favorite **Moments**

M Metro Stop
+ Church
(i) Information
⊠ Post Office
✿■ Synagogue

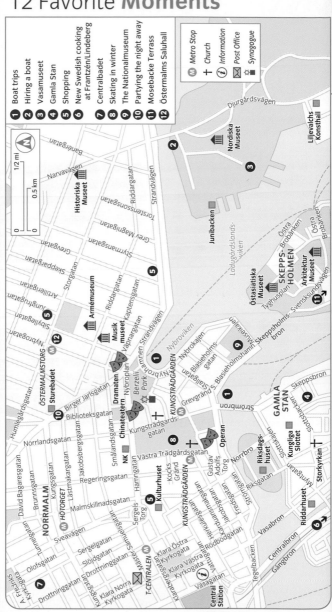

Previous page: The waterfront.

Y ou can just sit back and look at the views over one of the world's most beautiful cities. Alternatively, go back to the Middle Ages on a stroll through Gamla Stan, discover Stockholm's exciting new cooking, row a boat along a tree-lined canal in summer, or skate on the sea in winter. Stockholm is a city for all seasons. Here are some of my favorite things to do in Sweden's beautiful and elegant capital.

❶ Slipping through Stockholm on a boat. Getting on a boat and going anywhere—around the main islands, out to the Baltic Sea archipelago, or through the waterways onto Lake Mälaren—is the first thing I do when I arrive in Stockholm. If you take the trip in winter, the sound of ice breaking replaces the cries of gulls. *See p 7.*

❷ Hiring a boat and taking to the waters. The sea and Lake Mälaren fill up with boats in the summer. You can canoe, sail, zip up and down in a motorboat, or just paddle. I love hiring a rowboat from Djurgårdsbrons Sjöcafé with friends, getting a picnic and rowing along the canal that separates Ladugårdsgärdet from Djurgården. We park the boat and have an alfresco feast. *See p 7.*

❸ Walking into the Vasamuseet. No matter how many times I visit this museum, the hairs on the back of my neck always rise when I walk in from the bright sunlight to be confronted by this huge 17th-century wooden warship, raised from the dead and permanently moored in its own building. Go when the crowds are few and you can feel the ghosts of dead sailors as you pass the gun decks and gaze up at the ornately carved prow. *See p 8.*

❹ Wandering through the medieval streets of Gamla Stan. This may be Stockholm's most visited area, but catch it early in the morning when the light filters through the narrow alleyways and the shutters on the houses are still closed—you feel you've stepped back four centuries. Then walk down narrow Mårten Trotzigs Gränd, the 90cm (less than 3 ft) wide street where the drainpipes cling crazily to the peeling, damp walls. *See p 9.*

❺ Shopping for a new look. There's something about the strong shapes of furniture conceived by the Scandinavian icons of modern design that makes me want to transform my house. So I always spend time in Jacksons and Modernity. They stock mainly collectors' pieces; for something I can afford (and take home), I go to Design Torget and 10 Gruppen. *See p 89.*

❻ Sampling the new Swedish cooking. Many of Stockholm's

The medieval streets of Gamla Stan.

young chefs have had a French culinary training, but they've taken the classics and reinvented them. They use native ingredients such as Arctic char, lingonberries, and elk and put the tastes together in a unique way. Try the new Swedish cooking at Frantzén/Lindeberg from the two eponymous chefs and you'll see why Stockholm is rapidly becoming the latest gastronomic destination. *See p 145.*

7 **Spending the evening in Centralbadet.** The Jugendstil Centralbadet spa is a wonderful place to round off the day. I don't book a treatment but just get steamy in the sauna, swim in the outdoor pool, then sit in the leafy garden with a cup of coffee and let the world's troubles fade away. *See p 17.*

8 **Joining the skaters in winter.** Everybody, young and old, seems to take expertly to the ice in winter. You can join them on the little Kungsträdgården rink, or hire or buy your own skates and take to Lake

The leafy garden of Jugendstil Centralbadet spa.

Mälaren—and the sea if the temperature really plummets below zero. You can skate all the way to Sigtuna from Stockholm, but you may have to be Scandinavian to achieve that. *See p 45.*

9 **Discovering northern art at the Nationalmuseum.** A visit to the Nationalmuseum is a bit like taking an external art history degree. I come away ashamed at my ignorance of northern European artists and excited by the amount of great and unknown art that I've seen. *See p 33.*

10 **Partying the night away.** It's true that Stockholm is a clubber's paradise, but if you feel either too old or not well dressed enough, ignore the crowds outside the hippest places and pick a couple of bars or a jazz club for the evening. There's something about emerging at 3am into the light of day that seems to keep you going. *See p 123.*

11 **Looking at the view from Mosebacke Terrass.** Of all the magnificent views you get in Stockholm, I love sitting on Mosebacke Terrass with a glass of wine, often surrounded by musicians who are playing there that evening, looking out toward Skeppsholmen and down toward the Södermalm shoreline. This is one of the famous views Mikael Blomkvist and Lisbeth Salander enjoyed in Stieg Larsson's famous Millennium trilogy. *See p 50.*

12 **Shopping in Östermalms Saluhall.** This is one of Europe's great indoor food markets. It's relatively small, but packed full of infinite types of salmon and herring, and elk, sourdough and rye bread, conserves, preserves, and pastries. When you've done looking or shopping, settle down for the freshest sole or salted salmon with warm dill potatoes in Lisa Elmqvist. *See p 14.* ●

1 The Best **Full-Day Tours**

The Best **in One Day**

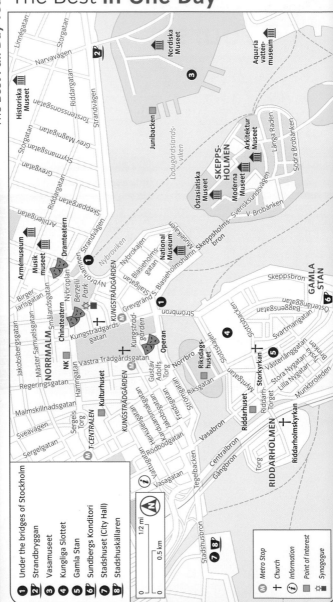

1 Under the bridges of Stockholm
2 Strandbryggan
3 Vasamuseet
4 Kungliga Slottet
5 Gamla Stan
6 Sundbergs Konditori
7 Stadshuset (City Hall)
8 Stadshuskällaren

- M Metro Stop
- † Church
- *i* Information
- ■ Point of Interest
- ✡ Synagogue

Previous page: The Mosebacke.

Stockholm's capital stretches out over 14 islands so you're **never far from the water,** which is the main attraction of this historic city. Start with a boat tour before visiting the blockbusters: the Kungliga Slottet (Royal Palace) and the impressive Vasamuseet. As you walk, you'll discover plenty of beautiful and different views over the water. START: **T-bana to Gamla Stan.**

❶ ★★★ kids Under the Bridges of Stockholm. With the sun—or the wind—in your face, take to the boats on a trip that shows you the city as people have seen it for centuries. You begin on the Baltic Sea side and then pass through the Slussen Lock into the shelter of Lake Mälaren, the third largest lake in Europe. As you slip under no less than15 bridges, your journey takes you past grand buildings and once-gritty, working-class areas. The commentary is full of useful and delightfully useless information and you'll come away knowing that performers at the Gröna Lund amusement park have included the Beatles and Jimi Hendrix, who was enjoying himself so much the organizers had to unplug his guitar to get him to stop. ⏱ *1 hr 50 min. Nybrokajen and Strömkajen.* ☎ *08-120 040 00. www.stromma. se. Tickets: Adults 200 SEK, children 6–11 years 100 SEK. Boats leave*

Strömkajen on the hour, from Nybro-kajen 5 minutes later. Daily May 1–27 10am–4pm (from Nybrokajen only), May 28–June 24 10am–6pm, June 15– Aug 28 10am–7pm, Aug 29–Sept 18 10am–5pm. Check on website for out-of-season dates and times. Tickets in advance from hotels, website, or the departure point booth. T-bana: Kungsträdgården.

❷ ★ Strandbryggan. It's a short walk along Strandvägen past the moorings to this cafe that floats on two boats. Order a coffee, meal— perhaps a plate of moules marin-ières—or drink at this all-day eatery, and look toward leafy Djurgården. The smug feeling of being a local and watching the tourists is irresist-ible (so what's wrong in pretend-ing?). *Strandvägskajen 27* ☎ *08-660 37 14. www.strandbryggan.se. Bus: 44, 47, Tram: 7. Moules marinières at 185 SEK.*

A different view of the capital.

③ ★★★ kids Vasamuseet. Nothing prepares you for the drama of Stockholm's blockbuster of a museum and the massive 17th-century **Vasa ship**. The ship was rediscovered in 1956 by wreck specialist, Anders Franzén, and lifted 5 years later. Walking into the darkened museum specially built to house the vessel, you get a very real impression of the might of the battleships that brought glory to the winners and horror to those who lost. *See minitour below. See also p 25, ①.*

Vasamuseet

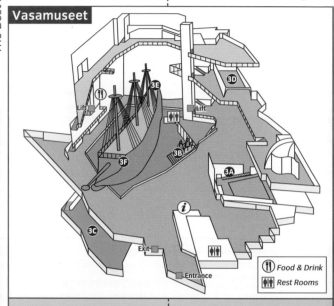

Food & Drink
Rest Rooms

You enter at sea level. Start with the 25-minute **③A film** of the discovery and raising of the *Vasa,* which sank in Stockholm's harbor on 10th August 1628 on its maiden voyage. Surrounding the great ship are different levels of exhibitions. At sea level you see an accurate **③B scaled-down model,** the history of *Vasa*, and the remarkable sculptures of the ship. Go down to level 2 where a **③C shipyard** shows how ships were built. Climb up to level 5 for **③D life on board,** which, for the ordinary seaman, was nasty, brutal, and short. The **③E stern** was wonderfully decorated with the Swedish national emblem; the ship was built to impress and its sculptures symbolized Sweden's power. You can walk around the entire ship, ending with a close look at the **③F gun ports and the lion figurehead** of the king who commissioned the ship, Gustav II Adolf (1594–1632), known as the Lion of the North. ⏱ *2 hr. Galärvarvsvägen 14. ☎ 08-519 548 00. www.vasa museet.se/en. Adults 110 SEK, free children 17 and under. Free with Stockholm Card (see p 11). Daily June 1–Aug 31 8:30am–6pm; Sept 1– May 31 10am–5pm (Wed to 8pm); Dec 31 10am–3pm. Closed Dec 23–25, Jan 1. Bus 47. Tram 7. Ferry to Djurgården (summer).*

The mighty Vasa warship.

❹ ★★★ kids Kungliga Slottet. Arrive early or late to miss the crowds. Built on the site of the Tre Kronor (*Three Crowns*) fortress, the Royal Palace was destroyed by fire in 1697. The whopping 608-room building—the largest working palace in Europe—was designed by the royal architect Nicodemus Tessin the Younger (1654–1728) and completed in 1754. It's imposing rather than beautiful so it's not surprising that the Royal Family prefers to live at Drottningholm (p 41, ❸) and use this palace for offices and state occasions only. Decorated by the main artists of the day and added to over the centuries, it gives an idea of Sweden's huge wealth and importance since the 18th century. There are various parts to visit (see the Kungliga Slottet tour, p 28), but if you have limited time, I suggest just visiting the State Apartments. In mid-summer the Royal Music Festival takes over the Royal Chapel and the Hall of Stage. ⏱ *3 hr. For details see p 28.*

❺ ★★★ kids Gamla Stan. With the story of Stockholm in mind, go back to the beginnings of the city here on Gamla Stan (*Old Town*). This tiny island once commanded the strategic entrance to Lake Mälaren from the Baltic Sea, protected by the Tre Kronor (*Three Crowns*) fortress. The crowded, medieval sprawl of houses largely burnt down in 1625 and a new city emerged with impressive waterfront stone buildings. Tourists choke the main streets in the summer but I'm amazed at how the herd instinct leaves many of the narrow alleyways and streets that criss-cross this timewarp of a quarter so undisturbed. Don't miss the tiny **Mårten Trotzigs Grand** alley, less than 90cm (3 ft.) wide, which runs up from Västerlånggatan, north of Järntorget. *See p 58.*

❻ ★ kids Sundbergs Konditori. You'll have to compete with locals and visitors to grab an outside table at Stockholm's oldest pâtisserie. Opened in 1785, Sundbergs Konditori remains totally traditional—cakes, coffee, and a slice of history are all served here. *Järntorget 83.* ☎ *08-10 67 35. Coffee and cake 75 SEK.*

The Best Full-Day Tours

❼ ★★★ Stadshuset (City Hall).
The tower of Stockholm's City Hall, at 106m (348 ft) high, dominates the skyline from all over the city, though there's new competition from the waterside city conference center and hotel. Even on a dull day, you can pick out the extravagantly gilded Tre Kronor—the three crowns that have been Sweden's heraldic symbol since the 14th century—atop the tower. The huge redbrick building was designed by the leading architect of the Swedish National Romantic style, Ragnar Östberg (1866–1945), and completed in 1923. City Hall is best known for the annual Nobel Prize banquet, held in

the palatial Blue Hall on December 10 for some 1,300 guests. You can only see the building on a guided tour; however, you can climb the 365 steps in the tower on your own (with an elevator taking you halfway if needed)—it's worth it for the fantastic view. ⏱ *1½ hr. Hantver-kargatan 1.* ☎ *08-508 290 59. www.stockholm.se/stadshuset. Tour: Adults 90 SEK, accompanied 12–17 year olds 40 SEK, free for 11 and under. Free with Stockholm Card (see p 11). 45 min tours in English on the hour (liable to change so check first). Daily Apr–Sept 10am–3pm, Oct–Mar 10am–noon. Tower Daily May–Sept 9am–4pm. Closed Oct–Apr. Adults 40 SEK, free for children 11 and under. Free with Stockholm Card (see p 11). T-bana: T-Centralen. Bus: 3, 62.*

Royal lions guard the Royal Palace.

Abba & the Tour

It began in June 1966 when Björn Ulvaeus of the Hootenanny Singers met Benny Andersson, then with the Hep Stars. They teamed up, recorded with Stig 'Stikkan' Anderson on his Polar label, met Agnetha Fältskog and Norwegian Anni-Frid Lyngstad and got married (Björn to Agnetha in 1971 and Benny to Anni-Frid in 1978). They became Abba, and in Brighton, U.K. in 1974, won the Eurovision song contest with the song 'Waterloo'. The rest, as they say, is history. One of the most successful groups ever (along with the Beatles), they last performed together way back in 1982—but the music goes on. Fans can take the ABBA walking tour, organized by the Stadsmuseum. It's around 1½ to 2 hours long and costs 120 SEK. You'll recognize the record covers from places on Gärdet, Djurgården, and Skansen, be entertained at Wallmans and more. Details and booking from the Stadsmuseum (p 75).

The Stockholm Card

The Stockholm Card is worth investing in. The card gives free admission to 80 museums and attractions; free travel by public transport on the T-bana, buses, commuter trains, and trams; free sightseeing by boat on the Historical Canal Tour (May to August), free trips on the hop-on hop-off sightseeing boat (May and beginning of September) (www.stromma.se); discounts on bus tours on Stockholm Panorama and Open Top Tours (www.stromma.se); discounts on boat trips to Drottningholm, and a guidebook. Adults: 1 day (24 hours) 425 SEK, 2 days (48 hours) 550 SEK, 3 days (72 hours) 650 SEK, 5 days (120 hours) 895 SEK. Children 7 to 17 years old: 1 day 195 SEK, 2 days 225 SEK, 3 days 245 SEK, 5 days 285 SEK. A child's card is only valid with an adult card. Cards are validated from the time and date you first use them, in 24-hour blocks. Buy in advance on the Internet (www.stockholmtown.com), or at the **Stockholm Tourist Center,** opposite the main railway station at Vasagatan 14. ☎ 08-508 28 508. www.stockholmtown.com. Open Jan 1–Apr 30; Sept 16–Dec 31 Mon–Fri 9am–6pm, Sat 10am–5pm, Sun 10am–4pm; May 1–Sept 15 Mon–Fri 9am–7pm, Sat 10am–5pm, Sun 10am–4pm. Closed Dec 24 and 25, Jan 1.

8 ★★ **Stadshuskällaren.** Underneath the splendors of the Stadshuset are some culinary delights. The Nobel banquet for 1,300 takes place every year in the Blue Hall, but mere mortals who are not invited can, from January the following year, order the previous year's Nobel banquet for dinner in the cellar restaurant. Otherwise have lunch from the salad buffet with soup, a main dish, and a coffee, or go a la carte. *Stadshuset, Hantverkargatan 1.* ☎ *08-506 322 00. www.profil restauranger.se/stadshuskallaren/. Lunch buffet for 100 SEK.*

Stadshuset from the water.

The Best **Full-Day Tours**

The Best **in Two Days**

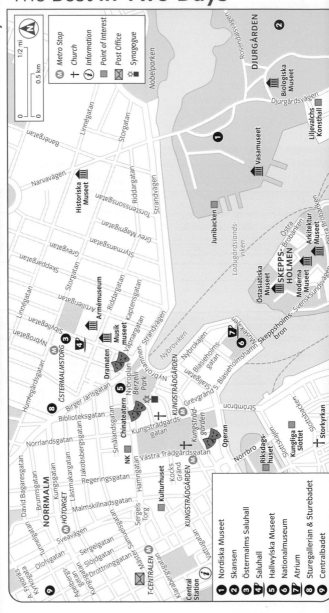

Legend:
- Ⓜ Metro Stop
- ✝ Church
- ⓘ Information
- ■ Point of Interest
- ✉ Post Office
- ✡ Synagogue

Scale: 0 – 1/2 mi / 0 – 0.5 km

DJURGÅRDEN

Nobelparken

Rosendalsvägen

Biologiska Museet ❷

Djurgårdsvägen

Liljevalchs Konsthall

Vasamuseet ❶

Junibacken

Ladugårdslands-viken

Linnégatan

Storgatan

Banérgatan

Narvavägen

Historiska Museet

Riddargatan

Strandvägen

Torstenssonsgatan

Grev Magnigatan

Styrmansgatan

Östasiatiska Museet

SKEPPS-HOLMEN

Moderna Museet

Arkitektur Museet

Östra Brobänken

Östra Brobänken

Svensksundsvägen

Skeppargatan

Artillerigatan

Riddargatan

Kaptensgatan

Valhallavägen

Storgatan

Armémuseum

Musik museet ❸

❹

Linnégatan

Sibyllegatan

Nybrogatan

Humlegårdsgatan

ÖSTERMALMSTORG Ⓜ

Dramaten

Nybroplan

Berzelii Park

Nybroviken

Nybrokajen

Blasieholms-gatan

Stallgatan

S. Blasieholmshamn

Skeppsholms-bron

Museivägen

❼

❻

Birger Jarlsgatan

Biblioteksgatan

Chinateatern ❺

Kungsträdgårds-gatan

KUNGSTRÄDGÅRDEN

Grevgränd

Strömbron

Norrlandsgatan

Smålandsgatan

NK

Kungsträdgården Ⓜ

Operan

Norrbro

Riksdagshuset

Kungliga Slottet

Slottsbacken

Slottskajen

✝ Storkyrkan

❽

Jakobsbergsgatan

Lästmakargatan

Regeringsgatan

Västra Trädgårdsgatan

Hamngatan

Kulturhuset

Kocks Grand

KUNGSTRÄDGÅRDEN

NORRMALM

David Bagaresgatan

Brunnsgatan

Kungsgatan

HÖTORGET Ⓜ

Malmskillnadsgatan

Sergels Torg

Sveavägen

Sergelgatan

Slöjdgatan

Drottninggatan

Samuel

Mäster Samuelsgatan

Olofsgatan

Klarabergsgatan

Vattugatan

Tunnelgatan

Apelbergsgatan

A. Fredriks Kyrkogata

T-CENTRALEN Ⓜ

❾

ⓘ Central Station

❶ Nordiska Museet
❷ Skansen
❸ Östermalms Saluhall
❹ Saluhall
❺ Hallwylska Museet
❻ Nationalmuseum
❼ Atrium
❽ Sturegallerian & Sturebadet
❾ Centralbadet

B y now you'll have your bearings, so, on this second day, **you should find the districts** of Norrmalm and Östermalm easy to navigate. Start with a rare treat, a dip into Scandinavian life and design at the Nordiska Museum. **START: T-bana to Kungsträdgården.**

1 ★★ **kids** **Nordiska Museet.** I love museums that show how people lived and the Nordic Museum gives a vivid picture of Sweden from the Middle Ages to today. The museum was created by teacher and folklorist, Artur Hazelius, also founder of Skansen (**2**). Designed in truly monumental style, it was opened in 1907. You're greeted in the Great Hall by an enormous statue by Carl Milles (1875–1955) of Gustav Vasa, the heroic king who won Swedish independence from the Danes in 1523. The 1.5 million objects encompass everything from 18th-century shoes that could come from today's creative designers to some remarkable headgear. It's like walking through a giant Nordic dolls' house with an incredible mix from folk art to 1860s Viking-style revival furniture when famine and the fear of Russian invasion sent Swedes back to their supposedly strong,

invincible ancestors. ⏱ *1½ hr. Djurgårdsvägen 6–16.* ☎ *08-519 546 00. www.nordiskamuseet.se. Admission: Adults 80 SEK, free children 17 and under. Free Wed 4–8pm (Sept–May). Free with Stockholm Card (see p 11). June 1–Aug 31 daily 10am–5pm; Sep 1–May 31 Mon–Fri 10am–4pm (Wed to 8pm), Sat, Sun 11am–5pm. Check opening hours over public holidays. Bus 44, 69 and 76. Tram 7. Ferry to Djurgården (summer)—4 min from Nybroviken; 3 min from Slussen.*

2 ★★★ **kids** **Skansen.** In 1891, Artur Hazelius (1833–1901) opened the world's first open-air museum. One hundred and fifty old buildings, farms, houses, shops, churches, and workshops were brought from all over Sweden to preserve and illustrate countryside traditions. This was a time when, according to 19th-century Romantics, the old way of life was rapidly disappearing. It's a

The Nordiska Museum was opened in 1907.

place to wander around, from the town quarter where you can see old crafts such as glass-blowing, to the turf shelters of the Sami camp. Nordic animals such as bears, wolves, and elk live in enclosures planted with native flora and fauna. There's plenty to see and cafes and restaurants to keep you going. In the summer, costumed guides show you round many of the buildings. Either spend a few hours here or all day on a separate tour (p 102). See also p 45, **2** for information on winter. 🕐 *2 hr. Djurgårdsslatten 49–51.* ☎ *08-442 80 00. www.skansen.se. Adults from 70–120 SEK; children 6–15 years 30–50 SEK, depending on time of year; free children 5 and under. Free with Stockholm Card (see p 11). Daily May 1–June 19 & Sept, 10am–8pm; June 20–Aug 31 10am–10pm. For other times, telephone or check the website. Bus: 47. Tram: 7. Ferry to Djurgården (summer).*

3 ★★★ **Östermalms Saluhall.** Östermalm's food market is gourmet Stockholm at its finest. The gastronomic temple, built in 8 months and opened by King Oscar II in 1888, has been supplying the capital's

Östermalms Saluhall.

Turf-roofed house at Skansen.

inhabitants with fresh bread, cakes, fish and seafood, vegetables, smoked, cured and fresh meat, and more ever since. For more information about stores, see p 37, **3**. 🕐 *1 hr. Östermalmstorg. www. ostermalmshallen.se. Mon–Thurs 9:30am–6pm, Fri 9:30am–6:30pm, Sat 9:30am–4pm. T-bana: Östermalmstorg.*

4 ★★★ **Saluhall.** Once you've done the rounds of the market, lunch with the ladies who do just that at Lisa Elmqvist (☎ 08-553 40 400, www.lisaelmqvist.se). Order a superb fish and seafood soup with all the trimmings (270 SEK). Or try Nyroe Smørrebrød for open sandwiches piled high with whatever takes your fancy (84–140 SEK). ☎ *08-662 23 20, www.nybroe.se.*

5 ★★★ **kids Hallwylska Museet.** It was a typical 19th-century marriage. Wilhelmina was the daughter of a very wealthy Swedish timber merchant; Swiss Walter van Hallwyl came from one of Europe's oldest families. Money won and he moved to Sweden. The Countess had a passion for collecting, so the couple commissioned Isak Clason (1856–1930)—who designed the Nordiska Museet (see p 13, **1**)—to create a winter home to house all her art. Behind the well-concealed entrance lies a Mediterranean palace. Finished in 1898, the house was a model of the modern age, kitted out with the latest central heating, electricity, elevators, bathrooms, and telephones. The ornately decorated rooms were filled with the vast and idiosyncratic collection of treasures, art, furniture, and silverware the Countess had amassed. Her plan was to leave the house as a museum; it opened to the public in 1938 and is preserved exactly as she left it. A costumed guide takes you back to the gilded past. Or wander by yourself around the first floor. ⏱ *1 hr. Hamngatan 4.* ☎ *08-519 555 99. www.hallwylskamuseet.se. Admission: Adults 90 SEK with guided tour; 50 SEK first floor and reception rooms only, free children 18 and under. Free with Stockholm Card (see p 11). July–Aug Tues–Sun 10am–4pm; rest of year Tues, Thurs–Sun noon–4pm, Wed to 7pm. Closed Mon. Guided tours in English Sat at 1:30pm. T-bana: Östermalmstorg.*

The Nationalmuseum.

Eat at Lisa Elmqvist in Östermalms Saluhall.

6 ★★★ **Nationalmuseum.** Designed by the German architect, August Stüler (1800–65) and finished in 1866, the National Museum houses Sweden's largest art collection. The staircase itself is a work of art with its frescoes by Carl Larsson (1853–1919). See works by artists like Rembrandt and Renoir, by relatively unknown north European painters such as David Klöcker Ehrenstrahl (1628–98), and an impressive applied arts section.

For minitour, see p 16.

Nationalmuseum

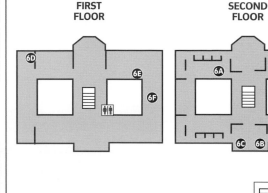

**FIRST
FLOOR**

**SECOND
FLOOR**

Stairs

Rest Rooms

On the top floor, paintings and sculptures from France, Holland, Flanders, and Sweden, plus a Renaissance section, include masterpieces such as **6A The Ill-Matched Couple** of 1532 by Lucas Cranach the Elder (1472–1553). Don't miss the seductive **6B portrait of the wife of Alexander Roslin** (1718–98), the leading 18th-century Swedish painter, and sculptures like **6C Cupid and Psyche** by Johan Tobias Sergel (1740–1814), the Swedish neoclassical sculptor who worked in Rome from 1767 to 1778.

Downstairs, turn left for applied art from 1500 to 1740. Monumental pieces such as the **6D chest of drawers by Georg Haupt** (1741–84), who became King Gustav III's cabinet maker (you can see many of his pieces in the Kungliga

Slottet, (see p 9)), show the spread of European influences to Sweden. Then move into the 20th century. Sweden was influenced by European designers like **Gerrit Rietfeld** (1888–1964) and his famous **6E red and blue chair.** Themed spaces take you through Pop Art and the craft tradition to industrial design. Of the striking glassware, don't miss **6F Ann Wåhlström's vases and Dante Marioni's delicate glass.** ⏱ *2 hr. Södra Blasieholmshamnen.* ☎ *08-519 543 00 www.nationalmuseum.se. Admission: Adults 100 SEK, free children 18 and under. Free admission to ground floor. Free with Stockholm Card (see p 11). Tues & Thurs 11am–8pm, Wed, Fri–Sun 11am–5pm (Sept–May 31 to 8pm on Thurs). Closed Mon & public holidays. T-bana: Kungsträdgården. Bus: 65.*

7 ★★ **Atrium.** The restaurant in the National Museum is a light, airy space, with granite floors and limestone walls (which make it quite noisy). It's a great place for coffee and a cake, or a glass of wine from their excellent list. ☎ *08-611 34 30. www.restaurangatrium.se. Coffee and cake 80 SEK.*

8 ★★ **Sturegallerian & Sturebadet.** Sturegallerian is where wealthy, upper-crust Stockholmers come to shop for international and Swedish names, and lunch in cafes and restaurants. The shopping complex was built around the original Sturebadet art nouveau swimming pool, opened in 1885 and restored in 1989 to provide a swish spa and gym as well. ⏱ *1 hr. See p 94 & p 100.*

9 ★★★ **Centralbadet.** Go on, after all that culture and exercise,

pamper yourself—and where better than in the newly renovated 1904 Jugendstil-style Centralbadet? On offer are all the treatments you expect, from facials to Swedish massage (book in advance); otherwise the entrance fee gives you access to the swimming pool, gym with free weights, warm water baths, bubble and thermal pools, and the sauna. You enter through a charming shaded garden where people sit and chat over cups of coffee and cakes at little tables under the shady trees. In summer there's a roof terrace and outdoor gym. *Drottninggatan 88. ☎ 08-545 213 00. www. centralbadet.se. Mon–Sat 11am–8pm. Entrance: Adults 180 SEK Mon–Thurs, 220 SEK Fri, Sat. Closed Sun. Age restriction 18 unless with an adult. See website for treatments (Swedish only). T-bana: Hötorget. Bus: 52.*

Centralbadet.

The Best **in Three Days**

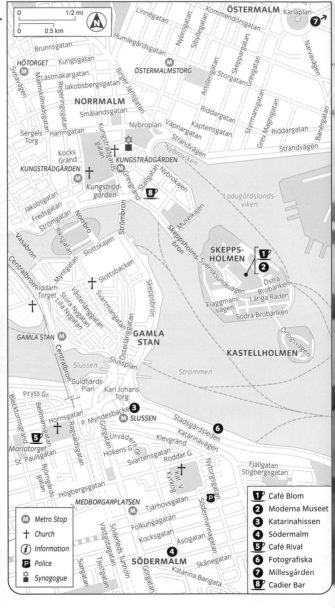

Legend:

- Ⓜ Metro Stop
- ✝ Church
- ⓘ Information
- 🅿 Police
- ✡ Synagogue

1. Café Blom
2. Moderna Museet
3. Katarinahissen
4. Södermalm
5. Café Rival
6. Fotografiska
7. Millesgården
8. Cadier Bar

For your third day try something different. Begin at the Modern Art Museum cafe before taking in one of Europe's great contemporary art collections. Finish the day with a trip out to see the stunning sculptures in Carl Milles's former home. It shows you how pleasant rural living outside the center could be. **START: Moderna Museum on Skeppsholmen.**

1️⃣ Café Blom. Tucked away in the Picasso Park of the Modern Art Museum (see below), take a strong coffee looking at Picasso's sculptures to get yourself into the mood. *Skeppsholmen.* ☎ *08-519 552 00. www.modernamuseet.se. Closed Mon. Coffee and cake around 60 SEK.*

2️⃣ ★★★ kids Moderna Museet. You know this is the Modern Art Museum by the crazy-colored Niki de Saint Phalle sculptures outside. The light modern building by Catalan architect Rafael Moneo (b. 1937) is large enough to display superb examples of every major modern artist and yet compact enough to keep your attention. This is now one of Europe's best contemporary art collections. It shows the history of modern art, starting with the early 20th century and works by Picasso, de Chirico, Dalí, Rauschenberg, Brancusi, and Chagall, as well as

videos and contemporary installations. You come across pieces such as Picasso's *Déjeuner sur l'Herbe*, Andy Warhol's *Mao* of 1973, and the most famous piece in the museum, the bizarre Robert Rauschenberg's *Monogram*, known as 'The Goat.' Take the guided tour for an in-depth visit. There's also a top photographic collection on view. 🕐 *1½ hr. Skeppsholmen.* ☎ *08-519 552 00. www.modernamuseet.se. Adults 100 SEK, free 17 and under. Free with Stockholm Card (see p 11). Tues 10am–8pm, Wed–Sun 10am–6pm. Closed Mon. Guided tour in English is included with admission July, Aug: Tues, Thurs, Sun at 1pm. T-bana: Kungsträdgården. Bus 65. Ferries from Djurgården and Nybroplan in summer.*

Catch the ferry to Slussen from the southern part of the island, or walk back over the bridge and take the 2, 55, 71 or 76 bus to Slussen.

Moderna Museet.

View to Riddarholmen and Stadshuset from Katarinahissen.

❸ ★ kids Katarinahissen. The steam-driven Katarinahissen elevator opened in 1883 and was replaced in the 1930s with an electric one to join the lower part of the town with the upper. From the 38m (125 ft.) high tower, the view is predictably grand. To prolong the experience, have an evening drink at Eriks Gondolen (p 127) and look down at the lights sparkling in the city below. In high summer you may have to wait in line for the lift. ⏱ *1 min (15 min wait at lift in summer). Stradsgården 6.* ☎ *08-642 47 86. Lift 10 SEK. Free with Stockholm Card (see p 11). Daily Sept–mid-May 10am–6pm; mid-May–Aug 8am–10pm. T-bana: Slussen.*

Café Rival.

❹ Södermalm. The laidback atmosphere of 'Söder,' as it is locally known, contrasts with the hustle and bustle of the center of the city. Södermalm is a large island, a surprising mix of urban grit and green parks, steep hills with great views, 18th-century cottages, gardens and allotments, plus an uninhibited nightlife and two of the more unconventional entertainment venues, the Folk Opera (p 139) and the Södra Teatern (p 51). Traditionally working-class, it's now vaunted as Stockholm's hippest area, revitalized by an influx of the young who come here for the new shops, cafes, and bars. The area that most typifies the change is SoFo (south of Folkungagaten and east of Gogatan). It's currently best known for Stieg Larsson's great trilogy of crime novels, and the Millennium Walk (see p 48). Check out one of the other Södermalm walks to discover the best parts of the island (p 70 and p 74). ⏱ *2 hr. T-bana: Slussen.*

❺ ★ Café Rival. Join the young and fashionable at the cafe that belongs to the Hotel Rival, owned by Benny Andersson—yes, he of colossal Abba fame. It has a summer terrace perfect for people-watching and good coffee, cakes, and sandwiches. And who knows? You may even spot Benny himself. *Marialorgel 3.* ☎ *08-545 789 25. www.rival.se.Coffee, cake & sandwich from 55 SEK.*

6 ★★★ Fotografiska. This contemporary photography gallery is one of Stockholm's most vibrant spaces. With six to seven major and many smaller exhibitions a year, it aims to bring world-class photographers like Annie Leibovitz and newer names to Sweden's capital. The redbrick, huge Fotografiska is housed in Stora Tullhuset, a former customs house, opened in 1906. There are guided tours in English and a bar and restaurant with good views. ⏱ *1½ hr. Stadsgårdshamnen 22.* ☎ *08-509 005 00. www.foto grafiska.eu. Adults 110 SEK, free children 11 and under. Free with Stockholm Card (see p 11). Daily 10am–9pm. Closed Dec 24 and 31, Jun 21. T-bana: Slussen.*

From Slussen take the T-bana (red line) to Ropsten (T13). From here either take the bus to Rorsvik, or **the delightful Lidingö train to Torsvik (both only one stop). From Torsvik it's a short walk (300 meters/328 yards) but uphill to Millesgården following the signs.**

7 ★★★ Millesgården. The former house and studio of sculptor Carl Milles is now the Milles Garden Museum. The modest approach doesn't prepare you for the hilltop garden full of spectacular sculptures overlooking the waters of Lilla Värtan. Some of the sculptures stand on high plinths; others are set in pools of water; some are massive; others delicate. From the garden, steps take you up to the house and studio. Milles was also a collector and on his travels he built up the largest private collection in Sweden of Greek and Roman statuary. It's a beautiful, tranquil place with a serenity you don't find in most museums. The house is just as delightful, with his wife Olga's painted furniture, and marble walls and mosaic floors in the gallery and the Red Room. When the couple returned here in 1950, Milles's half-brother Evert, an architect,

Millesgården is inspirational.

Carl Milles

Carl Milles (1875–1955) studied under Rodin in Paris before returning to Stockholm in 1906 and buying a plot of land in Lidingö to build his house and garden. In 1931 he left for the U.S.A. and built an international career. He became artist-in-residence at Cranbrook Educational Community in Bloomfield Hills, Michigan, and was commissioned to produce statues throughout the U.S.A.—in Detroit, Virginia, and St. Louis. All was not plain sailing, however; his playful, sometimes erotic, sculptures proved too much for some audiences and he employed a fig leaf maker on a retainer. He returned home in 1951 and spent every summer in Millesgården until his death in 1955. His burial here was courtesy of King Gustaf VI Adolf, who authorized it, overturning Swedish law that requires burial in sacred ground. The king, a keen gardener and friend, helped plant the garden at the site.

designed a second house on the lower terrace. If you want a small replica of one of the sculptures, the shop can oblige. In Stockholm, you can see many of his 26 public sculptures including the *Orpheus* fountain in front of Konserthuset and the arching *Gud på himmelsbågen* (God on the Rainbow) at Nacka Strand. ○ *1½ hr. Herserudsvägen 32.* ☎ *08-446 75 90. www.millesgarden.se. Adults 95 SEK, free 18 and under. Free with Stockholm Card (see p 11). Daily May 15–Sept 30 11am–5pm; Oct 1–May 14 Tues–Sun noon–5pm. Train: Torsvik.*

8 ★★ **Cadier Bar.** When you get back into central Stockholm, enjoy an early evening posh drink. The bar was named after King Oscar II's (1829–1907) head chef, Regis Cadier, who cannily founded the Grand Hotel in 1874. The high prices are worth it for the view and a glimpse of conservative Swedish society. Anyway, the Grand Hotel is an institution, and institutions should always be treasured. *Södra Blasieholmshamnen 8.* ☎ *08-679 35 00. www.grandhotel. se. T-bana Kungsträdgården. Drinks cost from 120 SEK.* ●

Stockholm & the Sea

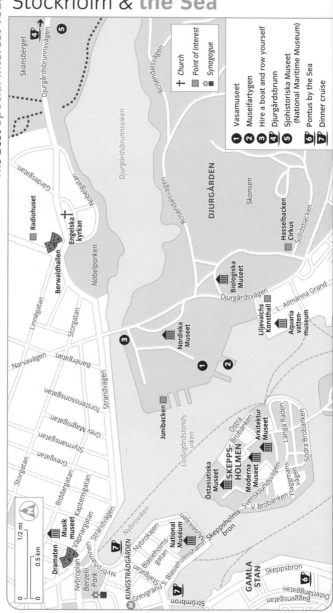

Legend
- † Church
- ■ Point of Interest
- ☼ Synagogue

1 Vasamuseet
2 Museifartygen
3 Hire a boat and row yourself
4 Djurgårdsbrunn
5 Sjöhistoriska Museet (National Maritime Museum)
6 Pontus by the Sea
7 Dinner cruise

Previous page: Musical statue.

Stockholm life has always been tied to the sea and it's this maritime love affair that makes the capital such an attractive city. The sea today is as important as ever, but it's a more peaceful relationship than in the past. In summer, the city empties as locals leave for their summer cottages in the archipelago islands, leaving the city for visitors. START: **Bus 47, tram 7, summer ferry to Vasamuseet.**

1 ★★★ kids **Vasamuseet.** It took 3 years to build the Swedish Navy's most expensive, powerful, and ornate ship. She was constructed on the island of Blasieholmen, and brought to the quay just below the Kungliga Slottet. News of the great warship traveled the length and breadth of an apprehensive Europe; she was, it seemed, invincible. On 10th August, 1628, watched by countless spectators in the harbor, she unfurled her sails and set off. After just 1,300m (4,365 ft.) the wind increased, the ship capsized, and the *Vasa* sank. The brackish waters preserved the ship until she was rediscovered and lifted from her watery grave 333 years later. 🕑 *2 hr. more information and a tour, see p 8,* **3**.

2 kids **Museifartygen.** More stories of Sweden's seafaring tradition are found on two nearby ships. The lightship **Finngrundet** (1903) was kept on the Finnbrung banks in the Gulf of Bothnia until lighthouses took over in the 1960s, and she was retired to a small berth here. Next door is the **St. Erik**, a seagoing icebreaker built in 1915. The technique is simple: the boat climbs onto the ice and crushes it as it moves slowly but noisily forward. 🕑 *40 min. Galärvarvet.* ☎ *08-519 549 00. www.vasamuseet.se/en/. Free admission. Daily end May–beg Sept 11am–6pm. Bus 47. Tram: 7. Ferry: Djurgården (summer only).*

3 ★★★ kids **Hire a boat and row yourself.** There's nothing more enjoyable and, until you have the hang of it, challenging than doing as the locals do and taking to the waters. Take a picnic and go at your own pace. Hire your boat at **Djurgårdsbrons Sjocafé** over the bridge on Djurgården and set off across the peaceful waters that lead onto the delightful canal and beyond. Stop here, or you'll find yourself all at sea! *Galärvarvsvägen 2.* ☎ *08-660 57 57. www.sjocafet.se. Hire rates vary according to the boat. A rowboat is 150 SEK per hour and 400 SEK for the whole day; kayaks are 100 SEK hourly and 400 SEK for the day. ID or passport required. Open mid-Apr–Sept. Bus 44, 47. Tram: 7.*

4 ★★ kids **Djurgårdsbrunn.** It's tempting to flop down into a deckchair and sit for hours on the terrace here, looking onto the bridge

Vasa's stern reconstructed in bold colours.

Sweden's Archipelago

Boats and boat trips are an essential part of a visit to Stockholm and there are plenty of options. For an overview of Stockholm, book an **Under the Bridges Tour** (see p 7, ❶). Those after a speed fix should try the 1hr 45 min **Archipelago Race,** a full-speed sightseeing tour at 26 knots (50 km/h) once out of the city. Adults 290 SEK, 6 to 11 years 145 SEK, free 5 and under (not recommended for 0–3 year olds); www.stromma.se. The 2½ to 3-hour **Archipelago** tour takes you out to sea for a glimpse of just a few of the 30,000 islands that make up this beautiful part of the world (adults 220 SEK, children 6–11 years 110 SEK, free for under 5 years). Or take the 11-hour **Thousand Islands Cruise** for a real sense of the island where the Swedes take their long summer holidays under the midnight sun. Adults 1,025 SEK to 1,160 SEK (lunch and one- or two-course dinner); children 6 to 11 years ½ price; free 5 and under. Summer only; www.stromma kanalbolaget.se for both archipelago tours.

over the canal. Their summer weekend BBQ lunch is perfect holiday eating (249 SEK adults, 95 SEK children). During the week, try classic veal meatballs (165 SEK). *Djurgårdsbrunnsvägen 68.* ☎ *08-624 22 00.* *www.djurgardsbrunn.com.*

❺ ★★ kids **Sjöhistoriska Museet (National Maritime Museum).** This is a dream for all those who love ships and the sea. The National Maritime Museum has more than 100,000 exhibits and an impressive 1,500 accurate model ships, all beautifully and painstakingly made. Get an idea of life on board in interiors such as the cabin and stern of the royal schooner *Amphion* built at the Djurgården shipyard in 1778, and Gustav III's flagship during the 1788 to 1790

Model ships sail endlessly in the Sjöhistoriska Museet.

The outside terrace at Pontus by the Sea.

war with Russia. There are films on destroyers, a Pirates' exhibition, and splendid maritime art, all housed in a building by Ragnar Östberg (1866–1945, architect of the Stadshuset, p 10 **7**) overlooking the water toward Stockholm. *For more information see p 67,* **3**.
🕐 1½ hr. Djurgårdsbrunnsvägen 24. ☎ 08-519 549 00. www.sjohistoriska se/en. Adults 50 SEK, free on Mon and for children 17 and under. June–Aug daily 10am–5pm; Sept–May Tues–Sun 10am–5pm. Guided tours daily 1pm (pre-book for the English tour). Bus: 69.

6 ★★★ **Pontus by the Sea.** This exquisite summer bar and restaurant draws in the crowds for its position on the waterfront, elegant but casual ambience, and comfortable wicker chairs. It's ideal for a drink at the end of the day, before slipping out into the archipelago for dinner (see below). *Tullhus 2, Skeppsbronn.* ☎ *08-20 20 95. www.pontusfrithiof. com.*

7 ★★ **Dinner Cruise.** Finish the day with a dinner cruise on a Stockholm summer 'white night'. In the late summer or autumn, you slip out into the archipelago to see the sunset. There are various options from a dinner of traditional prawns to a three-course dinner. *From Stadshusbron or Strandvägen. Book in advance on www.strommakanalbolaget.se. Various departures 5:30pm, 6pm, 7pm, depending on destination. Ticket 495 SEK. Drinks not included.*

The Vikings

We all grew up knowing about the fearsome Vikings; to us they may have been villains, but to the Swedes, Danes, and Norwegians, they were heroes and settlers. Only 1% of the population were those feared, rape-and-pillage chaps; 90% were peaceful farmers and 9% traders. Although the Vikings who raided Britain came mainly from Denmark, the old Norsemen were united by a common culture. Visit the Historiska Museet (see p 79, **2**) for a good section on Viking life, with models of their settlements, weaponry, and jewelry. There's always a great summer program for small would-be Vikings.

Kungliga Slottet

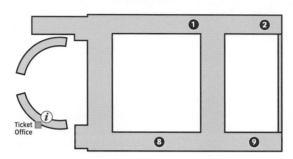

LOWER FLOOR

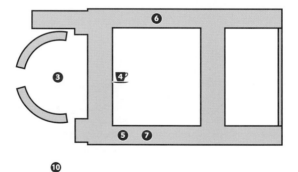

UPPER FLOOR

1. Museum Tre Kronor
2. Gustav III:s antikmuseum
3. Vaktavlosning (Changing of the Guard)
4. Palace Café
5. Representationsvåningarna (Royal Apartments)
6. Bernadotte Apartments
7. Slottskyrkan (Royal Chapel)
8. Skattkammaren (Treasury)
9. Livrustkammaren
10. Kungliga Myntkabinettet

The Royal Palace stands high above Gamla Stan, on a site that has defended access to Lake Mälaren since the 11th century. The present building, with its 608 rooms, was designed by the Royal architect, Nicodemus Tessin the Younger, and completed for King Adolf Frederik to move into in 1754. **START: T-bana Gamla Stan. Bus 2, 43, 55, 76.**

❶ ★ kids Museum Tre Kronor. For a proper historical introduction to the massive original 12th-century defensive architecture of the old Tre Kronor palace, go down into the dimly lit 16th- and 17th-century brick vaults. Two models and a short film tell you the story of the palace, along with artifacts that survived the fatal fire of 1697. ⏱ *30 min.*

❷ ★★ Gustav III:s antikmuseum. Don't dismiss this gallery by thinking it's going to be boring; it's a wonderful collection housed in the Greater and Lesser Stone Galleries. The black-and-white marble floor and classical columns make a suitably stark setting for the king's classical statuary. It's easy to imagine the monarch in this esoteric collection, walking slowly through his rogues' gallery of the antique world. Here are names to conjure with: the goddess Minerva, Lucrium Verus, Marcus Agrippa, Tiberius, Gaius Caligula, the child Britannicus, a suitably sensual Nero, Marcus Aurelius,

Jupiter, and a particularly evil-looking Pan. ⏱ *30 min.*

❸ ★★ Vaktavlosning (Changing of the Guard). This takes place daily at the Royal Palace. The Guard leaves from the Armémuseum and marches through the city along Slottsbacken to the outer courtyard of the palace with military bands in the summer. It's a low-key affair with a bit of marching and flag, although if you're lucky you might catch the mounted guards on one of their parades. ⏱ *30 min. Mon–Sat 12·15pm, Sun and holidays 1:15pm.*

❹ Palace Café. In the summer the small cafe looks out onto the palace's courtyard. Take a coffee and a bun and you might get a glimpse of the Royals as they drive themselves in and out of the palace. Or take the short walk down to Stortorget and its excellent cafes (p 59, ❹). *Coffee and bun 50 SEK.*

The Royal Palace's magnificent 'White Sea'.

⑤ ★★★ kids Representations-våningarna (Royal Apartments). Climb the entrance staircase to the rooms that make up the State Apartments and the smaller Guest Apartments used for visiting Heads of State. The splendid Hall of State where the King opened Parliament every year until 1975 is an opulent ceremonial room. In the State Apartments you go from the Council Chamber, where the King meets several times a year with the Government, to the theatrical State Bedchamber where Gustav III died after being shot at the Opera House in 1792. Karl XI's Gallery, modeled on Versailles and used for the annual honoring of the Nobel laureates, is magnificent; the saloon known poetically as 'The White Sea' is used at State banquets. Take the guided tour in English (included with the ticket) for a more detailed look at royal life. 🕐 *1 hr. Guided tours daily in English May 14–Sept 25 11am, 2pm, 3pm.*

⑥ ★★ kids Bernadotte Apartments. This fabulous suite of rooms includes the Pillar Hall and the rococo magnificence of the East Octagonal Cabinet. Named after the gallery of Bernadotte portraits, it's the place for receiving foreign ambassadors and ceremonial events. 🕐 *30 min.*

⑦ ★★ Slottskyrkan (Royal Chapel). If you're here on a Sunday, you can attend mass at the Royal Chapel. Otherwise, opening hours are restricted. The chapel, designed by Tessin the Younger, and completed by Carl Harleman in the mid-1700s is gorgeous. It has a painted ceiling, 17th-century bronze crowns, and items rescued from the original fortress such as the late 17th-century benches made by Georg Haupt. 🕐 *20 min.*

⑧ ★★★ kids Skattkammaren (Treasury). From the Royal

The Skattkammaren (Treasury).

Apartments, turn left outside and walk down to the entrance to the vaulted underground Treasury. This is another treat, a jewel box of regalia where some of the exquisite state symbols of power are on display. Don't miss Karl Gustav X's (1622–60) pale blue and gold crown with its distinctly Russian look, Erik XIV's (1533–77) crown made in Stockholm in 1561 with its huge ruby and pearls, and Gustav Vasa's (1496–1560) great sword of state. 🕐 *45 min.*

⑨ ★★★ kids Livrustkammaren. Turn left again and go down one further level to the Royal Armory. Started in 1633, it's a fascinating, gigantic toy box of a museum, which takes you through 500-odd years of Swedish regalia, weaponry, and clothing. Here you'll see ornate, heavily embroidered wedding dresses and the masked costume worn by King Gustav III when he was assassinated in 1792. You'll also see the elegant dresses of Crown Princess Victoria and the silver clothes of Gustav III (1746–92). Underneath, vaulted cellars house a formidable

Practical Matters—Kungliga Slottet

Royal Apartments, Bernadotte Apartments, Treasury, and Tre Kronor Museum: Jan 2–May 13 Tues–Sun noon–4pm; May 14–Sept 25 daily 10am–5pm; Sept 26–Dec 30 Tues–Sun noon–4pm. **Gustav III's Museum of Antiquities**: May 14–Sept Royal Armory (☎ 08-402 30 30; www.livrustkammaren.se): Sept–Apr Tues–Sun 11am–5pm, Thurs 11am–8pm; May–June daily 10am–5pm; July, August daily 10am–6pm. **The Royal Chapel** Jun–Aug Wed, Fri, noon–3pm, Mass Sun 11am.

Single attraction: Adults 100 SEK, children 7–18 years old 50 SEK, under-7s free. Combination ticket for Royal Apartments, Bernadotte Apartments, Treasury, Tre Kronor & Gustav III's Museum: Adults 130 SEK, children 65 SEK. Guided tour included in ticket price, free with the Stockholm Card (see p 11). You don't need a separate ticket; just go to whichever building you want to see. Gamla Stan ☎ 08-402 61 30. www.royalcourt.se. T-bana: Gamla Stan, Kungsträdgården. Bus: 2, 43, 55, 76.

The Royal Music Festival takes place from mid-August to mid-September in the Royal Chapel and Hall of State.

collection of royal vehicles and the stuffed bodies of the monarch's horses, including Streiff, Gustav II Adolf's mount when he rode fatally into battle in 1632. It's a ghostly place, with the sound of clopping hooves on cobbles accompanying you as you walk past the gilded carriages and winter sledges. ⏲ *1 hr.*

🔟 ★ **Kungliga Myntkabinettet.** The Royal Coin Cabinet is housed in a three-story building opposite the palace and tells the story of money from the 19th century to today. Here you'll see the first Swedish coin of the late 10th century from King Olof of Sigtuna and the world's largest 'coin,' the 'rai-stone' from Micronesia. ⏲ *30 min. Slottsbacken.* ☎ *08-519 553 04. Admission: Adults 50 SEK, free children 16 and under. Free on Mon, free with Stockholm Card (p 11). Daily summer 9am–5pm; winter 10am–4pm.*

The Royal Coin Cabinet.

Art & Design

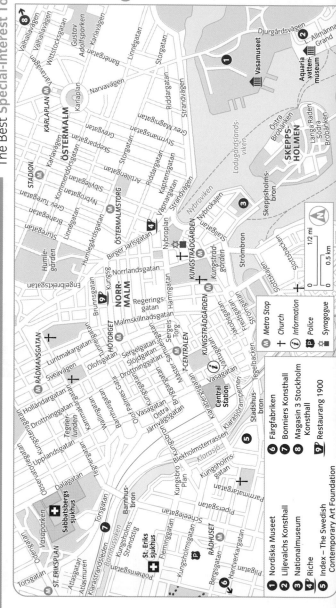

Metro Stop
Church
Information
Police
Synagogue

Sweden has a well-deserved reputation as a leader in art and design. At the 1925 World Exhibition in Paris, the clean lines, bold colors, and simple shapes using natural materials came as a revelation to a world still drowning in overblown country-house style. Liberation finally came when light wood furniture replaced heavy mahogany. START: **T-bana to Kungsträdgården.**

❶ ★★ kids Nordiska Museet. This museum places modern design in historical context, showing you the interiors of ordinary houses and how styles have changed over the decades. The small room settings are particularly evocative, charting what the younger generation saw as progress and the older lot saw as garish bad taste in design. ⏱ 1½ hr. See p 13, ❶.

❷ ★★ kids Liljevalchs Konst- hall. The Liljevalchs is renowned for its major exhibitions and collections of international, Swedish, and Nordic art from the 20th century. The highlight is the *Spring Salon* (end of Jan–mid-Mar) that showcases works by unknown artists. Built thanks to the wealth of industrialist Carl Fredrik Liljevalch (1837–1909), the gallery was designed by Carl G. Bergsten (1879–1935) and built in neoclassical style between 1913

and 1916. ⏱ 1 hr. *Djurgardsvägen 60.* ☎ *08-508-31 330. www.liljevalchs. se. Admission: Adults 80 SEK, free children 17 and under. Free with Stockholm Card (see p 11). Tues 11am–8pm, Wed, Fri–Sun 11am–5pm, Thurs 11am–8pm. Bus: 47. Tram: 7. Ferry to Djurgården (summer).*

❸ ★★★ Nationalmuseum. Walk around the exhibits in the Art and Design section to see the development of Swedish (and international) design over the past 100 years. It takes you from the 1900s through the movement for Arts and Crafts, industrial design, Pop Art and more into the 1990s when Sweden once again took the lead in modern design. It includes both the familiar and the unfamiliar and is a particularly interesting and comprehensive collection that brings out comments like 'Did we really like that?' ⏱ 2 hr. See p 15, ❻.

1976 Room Setting at the Nordiska Museet.

Liljevalchs Konsthall was designed by Carl Bergsten.

4 ★★ Riche. Über-fashionable, this is where design-conscious Sweden comes to graze. It's an old restaurant, originally conceived as a typical brasserie, but now jazzed up with leather banquettes and startling lights. Dress up, you're here to be seen. *Birger Jarlsgatan 4, Östermalm.* ☎ *08-679 68 42. www.riche. se, p 120.*

5 ★★ Index—The Swedish Contemporary Art Foundation. Originally a photographic gallery, the foundation puts on six to eight exhibitions a year, emphasizing the experimental by both international artists and Swedish unknowns. 🕐 *1½ hr. Kungsbrostrand 19.* ☎ *08-640 60 60. www.indexfoundation.se. Free admission. Tues–Fri noon–4pm, Sat, Sun noon–5pm. Closed Mon. T-bana: Rådhuset (exit Kungsholmsgatan).*

6 ★★ Färgfabriken. The Center for Contemporary Art, Architecture and Society, or 'laboratory of the contemporary,' has an experimental, cutting-edge approach. Founded

The Stockholm Art Scene

Stockholm is becoming known for its vibrant art scene, with both non-profit-making and commercial galleries playing a vital part. For young Swedish artists, visit Vasastaden. Go to the pioneering galleries of **Natalia Goldin** (www.nataliagoldin.com), and **Brändström & Stene** (www.brandstromstene.com). **Galleri Charlotte Lund** in Östermalm (www.gallericharlottelund.com) is a high-profile gallery for international and young artists. In Södermalm, try the art collective **Candyland** (www.candyland.se) and **ID:I** (www.idigalleri. org), a non-commercial cooperative of artists who each take over the gallery for 3 weeks at a time. For more information, pick up a copy of the free guide *Konstguiden*, available from most galleries. Most galleries are open Thursday to Sunday and many close from mid-June to mid-August.

Shopping for Swedish Design

As you'd expect, Stockholm has top interior design shops. For 20th-century Scandinavian furniture, lighting, ceramics, and glass from the master, try Andrew Duncanson's **Modernity** (p 98). The clean lines of furniture by Bruno Mathsson (1907–88) such as his laminated wood and plaited webbing chairs can be seen at **Studio B3;** while **Carl Malmsten** (1888–1972) (p 98) went against the prevailing trend and down the path of renewing traditional Swedish craftsmanship with his light wooden furniture. For an idea of what your home could look like on a large budget, go to the newly renovated Stockholm favorite **Svensk Tenn** (p 98); for colorful accessories, try **10 Gruppen** (p 98). Travel outside the center on the free shuttle bus from outside the Gallerian shopping center on Regeringshgatan to the biggest **Ikea** store in the world (www.ikea.com/se).

in 1995 in an old 1889 factory, its wide program of art, video, and installation events includes architecture and design in several exhibition spaces. ⏱ 1½ hr. *Lövholmsbrinken 1, Liljeholmenorsgatan 19.* ☎ *08-645 07 07. www.fargfabriken.se. Adults 40 SEK, free children 17 and under. Free with Stockholm Card (see p 11). Wed–Sun 11am–4pm. T-bana: Liljeholmen.*

❼ ★★ Bonniers Konsthall. This family-run, non-profit-making art gallery was set up by Jeanette Bonnier in memory of her daughter, Maria. The impressive building, designed by Swedish architect John Celsing, is a glass structure shaped like an upended iron, with light flooding into spaces devoted to innovative, often unknown, Swedish and international contemporary art. The restaurant, Spetsen, is run by chefs in charge of Carl Michael (p 114). ⏱ 1 hr. *Torsgatan 19.* ☎ *08-736 42 48. www.bonnierskonsthall.se. Adults 70 SEK, free children 17 and under. Free with Stockholm Card (see p 11). Wed–Fri noon–7pm, Sat, Sun 11am–5pm. T-bana: St. Eriksplan.*

❽ ★★★ Magasin 3 Stockholm Konsthall. This privately funded gallery has six to eight exhibitions a year, concentrating on three-dimensional work. The gallery also commissions site-specific installations. Previous exhibitions in this former 1930s' warehouse include photographs by Julia Margaret Cameron (1815–97), alongside those of Miroslav Tichy (1926–2011), Gilbert & George, Pipilotti Rist, and Jeff Koons. There are also talks, lectures, and film screenings. ⏱ 1 hr. *Frihamnen.* ☎ *08-545 680 40. www.magasin3. com. Adults 40 SEK, free children 19 and under. Admission includes a ticket to all that season's exhibitions. Thurs noon–7pm; Fri–Sun noon–5pm. Guided tours Sat 2pm. Bus: 1, 76.*

❾ ★★ Restaurang 1900. You have two options here: eat in the restaurant with its design echoes of 1900s' classics, or drink at the circular, contemporary, and very cool bar, which is highly rated for its cocktails (p 119). *Regeringsgatan 66.* ☎ *08-20 60 10. www.r1900.se.*

The Best Special-Interest Tours

Stockholm **for Foodies**

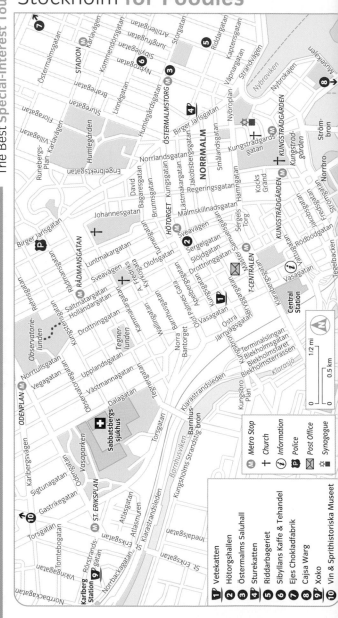

STADION

ÖSTERMALMSTORG

NORRMALM

KUNGSTRÄDGÅRDEN

Kungsträd-
gården

Ström-
bron

HÖTORGET

RÅDMANSGATAN

Observatorie-
lunden

Tegnér-
lunden

Norra
Bantorget

T-CENTRALEN

Central
Station

ODENPLAN

Sabbatsbergs
sjukhus

ST. ERIKSPLAN

Karlberg
Station

0   1/2 mi
0   0.5 km

M Metro Stop
+ Church
(i) Information
P Police
⊠ Post Office
✡■ Synagogue

1 Vetekatten
2 Hötorgshallen
3 Östermalms Saluhall
4 Sturekatten
5 Riddarbageriet
6 Sibyllans Kaffe & Tehandel
7 Ejes Chokladfabrik
8 Cajsa Warg
9 Xoko
10 Vin & Sprithistoriska Museet

at, drink, and be poor, but have fun on the way. Stockholm is one of Europe's gourmet capitals. As well as top restaurants, Stockholm's famous cafe life offers different venues from the cozily old-fashioned to the strikingly modern. The other surprise is the food markets where you can see, taste, and buy all kinds of local, seasonal produce. START: **T-bana to Kungsträdgården.**

1 ★★ kids **Vetekatten.** Start with a wonderful breakfast at this delightful old-fashioned cafe and pastry shop. It's all rather prim and proper, just as your great aunt would like. Sweet and savory, charcuterie, cheese and buns, teas and coffees are taken in a series of small rooms with old furniture and pretty textiles. The shop also sells all its cakes and bread, so you can stock up for a picnic. *Kungsgatan 55.* ☎ *08-20 84 05. www.vetekatten.se. T-bana: T-Centralen. Breakfast is 95 SEK.*

2 ★★ **Hötorgshallen.** Descend into the basement under the Filmstaden Sergel multiplex and you step into an international world. The food market was built in the 1950s and renovated in the '90s. What it lacks in soul it makes up for in choice. Whereas Östermalm (see **3**) is essentially Swedish, Hötorgshallen offers a varied stock—Indian spices, Turkish stuffed vine leaves, sweet Greek delicacies. If you want to eat, make for **Kajsas Fish** restaurant for its fish soup and grilled fresh fish (☎ 08-20 72 62). ⏲ *1 hr. Hötorget. www.hotorgshallen.se. Indoor market: June–Aug Mon–Fri 10am–6pm, Sat 10am–3pm; Sept–Apr Mon–Thurs 10am–6pm, Fri 10am–6:30pm, Sat 10am–4pm. Outdoor market: Mon–Fri 10am–7pm, Sat 10am–5pm, Sun noon–5pm. T-bana: Hötorget.*

3 ★★★ **Östermalms Saluhall.** At this food hall you can find fish that were happily swimming around a few hours before from **Melanders**

Cheeses on sale at Östermalms famous food hall.

Fisk, fresh truffles and seasonal game from **B. Andersson,** and rich, dark brown bread from the bakery of **Amandus Brödbrod.** This is one of Europe's great food halls, where you walk past stalls with moose heads staring down at you and chocolate stands groaning under the sweet weight. And it's full of excellent cafes and restaurants to tempt you. ⏲ *1 hr. Östermalmstorg, www.ostermalmshallen.se. Mon–Thurs 9:30am–6pm, Fri 9:30am–7pm, Sat 9:30am–4pm. T-bana: Östermalmstorg.*

4 ★★ kids **Sturekatten.** Enter through an archway and go upstairs to this little cafe. Here, in a series of different rooms all decorated with

Take an old-fashioned break at Sturekatten.

comfortable chairs and old paintings, you can settle down to traditional Swedish *prinsesstarta* (cream and marzipan mix) or the fabulous *äppelpaj* (apple pie). Service is as friendly as the surroundings. *Riddargatan 4. ☎ 08-611 16 12. T-bana: Östermalmstorg. Coffee and cake around 70 SEK.*

⑤ ★★ Riddarbageriet. Don't miss this famous bakery, which produces some of the best bread and cakes in Stockholm, with the highest praise going to Johan Sorberg's sourdough loaves. You can have tea or coffee (and those cakes) at the few small tables inside. *Riddargatan 15. ☎ 08-660 33 75. Mon–Fri 8am–6pm, Sat 8am–3pm. T-bana: Östermalmstorg.*

⑥ ★★ Sibyllans Kaffe & Tehandel. A real treat awaits you at this posh tea and coffee shop with its old-fashioned jars full of specialist blends. The shop has been here since World War I, as have, so it seems, some of its clients. *Sibyllegatan 35. ☎ 08-662 06 63. Mon–Fri 10am–6pm. Closed Sat & Sun. T-bana: Östermalmstorg.*

⑦ Ejes Chokladfabrik. Established in 1923 and supplying chocolates to the Royal Family, this is the place for upmarket chocolate. Everything is handmade here on the premises from the best Belgian ingredients, leaving nothing to chance. *Erik Dahlbergsgatan 25, Gärdet. ☎ 08-664 27 09. www.ejes choklad.se. Mon–Fri 10am–6pm, Sat 10am–3pm. T-bana: Karlaplan.*

⑧ ★★ Cajsa Warg. Named after Sweden's most famous cookerybook writer who lived from 1703 to 1769, this is a good choice for carefully sourced, organic foods (local, Swedish, and international). Staff test everything they stock, and provide a selection of cooked foods as

Top dessert chef makes the cakes at Xoko.

Swedish Food to Taste

The smorgasbord, a table full of small dishes, is most people's idea of typical Swedish food. Today, apart from at Christmas, most visitors will experience the smorgasbord at breakfast. As for typical Swedish dishes, even the most sophisticated restaurants in Stockholm usually include some in their menus. Try herrings done every which way; Swedish meatballs served with mashed potatoes and sharp lingonberry; Wallenbergers made from ground veal, egg yolk, cream and fried in breadcrumbs; Jansson's temptation (herring, potatoes, and onions baked in cream); pea soup, usually on a Thursday; and *pytt I panna* (fried diced meat cooked with onions and potatoes served with fried eggs and pickled beets). Stuffed cabbage rolls, as opposed to stuffed vine leaves, appeared in Sweden with the return of King Karl XII from Turkey. Summer brings riotous crayfish parties, washed down with copious servings of Swedish aquavit.

well. This is the place for a picnic: either make your own choice or buy one of their recommendations. (Also in Södermalm.) *St. Eriksplan 2.* ☎ *08-33 01 20. www.cajsawarg.se. Mon–Fri 8am–8pm, Sat, Sun 10am–7pm. T-bana: St. Eriksplan.*

☕ **Xoko.** Mecca for the sweet-toothed, Xoko is the inspiration of chocolatier and dessert chef, Magnus Johansson. He created the desserts for King Carl-Gustav's 60th birthday banquet and does the honors with the desserts at the Nobel Laureate banquet, so you know you can expect the best. The sublime desserts come at a price, but one well worth paying. *Rörstrandgatan 15.* ☎ *08-31 84 87. www.xoko.se. T-bana: St. Eriksplan. Cakes from 45 SEK.*

⑩ ★ **Vin & Sprithistoriska Museet.** In 1923, the building that now houses the Wine and Spirits Historical Museum was a warehouse; in 1989 it was converted into this quirky, interesting, and extensive

museum. The story is of Sweden's history of alcohol production—and consumption—from the Middle Ages when strong liquor (*brännvin*) was used for medicinal purposes and, more unusually, to make gunpowder. The route takes you past brewing equipment, a wine merchant's shop from around 1900 (patronized by playwright August Strindberg), and a home distillery of 1830 when potatoes were used to make schnapps. The audio tour in English brings it all alive. But the most enjoyable bit comes at the end when you can test your sense of smell with 55 spices and herbs used in vodka and liqueurs, and then move on to listen to 200 jolly drinking songs. The museum gets lots of requests for the songs and words (they have more than 2,000 songs in their archives) for the Midsummer celebrations. *Dalagatan 100.* ☎ *08-744 70 70. www.vinosprithistoriska.se. Adults 50 SEK, free children 16 and under. Free with Stockholm Card (p 11). Free audio guide in English. Tues 10am–7pm, Wed–Sun 10am–4pm. Closed Mon. Bus: 65, 73.*

Drottningholm

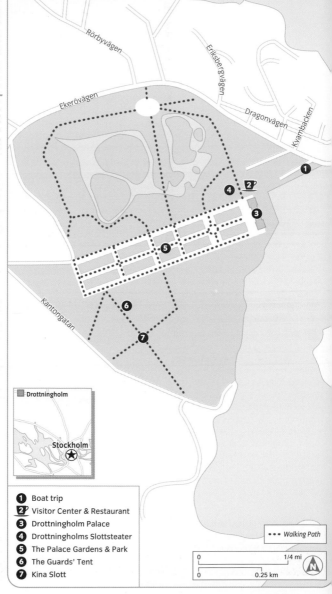

Drottningholm

Stockholm ★

1 Boat trip
2 Visitor Center & Restaurant
3 Drottningholm Palace
4 Drottningholms Slottsteater
5 The Palace Gardens & Park
6 The Guards' Tent
7 Kina Slott

••• Walking Path

0		1/4 mi
0	0.25 km	

Drottningholm Palace has been the Royal Family's home since 1981. There's plenty to see at this UNESCO World Heritage Site, 10km (6 miles) west of Stockholm on the island of Lovön. It's a great place for a picnic and makes a perfect excursion by boat, but if you're pushed for time, go by boat and return by bus and T-bana. START: **Boat from Stadshusbron on Kungsholmen.**

① ★★★ **kids** **Boat trip.** The skyline of Riddarholmen and the imposing Stadshuset recede into the distance as you slip away from central Stockholm. Smart residential areas give way to hidden creeks, marshland, and bays with moored boats during the 1-hour journey. The trip itself is a pleasure, particularly if you take an old 1900s' steamboat. ⏱ *1 hr. Stadshusbron. www.strommakanabolaget.se. By boat: buy tickets at the booth or online. Apr 10am, noon, 2pm. Return 11am, 1pm, 3pm. May 1–mid-Sept, daily and hourly 10am–3pm. Return daily and hourly 11am–4pm. Mid–end Sept some departures are only on Sat and Sun, so check first. Return ticket 165 SEK, one way 120 SEK. T-bana: Brommaplan, then bus 177, 178, 301, 323.*

② ★★ **kids** **Visitor Center & Restaurant.** Drop into the center for information and a detailed map, and grab a coffee to start the day. You'll also find the palace gift shop here. *May–Aug daily 9:30am–5pm; Sept 10:30am–4pm; Oct–Apr Sat, Sun 11am–4pm. Coffee 30 SEK.*

③ ★★★ **kids** **Drottningholm Palace.** The palace is a Royal Family home and so you see only one impressive part of it. Designed by the royal architect Nicodemus Tessin the Elder (1615–81), it was inspired by Versailles (see box, Royal Architects, p 43). Its State Rooms are decorated with polished marquetry floors, painted ceilings, lavish furnishings, and portraits of past kings. The central part is built

Take the old-fashioned 1900s steam boat to Drottningholm.

A battling Hercules faces the back of the palace.

around a huge stairwell with *trompe l'oeil* paintings giving an infinite perspective. *Levées* or morning receptions were held in Queen Hedvig Eleanora's **State Bedroom;** Queen Lovisa Ulrika's **Library** was decorated by Jean Eric Rehn (1717–93) in lavish style; and antique wood-burning porcelain stoves in some rooms add a domestic feel. ⏱ *1 hr.* ☎ *08-402 62 80. www.royalcourt.se. Adults 80 SEK, children 7–18 years 40 SEK, free children 6 and under. Including Chinese Pavilion in summer months adults 120 SEK, children 7–18 years 60 SEK, free children 6 and under. Free with Stockholm Card (see p 11). May–Aug daily 10am–4:30pm; Sept daily 11am–3:30pm; April & Oct Sat, Sun 11am–3:30pm; Nov–Mar Sat, Sun noon–3:30pm. Closed public hols. Guided tours (inc in entrance fee) in English: May Sat, Sun 10am, noon, 2pm, 4pm; Jun–Aug daily (same times); Sept noon, 2pm; Oct–Apr Sat & Sun noon, 2pm.*

④ ★★ **kids** **Drottningholms Slottsteater.** The 1776 Court Theater looks modest, but inside the world's oldest theater is a wonderful piece of design, the scenery all moved by wooden hand-driven machinery, still in working order.

Designed by architect Carl Fredrik Adelcrantz (1716–96), the theater retains its original 18th-century stage and hand-painted decorations. Sound effects may be simple but they work: a wooden box filled with stones makes thunder; other apparatus make waves and wind. Watch all this in action at the summer opera festival (p 139). ⏱ *30 min. www.dtm.se/eng. Adults 90 SEK, free children 15 and under. Free with Stockholm Card (see p 11). Guided tours in English: daily every hour May–Aug 11am–4:30pm; Sept noon–3pm.Check the website for opening hours as they vary with matinee performances.*

⑤ ★★★ **kids** **The Palace Gardens & Park.** Three baroque gardens stretch out from the back of the palace. The **Embroidery Parterre,** laid out in 1640, takes you past a dramatic statue of Hercules to the **Water Parterre** with its topiary and fountains. Beyond lies the enclosed **Theatre Bosquet.** The whole vista is flanked by rows of symmetrically cut chestnut trees. To the north, the **English Park** is dotted with lakes, small islands, and buildings such as the late 18th-century **Governor's Residence,** a small gatehouse, and a

Royal Architects

The Tessin family had a huge influence on Swedish architecture, town planning, and landscaping. **Nicodemus Tessin the Elder's** (1615–81) European travels gave him a passion for the new, flamboyant baroque style. His greatest work was Drottningholm Palace, which his son, **Count Nicodemus Tessin the Younger** (1654–1728) completed after his father's death. The younger Tessin also traveled around Europe, but under Swedish royal patronage, giving him such status that King Louis XVI turned on the fountains at Versailles especially for him to witness. When the Royal Palace in Stockholm was destroyed by fire, Tessin created its replacement, although it had not been completed when he died in 1728. He also drew up master plans for the development of Stockholm, designed various churches, and built his own magnificent home, Tessinska Palatset in Slottsbacken, which has been the residence of the Governor of Stockholm County since 1968.

Gothic Tower of 1792. With these wonderful follies and a perfect *rus in urbe* setting, I expect Marie Antoinette to pop out from behind a tree. ⏲ *1 hr.*

6 ★ The Guards' Tent. From afar it looks like an elaborate marquee, but this was built in 1781 as the quarters for Gustav III's dragoons. It was designed by Adelcrantz as a 'tent in a Turkish army camp.'

7 ★★ Kina Slott. The original Chinese Pavilion, pre-fabricated in Stockholm, was put up in secrecy for Queen Lovisa Ulrika's 33rd birthday in 1753 as a gift from her husband, King Adolf Frederik. It didn't last long and was replaced 10 years later by this pretty, low, curved building, restored to its original bright colors in the 1990s and furnished with Chinese and Japanese artifacts. Beside it stands 'The Confidence,' a separate building designed as a private dining room. No servants entered the room; instead a ready-laid table rose up through the floor from the underground kitchens. On the other side is

a 1760s' billiard room and King Adolf Frederik's lathe workshop—it was all the rage for 18th-century royals to practice woodturning. *As Palace, but closed Oct–Apr. Free with Stockholm Card (see p 11).*

The secret 'Confidence'.

Winter in Stockholm

Metro Stop
Church
Information
Police
Post Office
Synagogue

1 City Discovery boat trip
2 Skansen
3 Östermalms Saluhall
4 Ice skating at Kungsträdgården
5 Ice Bar
6 Ice hockey match
7 Observatoriemuseet
8 Café Piastowska

W inter in Stockholm, particularly at Christmas, can be a magical time. The sea freezes over and skaters take to the open-air ice rinks, the seasonal markets open, and the shops are decorated with some of the most beautiful winter windows. The days might be short but the city makes up for it with its sparkling lights and street lanterns. START: **T-bana to Kungsträdgården.**

1 ★★★ **kids** **City Discovery boat trip.** The ice crackles, the boat slowly moves forward; this is a boat trip with a difference because it's on a ship that can become an icebreaker if necessary. Slipping through the freezing sea as you edge out of Stromkajen toward the Fjäderholmarna islands, you get a totally different view of Stockholm from the wintery sea. It's a wonderful experience. ⏱ *1¼ hr. Strömkajen. City Discovery. www.city-discovery. com. Daily 10am, 11:30am, 1:30pm, 3pm. Contact them via the website for times and prices (from 214 SEK). T-bana: Kungsträdgården.*

2 ★★★ **kids** **Skansen.** During the winter months, Skansen is very quiet, with many houses closed and the animals hibernating during the winter months. But it comes into its own in December, with its Christmas markets, the annual Santa Lucia

celebrations on 13th December, its huge firework display lighting up the sky, and finally the New Year's celebrations. Walking through the buildings as the snow gently falls really takes you away from it all and you feel as if you have stepped back in time. It also makes you very happy to be living in the 21st century with all its creature comforts. ⏱ *2 hr. See p 13.*

3 ★★★ **Östermalms Saluhall.** In winter this food hall is full of game and seasonal delights. It's particularly attractive in the run up to Christmas. And it's the perfect place for unusual presents of food to take home. ⏱ *1 hr. See p 37,* **3**.

4 ★★ **Ice skating at Kungsträdgården.** There's a small open-air ice rink here in winter, which is best at night when you can skate under the floodlights. It's popular and well-established (it's been

Keeping warm in Skansen.

Christmas Markets

Stockholm's Christmas markets are as colorful as anywhere in Europe. Particularly worth looking out for are Swedish Christmas candy, reindeer meat, and smoked sausages. Keep warm with copious mugs of *glogg* (mulled wine). The market at **Skansen** (p 13) is held at weekends in December until Christmas Eve. It's a good source for craft products, from handmade candles and Christmas food to traditional Christmas ornaments, and the famous Dala horses, originally carved by lumberjacks when they weren't cutting down the forests in the Dala region. **Stortorget** in Gamla Stan is another place to make for, with the historic surroundings adding to the atmosphere. The market runs from November 24 to December 24. **Sigtuna** has a fair on the four Sundays before Christmas (see Sigtuna, p 154). For that royal touch, go to **Drottningholm Slott** on the first weekend in December (p 139).

running here since 1962) and it's free to use so you only pay for skate rental. ⏱ *1 hr. Mid-Nov–Mar. Mon, Thurs, Fri 9am–6pm; Tues, Wed 9am–9pm; Sat, Sun 10am–6pm. Skate rentals* ☎ *08-20 01 77. Adults per hour 40 SEK, children 17 and under 20 SEK per hour. T-bana: Kungsträdgården.*

5 **Ice Bar.** On the basis that you're so cold already nothing will affect you, try the Ice Bar. At –5°C (23°F) you'll be grateful for the fur-lined coats and warm boots that come with the ice-cold vodka. *Nordic Sea Hotel.* ☎ *08-505 630 00. See p 128.*

Ice skating at Kungsträdgården.

Long-Distance Ice Skating

Inspired by what you've seen, take lessons in long-distance ice skating with experts. On the best natural ice on Lake Mälaren, you can choose between a 2½ hour lesson, a half or a whole day. Everything is included from transportation to equipment. Just think you could be halfway to Sigtuna (see p 154) before you know it.
Ice Guide, *Slåttervägen, Tyresö.* ☎ *07-308 947 63. www.iceguide.se. From 300 SEK to 6,500 SEK.*

6 ★★ **kids** **Ice hockey match.** It's fast and furious as native teams such as Djurgården IF and international names like the NHL Pittsburg Penguins and the Ottawa Senators battle it out in front of capacity crowds. Matches take place at Hovet, the old ice hockey stadium within the Globen complex and in Globen itself, the huge spherical construction that stands out for miles. Djurgården IF is the major Stockholm team and plays in the Elitserien, the Swedish Elite League, one of the top European leagues. *Arenavägen, Johanneshov. Tickets* ☎ *07-713 100 00. www.globen arenas.se/en. T-bana: Globen.*

7 ★ **kids** **Observatoriemuseet.** The small, old Observatory Museum is at its best on a winter evening when the sky is dark enough to see the stars. The museum is housed in a hilltop observatory built for the Royal Swedish Academy of Sciences in the late 1740s, and opened in 1753. Guided tours take you through the observation rooms furnished with 18th-century instruments belonging to astronomer Pehr Wargentin (1717–63) who lived and worked here. Climb the narrow staircase to the dome to see the city spread below you. On Tuesdays and Thursdays you can gaze at the heavens through a telescope, weather permitting. In 1931, the observatory moved its scientific research to Saltsjobaden in the Stockholm archipelago. ⏱ *1 hr. Drottninggatan 120.* ☎ *08-545 483 90. www. observatoriet.kva.se. Adults 50 SEK, children 7–18 years 25 SEK. Free with Stockholm Card (p 11). Sun open noon–3pm, guided tours noon, 1pm, 2pm. Oct–Mar Tues, Thurs 6–9pm; guided tours on the hour (in Swedish) with observations from the telescope, weather permitting. T-bana: Rådmansgatan.*

8 **Café Piastowska.** A warming bowl of *borscht* or a plate of Swedish meatballs is just what you should order at this tiny, cozy, friendly venue. There are tables outside in summer, but the point of the place is the cluttered interior, hearty food, and good beer. The last time I was there, a suitably laid-back and somewhat old-fashioned couple performed—he on the guitar, she singing the equivalent of Blowing in the Wind. Perfect for a melancholy winter evening. *Tegnergatan 5.* ☎ *08-21 25 08. Main dishes under 200 SEK.*

Stieg Larsson's Millennium Tour

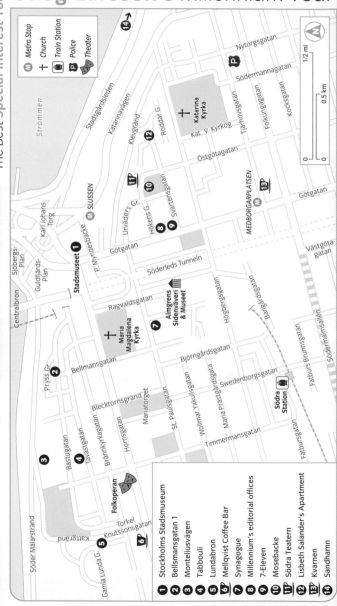

Legend:
- Ⓜ Metro Stop
- ✝ Church
- 🚉 Train Station
- 🅿 Police
- 🎭 Theater

Strömmen

Stadsgårdsleden

Katarina Kyrka

Kat. V. Kyrkog.

Östgötagatan

SLUSSEN

MEDBORGARPLATSEN

Götgatan

Söderleds Tunneln

Stadsmuseet ①

Almgrens Sidenväveri & Museet ⑦

Ragvaldsgatan

Maria Magdalena Kyrka

Björngårdsgatan

Swedenborgsgatan

Södra Station

Bellmansgatan

Blecktornsgränd

Mariatorget

Timmermansgatan

Hornsgatan

Folkoperan

Torkel Knutssonsgatan

Söder Mälarstrand

① Stockholms Stadsmuseum
② Bellmansgatan 1
③ Montelliusvägen
④ Tabbouli
⑤ Lundabron
⑥ Mellqvist Coffee Bar
⑦ Synagogue
⑧ Millennium's editorial offices
⑨ 7-Eleven
⑩ Mosebacke
⑪ Södra Teatern
⑫ Lisbeth Salander's Apartment
⑬ Kvarnen
⑭ Sandhamn

Millennium fever has hit Stockholm big time, and the whole world, it seems, wants to see where the characters of Mikael Blomkvist and Lisbeth Salander, created by author Stieg Larsson, played out their particular drama. Take a walk around the streets, bars, and cafes of the Millennium trilogy books and films for a different view of gritty Södermalm. **START: T-bana to Slussen.**

Take in the view from Monteliusvägen.

1 ★★★ kids **Stockholms Stadsmuseum.** What better place to start than with the film set of the Millennium editorial office? It should get you in the mood. Buy the official map of the Millennium tour here (40 SEK). See box for Millennium tours. *See p 75,* **1**.

2 ★★★ **Bellmansgatan 1.** Now one of Stockholm's most famous addresses, this is where Blomkvist lived in an attic apartment. It's a Gothic fantasy of a building with a private bridge and wonderful views. The real entrance is at street level, but the entrance at the walkway depicted in the film is much more picturesque. *T-bana: Slussen. Bus: 43, 55.*

3 ★★★ **Monteliusvägen.** Take in the view, but also look over to Kungsholmen island and the **Rådhuset** with its light brown tower and green roof. This is the courthouse where Blomkvist is convicted of slander against Hans-Erik Wennerström and it all kicks off.

4 ★★★ **Tabbouli.** It's better known to Larsson aficionados as Samir's Cauldron, the Bosnian restaurant where the famous shoot-out takes place. It's shut during the day, but you might want to come back here for a thoroughly satisfying *meze* in the garden in the evening, without the guns. *Tavastagatan 22.* ☎ *08-429 82 55. www.tabbouli.eu.*

5 ★ **Lundabron.** It's not particularly attractive, nor is it meant to be. The Lunda bridge is between Blomkvist's apartment and Salander's, which was in an old building with no comforts. Most of these tenements were swept away in the 1970s when new apartments were built for the inhabitants, with running water and inside toilets. The bridge spans one of the places deliberately blown apart by dynamite in the 1880s (Nobel's great invention).

6 ★ **Mellqvist Coffee Bar.** One of the most important places in the

Millennium Tours

Guided Millennium tours take place in English on Saturdays at 11:30am and Wednesdays at 6pm from May through the summer. Winter walks in English leave on Saturdays at 11:30am. Tickets cost 120 SEK. Book at the Stadsmuseum, Slussen, ☎ 08-508 31 600, www.stadsmuseum.stockholm.se, or at the Stockholm Tourist Center, Vasagatan 14 or online at www.ticnet.se. The walk starts at Bellmansgatan 1 and takes between 1½ and 2 hours. For a private tour ☎ 08-508 316 59 or e-mail bokning.stadsmuseum@stockholm.se.

books where Blomkvist takes his various women. Larsson himself used it extensively when working at Expo's editorial offices in the same building and could be seen tapping away at his laptop. Despite the fame, it's friendly, laidback, and local with an outside terrace for winter and summer. *Hornsgatan 78. Small latte 30 SEK.*

7 ★★ **Synagogue.** Walk through Mariatorget, also used in the Swedish film, along St. Paulsgaten to the discreet building that is the Adat Jisrael Synagogue, one of Stockholm's oldest Orthodox synagogues set in an 18th-century building. Jewish Inspector Bublanski is a regular worshipper and meets with Dragan Armansky, CEO of Milton Security, here. *St. Paulsgatan 13.*

8 ★★ **Millennium's editorial offices.** This must be one of Stockholm's most photographed buildings. It's where Millennium has its editorial office, located above what was once Greenpeace's. *Corner of Götgatan and Hökens Gata.*

9 ★★ **7-Eleven.** Go in and buy a package of Billy's Pan Pizza and you must be the…well, 1,000th, 5,000th? visitor to do this. It has to be keeping Billy in business. This is where Salander shops after buying

her fantastic new apartment. *Götgatan 25.*

10 ★★ **Mosebacke.** The square was already pretty famous due to the Mosebacke theater, but it took Salander to bring the Nils Sjögren statue of *The Sisters* to general notice. It was inspired by the suicide of two girls in Hammarby Lake in the early 1900s. The official story is that they were in love with the same man; the more likely one was that they were in love with each other—of course, thoroughly impossible at the time.

Mellqvist Coffee Bar.

11 **Södra Teatern.** This is a wonderful bar and the place where Salander and her lawyer, Blomkvist's sister Giannini, have a beer at the end when all the drama is over. But was it? As Larsson intended many more books, it could have been the beginning of something… Have another beer and speculate. *Mosebacke torg 1–3.* 📞 *08-531 99 400. www.sodrateatern.com. Beer from 65 SEK.*

Nils Sjögren statue of The Sisters in Mosebacke.

12 ★★ **Lisbeth Salander's Apartment.** Who says that crime doesn't pay? Lisbeth Salander's apartment, bought out of the 3 billion dollars she makes through computer hacking, is a wonderful 21 rooms on the top floor of the building that you can see from all over Stockholm. When built in the 1920s it obscured the view of Katarina Church from the sea and was named the Scandal House as a result. Salander lives here under the name of V. Kulla, which, as fans will know, is short for Villa Villakulle, the name of Pippi Longstocking's house (see p 53). 🕐 *1 hr. Fiskargatan 9.*

13 **Kvarnen.** A lot happens at Kvarnen with Salander and the girls' rock band Evil Fingers, and it's also where Lisbeth kisses Miriam Wu. Pretty well anything goes here. (See p 128). *Tjarhovsgatan 4.* 📞 *08-643 03 80. www.kvarnen.com. Beer from 63 SEK.*

14 ★★★ **Sandhamn.** Hard-core fans can take the boat out into the archipelago to Sandhamn, where Blomkvist goes to escape the city. But his summer cottage is not marked, so go for the atmosphere and a good day out. *Cinderella boats leave from Strandvägen from mid-Apr to mid-June. www.cindarella batarna.com. For information on Sandhamn: www.sandhamn.com.*

Stieg Larsson

Stieg Larsson (1954–2004) was a Swedish writer and journalist known for his left-wing views. He was the driving force behind the Expo-foundation which aimed to expose neo-Nazi activity in Sweden and was editor-in-chief of the antiracism magazine *Expo* from 1999. He wrote three detective novels in his Millennium trilogy: *The Girl With The Dragon Tattoo*, *The Girl Who Played With Fire*, and *The Girl Who Kicked the Hornets' Nest* but died of a heart attack just after delivering the final manuscript. More than 50 million books have been sold; three Swedish films have been made, and the American versions, appearing in December 2011, 2012, and 2013, star Daniel Craig as Mikael Blomkvist and Rooney Mara as Lisbeth Salander. For more information go to www.stieglarsson.com. For the Swedish film producer of the first Millennium trilogy: www.yellowbird.se.

Stockholm with Kids

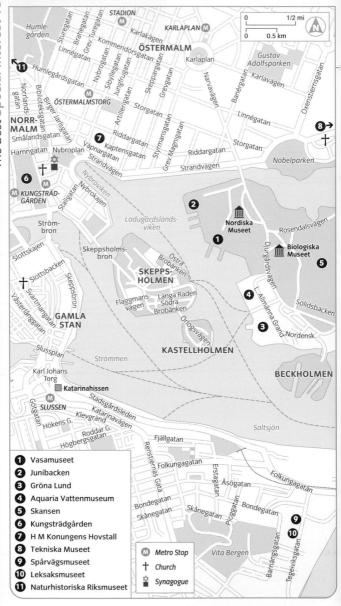

0   1/2 mi
0   0.5 km

STADION
KARLAPLAN
Humle-gården
Sturegatan
Brahegatan
Grev Turegatan
Karlakägen
Kommendörsgatan
ÖSTERMALM
Linnégatan
Karlaplan
Gustav Adolfsparken
Karlavägen
Humlegårdsgatan
Nybrogatan
Sibyllegatan
Skeppargatan
Grevgatan
Narvavägen
Banérgatan
Oxenstiernsgatan
Nordlandsgatan
Biblioteksgatan
Birger Jarlsgatan
ÖSTERMALMSTORG
Artillerigatan
Riddargatan
Storgatan
Styrmansgatan
Grev Magnigatan
Linnégatan
NORR-MALM
Smålandsgatan
Väpnargatan
Kaptensgatan
Riddargatan
Storgatan
Hamngatan
Nybroplan
Strandvägen
Strandvägen
Nobelparken
Nybroviken
KUNGSTRÄD-GÅRDEN
Stallgatan
Nybrokajen
Ladugårdslands-viken
Nordiska Museet
Rosendalsvägen
Biologiska Museet
Ström-bron
Skeppsholms-bron
Östra Brobänken
Djurgårdsvägen
L. Allmänna Grand
Slottskajen
SKEPPS-HOLMEN
Solidsbacken
Slottsbacken
Skeppsbron
Flaggmans-vägen
Långa Raden Södra Brobänken
Nordensk.
Svartmangatan
Västerlånggatan
GAMLA STAN
Örlogsvägen
KASTELLHOLMEN
BECKHOLMEN
Slussplan
Strömmen
Karl Johans Torg
Katarinahissen
SLUSSEN
Götgatan
Hökens G.
Stadsgårdsleden
Katarinavägen
Klevgränd
Roddar G.
Högbergsgatan
Fjällgatan
Saltsjön
Renstiernas Gata
Folkungagatan
Erstagatan
Åsögatan
Folkungagatan
Bondegatan
Skånegatan
Skånegatan
Picgatan
Bondegatan
Barnängsgatan
Tegelviksgatan
Vita Bergen

1. Vasamuseet
2. Junibacken
3. Gröna Lund
4. Aquaria Vattenmuseum
5. Skansen
6. Kungsträdgården
7. H M Konungens Hovstall
8. Tekniska Museet
9. Spårvägsmuseet
10. Leksaksmuseet
11. Naturhistoriska Riksmuseet

Ⓜ Metro Stop
✝ Church
⛩ Synagogue

S tockholm is one of the most child-friendly cities in Europe. Even museums are fun with entertainment and special rooms for drawing, painting, and dressing up. If all else fails, the great outdoors beckons at Gröna Lund, Sweden's oldest amusement park. This is a long day; I recommend you pick and choose. **START: Bus 47, Tram 7, ferry to Djurgården (summer).**

① ★★★ **kids Vasamuseet.** If you take them to only one 'grown-up' museum, make it the Vasa, where the old ship looms, huge and apparently invincible, above us mere mortals. ⏱ 1½ hr. See p 8, ③.

② ★★★ **kids Junibacken.** Even if your child hasn't heard of Astrid Lindgren (1907–2002), Sweden's most famous children's author, they'll love it here where her famous characters, Pippi Longstocking, Emil and the Lionheart Brothers, and others, live in their own wonderland. In Pippi's Villa Villekulla, children can ride her horse and play in her kitchen. The main action is a minitrain journey through some enchanted scenes in the stories. Ask for the English commentary. Take some distractions of your own because the lines in summer can be long. There's a good cafe and a

well-stocked shop. ⏱ 1 hr. *Galärvarvsvägen, Djurgården ☎ 08-587 230 00. www.junibacken.se. Adults 125 SEK (145 SEK at Christmas and summer holidays); children 2–15 years 110 SEK (125 SEK during Christmas and summer holidays); under-2s free. Free with Stockholm Card (see p 11). Jan–May, Sept–Dec, Tues–Sun 10am–5pm; June, Aug 10am–5pm; Jul 9am–6pm. Bus: 4, 69. Tram: 7. Ferry to Djurgården (summer).*

③ ★★★ **kids Gröna Lund.** This is a real favorite with children, so keep this one for the afternoon if you want to visit other attractions. Although many rides are not as terrifying as some modern parks (built in 1883 this family-owned amusement park is Sweden's oldest), the free-fall 'Power Tower', at 80m (262 ft) high and Europe's highest, challenges even the very brave. New

Thrills at Gröna Lund.

Wild brown bear and her cub in Skansen.

attractions include Twister, a wooden rollercoaster. Older rides are gentler and there are some for kids under 3 with parents. Evening concerts are held once a week. ⏲ *2 hr. Allmanna Grand 9.* ☎ *08-587 502 00. www.gronalund.com. Admission 90 SEK ages 7–64 years (more for evening concert); over-65s and under-7s free. Individual ride 20 SEK, multi-ride, all day passes from 299 SEK, under-3s free rides (height restrictions may apply). Free with Stockholm Card (see p 11). Summer times (May–Sept) vary between 11am–10pm and 11am–11pm; call for details. Closed end Sept–end Apr. Bus: 47. Tram: 7. Ferry to Djurgården (summer).*

④ ★ kids Aquaria Vattenmuseum. This imaginative aquarium takes you through different ecosystems. Step into a rainforest complete with thunderstorms and then walk over a rope bridge looking down at piranhas and catfish. There's a Nordic waters' display, and a glass tunnel where you're inches away from the sharks swimming. The intrepid can climb down into a sewer for a fish eye's view of what goes on underground—but you might prefer not to know. ⏲ *1 hr. Falkenbergsgatan 2.* ☎ *08-660 90 89. www.aquaria.se. Adults 90 SEK, children 6–15 years 50 SEK, children 3–5 years 25 SEK. Free with Stockholm Card (see p 11). Mid-June–end Aug 10am–6pm; Sept–mid-June Tues–Sun 10am–4:30pm. Bus: 47. Tram: 7. Ferry to Djurgården (summer).*

⑤ ★★★ kids Skansen. This will be the other attraction vying for your older children's attention; and the young ones will be enchanted by the zoo and particularly the bears. ⏲ *2 hr. See p 13.*

⑥ ★★ Kungsträdgården. The long esplanade that goes down to the water was once the royal kitchen garden. Today it's a delightful park with summer concerts, mime artists, and children's activities, such as a summer trampoline (50 SEK for 5 minutes). ⏲ *1 hr.*

⑦ ★★ H M Konungens Hovstall. Meet just before 2pm for a guided tour of one of the Royal

Mews, a working royal department. The King's coachmen show you around the beautiful working harnesses, the 40 19th- and 20th-century carriages, and the 14 large Swedish half-blood horses that you see exercising in the riding arena (they may be resting in the countryside in the summer). Plus, there's the garage with 11 royal cars. ⏲ *1 hr. Väpnargatan 1.* ☎ *08-402 61 06. www.kungahuset.se. Adults 50 SEK, children under 18 20 SEK. Free with Stockholm Card (see p 11). Guided tours only. End Jun–mid-Aug Mon–Fri 1pm; Aug 20–Dec 11, mid-Jan–end May Sat, Sun 2pm. T-bana: Östermalmstorg/Kungsträdgården. Bus: 47, 62, 69.*

⑧ ★★ kids Tekniska Museet. The Museum of Science and Technology is full of interactive exhibits geared to children, particularly in the Space section. When they're tired, take them to Cino 4 for a 4-D movie. The 4th dimension involves extra technical effects (see p 68, ⑤). ⏲ *1½ hr. Museivägen 7, Norra Djurgården.* ☎ *08-450 56 00. www.tekniskamuseet.se. Admission: Adults 160 SEK, children 7–18 years 95 SEK, free children 6 and under. Cino 4: adults 70 SEK; children 7–19 years 40 SEK. Free with Stockholm Card (p 11). Daily 10am–6pm (Wed to 8pm). Guided tours daily. Bus: 69.*

⑨ ★★ kids Spårvägsmuseet (Transport Museum). The 60 vehicles—from an 1877 horse-drawn tram to the transport of the future—really do keep children entertained. You can pretend to drive a 1960s' tram, ride a miniature underground, and buy Brio trains in the shop. ⏲ *1 hr. Tegelviksgatan 22.* ☎ *08-686 17 60. www.sparvags-museet.sl.se. Admission: Adults 40 SEK, children 7–18 years 20 SEK, free children 6 and under. Free with Stockholm Card (see p 11). Mon–Fri 10am–5pm, Sat, Sun 11am–4pm. T-bana: Slussen then bus 2, 66.*

⑩ ★★ kids Leksaksmuseet. At Stockholm's Toy Museum, exhibits change all the time, with new toys appearing like magic. Musical instruments, mechanical toys, models, dolls' houses, there's something from everybody's childhood here. It shares an entrance with the Transport Museum (see above). ⏲ *1½ hr. Tegelviksgatan 22 (same entrance as Spårvägsmuseet).* ☎ *08-641 61 00. www.leksaksmuseet.se. Admission: Adults 40 SEK, children 7–18 years 20 SEK, free under-7s. Free with Stockholm Card (see p 11). Mon–Fri 10am–5pm; Sat, Sun 11am–4pm. T-bana: Slussen then bus 2, 66.*

⑪ ★★ kids Naturhistoriska Riksmuseet. You can't miss the

Games in the energy section of the Tekniska Museet.

Huge creatures at the Natural History Museum.

enormous Natural History Museum. This huge building, designed by Axel Anderberg (1860–1937), who also designed the Royal Opera House (see p 83), is certainly dramatic. Completed in 1916, it's one of the 10 largest museums of its kind in the world with more than nine million objects, consisting of fungi, animals, minerals, and plants from all over the planet. It's divided into different exhibitions: *Life in Water* brings you up close to giant squid; meteorites from outer space are revealed in *Treasures from the Earth's Interior*; while *4.5 Billion Years* is quite simply the history of life on Earth, with dinosaurs to keep the children amused. The other excellent attraction is **Cosmonova**, Sweden's only IMAX 3-D cinema (see p 138). *Frescativägen 40.* ☎ *08-519 540 40. www.nrm.se. Tickets: Adults 80 SEK, free under-18s. Free with Stockholm Card (see p 11). Cosmonova: Adults 90 SEK, children 5–18 years 50 SEK. Exhibitions + one Cosmonova show: Adults 135 SEK, children 5–18 years 50 SEK. Tues–Fri 10am–6pm, Sat, Sun 11am–6pm. Last show at Cosmonova starts 1 hr before the museum closes. T-bana: Universitetet; bus 40, 540.* ●

Globen's Skyview

Take the family skyward in a 20-minute ride in a glass gondola on the outside of Globen, the largest spherical building in the world. You'll appreciate the views; and the family will get a kick from just looking down. Globen is the venue for rock concerts and ice hockey matches (see p 140). Globentorget 2. ☎ 07-718 110 00. www. globenarenas.se. Summer: June to August daily 9am to 9pm, rest of the year Monday to Friday 10am to 7pm, Saturday and Sunday 9:30am to 6pm. Tickets: Adults 120 SEK, children 3 to 12 years 90 SEK. Buy online to avoid queues or ☎ 07-714 546 00.

Gamla Stan & Riddarholmen

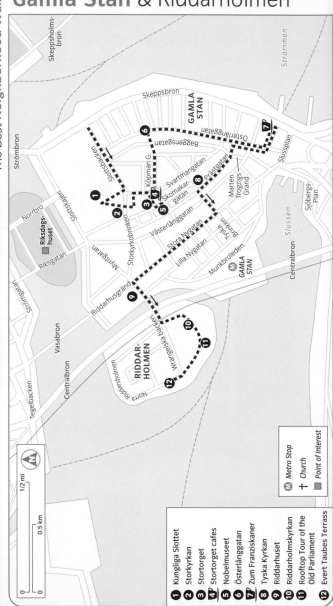

Metro Stop

† Church

■ Point of Interest

Previous page: St. Jacobs Kyrka.

In the 13th century the whole city, protected by a defensive castle, crowded onto the tiny island of Gamla Stan (Old Town). By the 18th century, 10,000 people lived in the city. Today it's a wonderful area of restored medieval and 18th-century houses, dominated by the huge Kungliga Slottet (Royal Palace). **START: Bus 2, 43, 55, 71, 76 to Kungliga Slottet. T-bana to Kungsträdgården and walk.**

❶ ★★★ kids Kungliga Slottet. Walk up to the Royal Palace from Skeppsbron and the statue of Gustav III, sculpted in 1799 in memory of the 'charming king' who was murdered in 1792. The magnificent palace should be on your must-do list (see p 9). 🕐 *2 hr.*

❷ ★★ Storkyrkan. Stockholm's 700-year-old cathedral is a striking, lofty building. Inside, it's a mix of styles: the medieval red tiles a background for the baroque royal chairs designed by Nicodemus Tessin the Younger (1654–1728) in 1684. Treasures include the 1489 *St. George and the Dragon* by Berndt Notke of Lübeck carved from oak and real elk antlers, and *The Parhelion* painting showing an extraordinary light phenomenon over Stockholm in 1535 with six sparkling rings of light in the skies—a sure sign, to superstitious medieval minds—of the end of the world. 🕐 *30 min. Trångsund 1.* ☎ *08-723 30 16.*

www.stockholmsdomkyrkoforsamling. se. Adults 40 SEK; free children 17 and under. Free with Stockholm Card (see p 11). Jan 1–Jul 1 & Sept 1– Dec 31 daily 9am–4pm; Jul 1–Aug 30 Mon–Fri 9am–6pm, Sun 9am–4pm. Services Sat, Sun 11am. T-bana: Gamla Stan. Bus: 2, 43, 55, 71, 76.

❸ ★★ Stortorget. This pretty medieval square was the scene of the notorious Stockholm Bloodbath. In November 1520 the Danish King Kristian II, who had defeated the Swedish Sten Sture the Younger, betrayed his promise of an amnesty. A feast at Tre Kronor Fortress ended with the arrest and execution the next day of more than 80 noblemen. Today the Nobel Museum (see below) looks over the square's cafes and terraces. 🕐 *15 min.*

❹ ★ Stortorget cafes. Forget the infamous Bloodbath over a fortifying cup of hot chocolate and a cake at **Chokladkoppen** (Stortorget 18

The cathedral from the narrow streets.

Mårten Trotzigs Gränd is the city's narrowest street.

☎ 08-20 31 70) or, if it's raining, dive into the next door Café Kaffekoppen. *Stortorget 20* ☎ *08-20 31 70. Hot chocolate and cake at both from around 60 SEK.*

⑤ ★★ kids Nobelmuseet. You start with an ingenious display of Nobel prizewinners whose biographies, printed on large banners, slowly circle the ceiling. There's plenty to occupy you in this small museum: short films about the laureates and TV clips on sets located in the floor. Listen to some of the acceptance speeches on headphones—don't miss the highly entertaining speech by Isaac Bashevis Singer (1902–91), who received the Nobel Prize for Literature in 1978. ⏰ *45 min. Börshuset, Stortorget.* ☎ *08-534 818 18. www. nobelmuseet.se. Adults 70 SEK; free*

children 17 and under. Free with Stockholm Card (see p 11). Daily guided tours in English 11:15am & 3pm. Mid-May–mid-Sept daily 10am– 6pm (Tues to 8pm); mid-Sept–mid-May Tues 11am–8pm, Wed–Sun 11am– 5pm. Closed public hols. T-bana: Gamla Stan. Bus: 2, 43, 55, 71, 76.

⑥ ★★ Österlånggatan. While tourists stick to Västerlånggatan, locals prefer to shop in and around Österlånggatan for its small boutiques. Don't miss the tiny alleyway that's a mere 90cm (less than 3 ft.) wide, called **Mårten Trotzigs Gränd** after a German merchant who cannily married the mayor's daughter and so ensured his place in history. ⏰ *30 min.*

⑦ ★ Zum Franziskaner. Claiming its place in history as Stockholm's oldest restaurant (1421), this rebuilt 1906 version looks pretty good with wooden floors, paneling, and 19th-century artifacts. Lunch, around 90 SEK, comes with a hot dish, bread, salad, and coffee. *Skeppsbron 44.* ☎ *08-411 83 30.*

⑧ ★★ Tyska Kyrkan. The splendid German church, also called St. Gertrude's, testifies to the power of the German Hanseatic League, whose trading empire from the 13th to late 17th century included Gamla Stan. The church, built between 1638 and 1642, has a royal gallery,

Parliament Tours

You can tour the present Parliament (Riksdag)—join in one of the free tours from late June to late August, every weekday at noon, 1pm, 2pm, and 3pm, and from October to early June, in English on Saturdays and Sundays at 1:30pm. Riksgatan 3, ☎ 08-786 48 62 (Mon–Thurs 9–11am), www.riksdagen.se.

a 1660s' pulpit, and a beautiful altar. ⏱ *30 min. Svartmangatan 16A.* ☎ *08-411 11 88. Wed, Fri, Sat noon–4pm, Sun 12:30–4pm. T-bana: Gamla Stan. Bus: 2, 43, 55, 71, 76.*

⑨ ★★ Riddarhuset. The House of the Nobility, one of northern Europe's most beautiful buildings, was built in the Dutch Renaissance style (1642–74) for the nobility. The inside is as beautiful as the exterior, with several halls, a magnificent double staircase, and the Knights' Room with a ceiling painted by David Klöcker Ehrenstrahl (1628–98). Approximately 2,320 coats-of-arms of the noble cover the walls. It's also a wonderful concert venue (p 137). ⏱ *30 min. Riddarhustorget 10.* ☎ *08-723 39 90. www. riddarhuset.se. Admission 50 SEK. Free with Stockholm Card (see p 11). Mon–Fri 11:30am–12:30pm. T-bana: Gamla Stan.*

⑩ ★★ Riddarholmskyrkan. Walk over Riddarholmsbron bridge onto tiny Riddarholm, deserted when the offices in the magnificent 17th-century noble palaces close. The ghost town feel extends to the 14th-century **Riddarholm** church where many of Sweden's monarchs lie buried. The walls are decorated with coats-of-arms, but also seek out the chapels. The Carolean chapel, built between 1671 and 1743, houses

Riddarholm is a tiny island.

Evert Taube entertains.

small ornate tombs to remind you of the frailty even of royal life. The tomb of the founder of the Bernadotte dynasty (the present Royal Family) and of Gustav Adolphus Magnus are particularly bombastic. ⏱ *40 min. Birger Jarls Torg.* ☎ *08-402 61 30. www.royalcourt.se. Adults 30 SEK; children 7–18 years 15 SEK, free aged 6 and under. Free with Stockholm Card (see p 11). Mid-May–mid-Sept 10am–5pm. Tours in English 2pm. T-bana: Gamla Stan.*

⑪ ★★ Rooftop Tour of the Old Parliament. If you've a head for heights and want to see the city from a bird's eye view, take a guided rooftop tour of the former Parliament building, complete with hard hats and harnesses. ⏱ *1¼ hr. Meet at Birger Jarls statue, Riddarholmen. Tickets only through www. upplevmer.se—book well in advance. Tickets 525 SEK (weight and height limits apply). Tours in English and/or Swedish/German Apr–end June Fri; July 1–Aug 31, Mon, Thurs, Fri, Sun. T-bana: Gamla Stan.*

⑫ ★★ Evert Taubes Terrass. End on the terrace steps, looking out onto the waters and Stadshuset (City Hall, p 10, ⑦). Romantics hang out here with a bottle of fizz beside the statue of Evert Taube (1890–1976), Sweden's much-loved singer and writer. ⏱ *40 min. Norra Riddarholmshamnen. T-bana: Gamla Stan.*

Djurgården

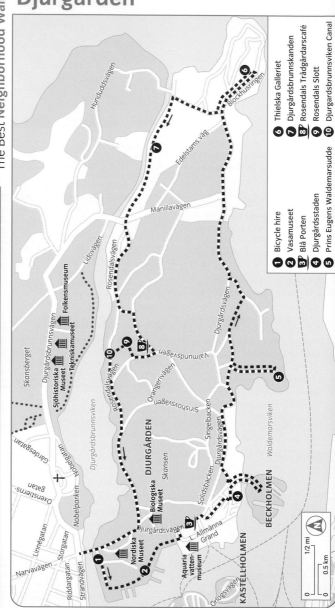

1 Bicycle hire
2 Vasamuseet
3 Blå Porten
4 Djurgårdsstaden
5 Prins Eugens Waldemarsudde
6 Thielska Galleriet
7 Djurgårdsbrunnskanden
8 Rosendals Trädgårdarscafé
9 Rosendals Slott
10 Djurgårdsbrunnsviken Canal

The former royal hunting ground on the delightful island of Djurgården (pronounced 'your-gore-den') is a green, forested area with very few houses. However, it does have some of Stockholm's best museums. To do the whole island, hire a bicycle. Or divide it into two parts and take public transport for part of it. **Bus 44, 47, tram 7, summer ferry to Vasamuseet.**

❶ Bicycle hire. Djurgårdsbrons Sjocafé just over the ornate iron bridge connecting Östermalm and Djurgården is a good place to hire a bicycle. Then cycle off down the relatively traffic-free roads and cycle paths around the island. *Galårvarvsvägen 2. ☎ 08-660 57 57. Open Mar–Oct 9am–9pm. Bikes are 80 SEK an hour, or 275 SEK for the day. ID required so take your passport. Bus: 47. Tram: 7. Ferry to Djurgården (summer).*

❷ ★★★ kids Vasamuseet. No matter how many times I see this ship, walking into the *Vasa* museum always sends a shiver down my spine. It's one of the world's great sights and I always find something new to discover on the ship itself or in the surrounding displays that explain what is an incredibly romantic story. 🕐 *2 hr. See p 8,* ❸.

❸ ★★ kids Blå Porten. The 'Blue Door' is well worth seeking out, hidden beside the contemporary art gallery, Liljevalchs Konsthall (see p 33, ❷). It's a delightful cafe with a wonderful secret garden, and is perfect for families. Get your food inside and your cakes from a groaning table and find a place outside. It's one of the best short stops if you're visiting any of the nearby museums. *Djurgårdsvägen 64. ☎ 08-663 87 59.www.blaporten.com. Coffee and cake around 60 SEK.*

❹ ★ Djurgårdsstaden. Get away from the crowds down the small streets on the south of the

Blå Porten is one of the city's most delightful outdoor cafes.

island. There aren't many old wooden houses left and most of them seem to be occupied by hi-tech firms, but the area gives you a very real idea of old Stockholm. Cross over to **Beckholmen**—a small island with dry docks used first for commercial boats and subsequently by the Swedish navy—where a local pitch boilery gave the island its name. It's still a working area, and with its old equipment recalls its former days.

❺ ★★ Prins Eugens Waldemarsudde. Go past the impossibly handsome and huge Italian Embassy, located in a house called Oakhill down beside the water, to this other huge waterside mansion, designed by Ferdinand Boberg

The garden at Prins Eugens Waldemarsudde.

(1860–1946) who also designed the NK Department Store (p 94). It was owned by Prins Eugens (1865–1947), the son of Oscar II and the younger brother of King Gustav V. Eugens was a noted artist and his former mansion is full of the landscapes for which he rightly became famous. He was also a great patron and so this patrician house is full of early 20th-century Swedish art. Temporary exhibitions of important artists are held on the upper floors. Even if you don't go for the art, the house is a tour in itself, and there's an excellent shop. ⏲ *1 hr. Prins Eugens Vag 6.* ☎ *08-545 837 00. www.waldemarsudde.se. Adults 90 SEK, free children 18 and under. Tues–Sun 11am–5pm (Thurs to 8pm). Closed Mon. Park open daily. Free with Stockholm Card (see p 11). Bus: 47. Tram: 7.*

If you're tired or have limited time, from here you can walk up to ⑧ and continue back to ⑩.

⑥ ★★ **Thielska Galleriet.** Seek out this wonderful example of a villa by architect Ferdinand Boberg (1860–1946) and its fascinating collection of Nordic art from the late 19th and early 20th centuries. Both belonged to the remarkably rich banker Ernest Thiel (1860–1947), who described himself as 'Something extremely surprising and dangerous for my time: a thinking banker.' However, all his intellect didn't save him from bankruptcy shortly after World War 1. The Swedish state then stepped in and bought both the house and the collection. All the major Swedish artists of Thiel's time are displayed here, plus works by Thiel's friend, Edvard Munch. It makes a fascinating gallery of works by—to foreign visitors at least—relatively unknown artists. ⏲ *1 hr. Sjötullsbacken 8.* ☎ *08-662 58 84. www.thielska-galleriet.se. Adults 80 SEK, free children 17 and under. Free with Stockholm Card (see p 11). Daily noon–4pm. Bus: 69.*

⑦ ★★ **Djurgårdsbrunnskanden.** Make your way north to where the Djurgårds canal empties into the sea. The route takes you beside the small canal, flanked by trees that turn the scene into an Impressionist painting. If you're tired and have no bicycle, the no. 69 bus from the Thielska Gallery will take you to the canal bridge. From here it's a short stroll to the next stop.

8 ★★ **Rosendals Trädgårdarscafé.** This pretty organic market garden, shop, and superb cafe seem to be in the middle of the countryside. The cafe is housed in a greenhouse and you can take your home-cooked meal or coffee into the garden and relax in a thoroughly rural setting, disturbed only by birdsong and children's voices. *Rosendalsterrassen 12.* ☎ *08-545 812 70. www.rosendalstradgard.se. Lunch dishes from 85 SEK.*

Stop for a coffee and organic food at Rosendals Trädgårdarscafé.

9 ★★ **kids** **Rosendals Slott.** The small, two-story high, royal summer retreat, built in the 1820s, was turned into a museum about the life of Karl XIV Johan (1818–44) in 1913. The palace was prefabricated in Norrmalm and constructed here. It's well worth visiting (guided tours only) for its Swedish furniture and textiles. Fabric in the dining room is pleated to make the room resemble a tent. You'll find wonderfully painted ceilings, tiled stoves, and odd, interesting artifacts throughout. ◷ *1 hr. Rosendalsvägen.* ☎ *08-402 61 30. www. royalcourt.se. Adults 70 SEK, children 7–18 years 35 SEK, free for 6 and under. Free with Stockholm Card (see p 11). End May–Aug 31 Tues–Sun guided tours only at noon, 1pm, 2pm & 3pm. Bus: 44 or 69.*

10 ★ **Djurgårdsbrunnsviken Canal.** From here walk or cycle along the quiet paths to the north of the island. Rosendalsvägen will take you back to the Djurgårds Bridge and over to Strandvägen, one of Stockholm's great boulevards.

Rosendals Slott.

Ladugårdsgärdet

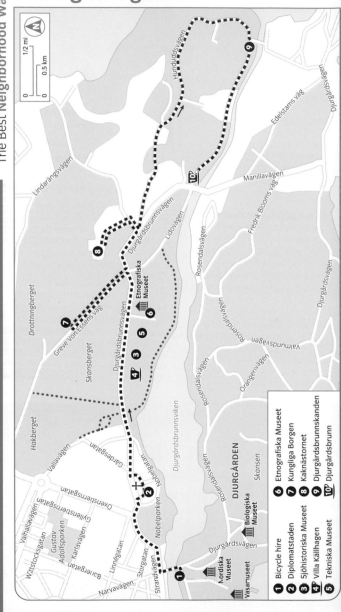

0 1/2 mi
0 0.5 km

1 Bicycle hire
2 Diplomatstaden
3 Sjöhistoriska Museet
4 Villa Källhagen
5 Tekniska Museet
6 Etnografiska Museet
7 Kungliga Borgen
8 Kaknästornet
9 Djurgårdsbrunnskanden
10 Djurgårdsbrunn

Ladugårdsgärdet is the greenest part of Gärdet, an extensive residential neighborhood mainly built up in the 1920s and 1930s with Functionalist apartments for workers. Along the south shore lies a series of good museums. **START: Bus no. 69 to Nobelparken for Diplomatstaden. Bus 47, tram 7 or summer ferry to Djurgården for bicycle hire.**

1 ★★ **kids** **Bicycle hire.** See p 25, **1** for details on the Djurgårdsbrons Sjocafé on Djurgården, just over the bridge from Östermalm, which is the nearest place for bicycle rental. *Galärvarvsvägen 2.* ☎ *08-660 57 57. Open Mar–Oct 9am–9pm. Bus 47. Tram 7. Ferry to Djurgården (summer).*

2 **Diplomatstaden.** As you can guess from the name, you'll find various foreign residencies in this area, a move that started when the British ambassador took over Nobelgatan 7 in 1910. To the south lies the small **Nobelparken**, named after Alfred Nobel (1833–96); a little farther along Dag Hammarskjölds Vag you come to the brick **Engelska Kyrkan** (English Church) that was moved from the city center out to here in 1913, although it was only finished in the 1980s. ⏱ *30 min.*

3 ★★ **kids** **Sjöhistoriska Museet.** This lovely building housing the National Maritime Museum stands beside a quiet stretch of water. The peaceful setting seems a far cry from the warlike maritime history that made Sweden the ruling power in much of northern Europe and the Baltic Sea from 1611 to 1721. As well as Sweden's maritime history, the museum tells the stories of shipbuilding in Sweden and of life on board. There's also a splendid maritime art collection as well as regularly changing exhibitions. ⏱ *1½ hr. See p 26,* **5**.

4 ★★ **kids** **Villa Källhagen.** Double back a few hundred meters to the delightful hotel and restaurant for a proper lunch looking out over the sea. Or just take the

Sculpture in Nobelparken.

Royal Connections

This leafy green area's royal associations began in the 15th century with a royal farm. It lost its original purpose and King Karl XI (1655–97) built a fort, the Kungliga Borgen, here in 1672. The area was subsequently used for military training of royal troops. In 1820 Karl XIV commissioned another building from the soldier-architect Fredrik Blom which burnt down in 1977 but was entirely rebuilt in the old style. The area is now a summer playground, used for fun runs and kite-flying and you'll always see horse riders and dog walkers here. It forms part of the Nationalstads park and is one of the main places on the Historical Bike Ride route (see p 108).

excellent shrimp sandwich (185 SEK). *Djurgårdsbrunnsvägen 10.* ☎ *08-665 03 00. www.kallhagen.se. Main dishes from 185–310 SEK.*

⑤ ★★ kids Tekniska Museet. The National Museum of Science and Technology is designed with families in mind. It presents the history of Swedish technology and industry in an exciting way in a series of changing exhibitions. You'll discover commercial aircraft, early Swedish cars from Saab, Scania, and Volvo, motorbikes, and a working model railway. Most families gravitate toward Teknorama, the museum's science center, where you can try various experiments at your own pace. The *Inventions of Women* exhibit shows inventions by women, both world-famous and those by housewives. Then it's on to the Mine, which is suitably spooky and underground. Finally, Sweden's only 4-D cinema, Cino 4, has daily shows in English. ⏲ *2 hr. See p 55,* **⑧**.

⑥ ★★ kids Etnografiska Museet. One of the first things you see at the National Museum of Ethnography is a sculpture made out of old suitcases. In an increasingly technology-dominated world, it's a nice reminder of how so many of the valuable artifacts displayed in the museum were painstakingly brought back by travelers and scientists from

The Japanese Teahouse at the Etnografiska Museet.

The lofty Kaknästornet tower dominates the skyline.

the 18th century on—the explorer Sven Hedin (1865–1952) was one of the main contributors of Buddhas and Chinese artifacts. The museum is inventively laid out, placing its masks and ceramics, totem poles and statues, canoes and huts in delightful settings. The *First Nations of North America* exhibit has the expected history but also shows odd aspects such as schooling Native American children to be white. In the gardens the secluded **Japanese Teahouse,** Zui-Ki-Tei (Pavilion of Auspicious Light), following the designs of a Japanese professor, was built here in 1990. ⏱ *1½ hr. Djurgårdsbrunnsvägen 34.* ☎ *08-519 550 00. www.etnografiska. se. Free admission. Mon–Fri 10am– 5pm (Wed to 8pm), Sat, Sun 11am– 5pm. Closed public hols. Bus: 69.*

❼ Kungliga Borgen. If you have the time and energy, strike north along Greve von Essens Vag to Kungliga Borgen, originally the fortress where generations of monarchs trained their troops. Today there's a restaurant on the site used for receptions and parties. ⏱ *30 min.*

❽ Kaknästornet. On a clear day, this dominant tower, 155m (508 ft.) high, gives a dramatic view across 60km (37 miles) of capital and countryside from its observation points

30 and 31 floors up. The huge tower was opened in 1967 as the major broadcast beacon for almost all radio and TV signals in the country and now provides satellite connections between European cities via five huge and daunting-looking dishes on the ground. To savor the view, you can linger over a coffee or a meal in the 28th-floor restaurant. ⏱ *30 min. Mörka Kroken 28–30.* ☎ *08-667 21 05. www.kaknastornet.se. Adults 45 SEK, children 7–15 years 20 SEK. Free with Stockholm Card (see p 11). Free with restaurant booking. Mon–Sat 10am–9pm, Sun to 6pm. Bus: 69.*

❾ Djurgårdsbrunnskanden. From here you can do a circular walk, taking around 25 to 30 minutes, along Hundudsvägen to where the Djurgård canal reaches the sea, and return beside the still waters of the canal to a small bridge that connects this area with Djurgården. ⏱ *25–30 min.*

🔟 ★★ kids Djurgårdsbrunn. This is just the place for a coffee beside the canal, feeling away from it all. It's remarkably relaxed and you might see the odd horse and cart trot by. Then take the no. 69 bus back into town. *Djurgårdsbrunnsvägen 68.* ☎ *08-624 22 00. www.djurgardsbrunn.com. Coffee and cakes around 70 SEK.*

Chill out at Djurgårdsbrunn.

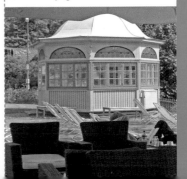

Eastern **Södermalm**

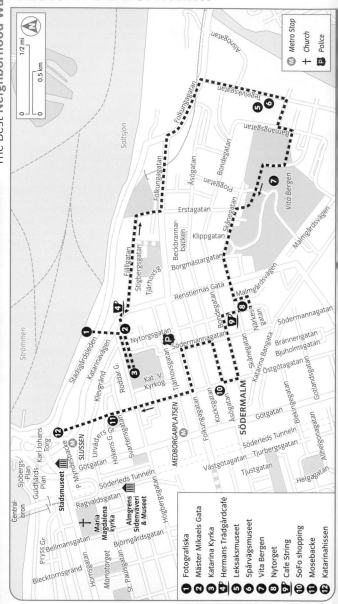

Metro Stop
+ Church
P Police

1 Fotografiska
2 Mäster Mikaels Gata
3 Katarina Kyrka
4 Hermans Trädgårdcafé
5 Leksaksmuseet
6 Spårvägsmuseet
7 Vita Bergen
8 Nytorget
9 Cafe String
10 SoFo shopping
11 Mosebacke
12 Katarinahissen

Södermalm, familiarly known as 'Söder', is a large island and traditionally was the working-class area of Stockholm. Then industry left and the place declined until its discovery first by artists, then the young. This long walk will take you to Söder's small boutiques, cafes, restaurants and late-night clubs. **START: T-bana to Slussen.**

❶ ★★★ Fotografiska. Walk from Slussen along Stadsgårdsleden to this huge new museum housed in an Art Nouveau industrial building of 1906. Both international names and up-and-coming photographers are showcased in a dynamic changing series of exhibitions. Fotografiska is adding hugely to Stockholm's reputation as a European cultural center. There's also a very good restaurant with views over to Djurgården and beyond. ⏱ 1½ hr. See p 21, ❻.

❷ ★★ Mäster Mikaels Gata. Walk up the steep steps just to the west of the museum on the opposite side (ask at the gallery for directions) to Karlinavägen and great views of Stockholm's waterside below. Walk along Mäster Mikaels Gata (named after the city's first employed executioner) for a glimpse of the 18th-century houses built after the disastrous fire in 1723. ⏱ 20 min.

❸ ★★ Katarina Kyrka. The modern altar is the only outward sign of the complete rebuild of this church in 1995, after a disastrous fire in 1990 destroyed its impressive baroque interior. The reconstruction used 17th-century building techniques to reproduce the original church, designed by Jean de la Vallée (1620–96), as faithfully as possible. It followed the central plan established in Maria Magdalena (see p 75, ❹) where both altar and nave are located in the middle of the building. Outside, the peaceful cemetery contains the simple grave of Anna Lindh, Sweden's foreign minister murdered in 2003. In summer, the church puts on a good program of concerts, or visit at lunchtime to listen to the organ and take in the beauty of your surroundings. ⏱ 20 min. Högbergsgatan 13. ☎ 08-743 68 40. www.svenskakyrkan.se/ katarina. Mon–Fri 11am–5pm, Sat, Sun 10am–5pm. Free admission. T-bana: Medborgarplatsen.

Katarina Kyrka high on Södermalm.

4 ★ **Hermans Trädgårdcafé.**
Walk back to Fjällgatan. Freshly
made, inventive salads at the lunchtime buffet and a spectacular view
make Herman's a real attraction. Or
just sit with a coffee and cake taking
in the sight of Djurgården and Gröna
Lund opposite. *Fjällgatan 23.*
☎ *08-643 94 80. www.hermans.se.*
Buffet 88–100 SEK.

5 ★★ **kids Leksaksmuseet.** No
matter where you come from—
Sweden, the U.S.A., Mars—children's toys are pretty universal and
so the well-established Toy Museum
will delight everyone. It's a large collection arranged in sections of
steam engines, trains (always a
favorite), cars, airplanes, peep-
shows, teddy bears, and dolls,
including 16th-century dolls'
houses. 🕐 1½ hr. See p 55, **10**.

6 ★ **kids Spårvägsmuseet.**
From the early days of public transport in Stockholm and the first
horse-drawn tram of 1877 to the
future of transport; it's all here.
You'll also find information on the
T-bana stations that have been decorated by artists, turning them into
their own artworks. The museum
itself is housed in an old bus station
and, as at all transport museums,
the sight of more than 60 trams,
buses, and carriages from the late
1880s on captivates a child's imagi-
nation. 🕐 1 hr. See p 55, **9**.

7 ★★ **Vita Bergen.** Walk down
Renstiernasgata, turn left on Bondegatan and right on Borgmästergatan
to Skånegatan. Ahead of you is a hilly
park (translated as 'White Moun-
tains'). It's crowned by **Sofia Kyrka,**
the church named after Sofia of Nas-
sau (1836–1913), Queen Consort of
Sweden from 1872 to 1907. The
design won an architectural contest
in 1899 and it opened in 1906. It's
surrounded by a handful of old

red-painted, wooden houses once
owned by the working classes. Today
they are highly desirable, particularly
as they are near that sought-after
accessory of the young professional,
an allotment. 🕐 45 min.

8 ★ **Nytorget.** Stop in this pretty
garden square that has a street of
old houses running off it. The little
park is a local hit, full of children playing and parents organizing picnics.

9 ★ **Café String.** As laidback as
you could ever want, the last time I
was at this cafe I shared the place
with a group of friends, locals playing an endless game of cards, a guy
on his laptop perched on a chair on
(yes, on) the windowsill, and a couple who were clearly in the throes
of a burgeoning love affair. This
attractive, quirky venue offers sandwiches, drinks, and coffee—and all
the furniture to buy and take home
should you need a table and chairs
or even a motorbike to go with your
latte. *Nytorgsgatan 38.* ☎ *08-714
85 14. www.cafestring.com. Sandwiches 40–50 SEK.*

*The laidback Café String where every-
thing is for sale.*

Great plastic kitsch at coctail.

⑩ ★★ **SoFo shopping.** Okay, you've heard all about it, so now's the time to go shopping in the area. My advice is to wander at will in the streets. If you're a fan of the past, head to **Bondegatan.** For a good selection of secondhand and vintage clothing try the famous **Lisa Larsson Secondhand** (no. 43). Also worth seeking out is **coctail** (no. 34) for some honest-to-goodness kitsch. Get your sweet fix at **Chokladfabriken** at Renstiernas Gata 12, and for one of the best art and architecture bookshops in Stockholm, try **konst-ig** at Asögatan 124. ⏱ *1½ hr.*

⑪ ★ **Mosebacke.** This small area high up at the top of the Katarinahissen elevator became famous for entertainment in the 1850s with carousels, a summer theater, and open-air dance floors. A permanent theater was put up in 1859 along with the gateway leading onto Mosebacke Terrass. The theater's fortunes waxed and waned until it closed in 1958 for complete renovation. It reopened in 1967 as **Södra Teatern** and has never looked back. Beside it stands **Mosebacke Etablissement,** one of Stockholm's best live music and performance venues. The cafe/bar provides a great summer spot on the outside terrace—I like to order a glass of wine or a coffee, mingle with the musicians who are invariably hanging out here, and look out over the stunning view. ⏱ *15 min.*

⑫ ★★ **Katarinahissen.** Take in the view from this huge elevator then take it down to Slussen. ⏱ *1 min (plus 15 min wait). See p 20, ❸.*

West Södermalm & **Långholmen**

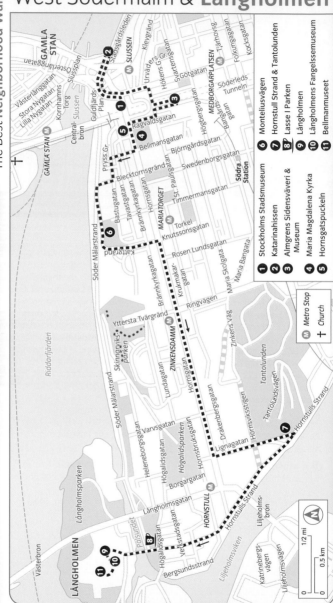

GAMLA STAN

Österlånggatan

Västerlånggatan
Stora Nygatan
Lilla Nygatan

Kornhamns
Torg

SLUSSEN

Stadsgårdsleden

Klevgränd

Urväders Gränd

Hökens G.

Svartensgatan

Götgatan

MEDBORGARPLATSEN

Tjärhovsg.

Folkungagatan

Kocksgatan

Söderleds
Tunneln

Central-
bron

Slussen

Guldfjärds
Plan

Rågvaldsgatan

Bellmansgatan

Björngårdsgatan

Högbergsgatan

Bangårds-
gatan

Bangård

GAMLA STAN

Pryss Gr.

Blecktornsgränd

Swedenborgsgatan

Södra
Station

Bastugatan

Tavastgatan

Brännkyrkagatan

Hornsgatan

St. Paulsgatan

Timmermansgatan

MARIATORGET

Riddarfjärden

Söder Mälarstrand

Kattgränd

Torkel
Knutssonsgatan

Rosen Lundsgatan

Yttersta Tvärgränd

Skinnarviks-
parken

Lundagatan

ZINKENSDAMM

Hornsgatan

Brännkyrkagatan

Krukmakar-
gatan

Maria Skolgata

Ringvägen

Zinkens Väg

Maria Bangata

Tantolunden

Tantolundsvägen

Långholmsparken

Söder Mälarstrand

Heleneborgsgatan

Varvsgatan

Högalidsparken

Hornsbruksgatan

Drakenbergsgatan

Hornsviksstigen

Lignagatan

Hornstulls Strand

Hornstulls Strand

Borgargatan

Högalidsgatan

HORNSTULL

Långholmsgatan

Västerbron

LÅNGHOLMEN

Pålsundet

Högalidsgatan

Verkstadsgatan

Bergsundsstrand

Katrineberg-
vägen

Liljeholms-
bron

Liljeholmsviken

Liljeholmsvägen

Metro Stop ⓜ

Church ✝

1/2 mi

0.5 km

N

1 Stockholms Stadsmuseum
2 Katarinahissen
3 Almgrens Sidensväveri & Museum
4 Maria Magdalena Kyrka
5 Hornsgatspuckeln

6 Montelíusvägen
7 Hornstull Strand & Tantolunden
8 Lasse I Parken
9 Långholmen
10 Långholmens Fangelssemuseum
11 Bellmanmuseet

Whereas eastern Södermalm is the edgier part of the island, western Söder is more residential. It's very green as well, with the large Tantolunden Park in the southwest corner. This is where Stockholmers gather to picnic and swim in summer and bring their sledges in winter. You can combine this with Stieg Larsson's Millennium trilogy walk (p 48). START: T-bana to Slussen.

Steep streets characterize Södermalm.

① ★★ kids Stockholms Stadsmuseum. Appropriately for a city museum, the building, completed in 1685, has served as the City Hall, then as law courts and prison, schools, and a tavern. It was designed by Nicodemus Tessin the Elder (1615–81) and became a museum in the 1930s. This imaginative museum uses smells and sounds, as well as artifacts, pictures, and maps to demonstrate Stockholm through the centuries, from the Stockholm Bloodbath of 1520 to huge growth in the 20th century. ⏱ *45 min. Ryssgården. www.stadsmuseum.stockholm.se. ☎ 08-508 316 00. Free admission. Tues–Sun 11am–5pm, Thurs to 8pm. Closed Mon. T-bana: Slussen.*

② ★★ Katarinahissen. Most visits to Söder start or end at the top of the 37m (124 ft.) high elevator that whisks you up in a few seconds to a glorious view over Stockholm laid out below you. ⏱ *1 min (plus 15 min wait). See p 20, ③.*

③ ★ kids Almgrens Sidensväveri & Museum. You normally don't associate Sweden with silk weaving, but in 1833, the enterprising Knut August Almgren opened a factory based on a secret technique of silk weaving that he ingeniously stole from the French while visiting Lyon. For decades he was the largest employer of female labor, offering his workforce healthcare, pensions, and a cooperative shop. Swedish high society adored the sensuous new material and the Almgren family carried on satisfying their fashionable clientele until 1974 when the factory closed. In 1991, a descendant of the original owner reopened the factory as a working museum. Today you can discover the story and watch the 170-year-old looms in action. The shop sells silk scarves and fabric. ⏱ *45 min. Repslagargatan 15. ☎ 08-642 56 16. www.kasiden.se. Adults 65 SEK, free for children 11 and under. Free with Stockholm Card (see p 11). Summer Mon–Sat 11am–3pm; Winter Mon–Fri 10am–4pm, Sat, Sun 11am–3pm. Guided tours (in Swedish) Wed, Sat, Sun 1pm, Mon 1pm, 6pm. T-bana: Slussen.*

④ Maria Magdalena Kyrka. Söder's oldest church was started in 1580, but not completed until the early 17th century. Its central plan is the model for all of Stockholm's later glorious baroque churches. Today it is rather marooned in its commanding position but the short distance away from the main road gives its graveyard a particularly peaceful feel. Some of Sweden's poets are buried here, the best known outside Sweden being the troubadour, Evert Taube (see p 61, **12**). 🕐 *15 min. St. Paulsgatan 10.* 📞 *08-462 29 40. www.maria magdalena.se. Mon, Tues, Thurs–Sun 11am–5pm, Wed to 7:30pm. T-bana: Slussen.*

5 **Hornsgatspuckeln.** Cross over the road to the small elevated, traffic-free section of Hornsgatan for a good selection of art and design galleries. Try **blås&knåda** (no. 26) for a wide variety of modern ceramics and jewelry; **Gallery Kontrast** (no. 8) for photography, and **The Glassery** (no. 38) for some startling and innovative glass items. The glamorous **Efva Attling** (no. 42) designs modern jewelry, and counts Madonna among her clients. 🕐 *45 min.*

6 **Monteliusvägen.** Walk down Guldfjardsterrassen to the sheltered path along Monteliusvägen, high above Söder Mälarstrand. You're

Unusual glass at blås&knåda.

rewarded with great views over the water and an idea of what old Södermalm was like. Small stone houses cluster in the narrow streets and alleyways and there's a little park full of mothers and children in the summer months. 🕐 *30 min.*

7 ★★ **kids** **Hornstull Strand & Tantolunden.** Take the T-bana from Mariatorget to Hornstull and walk south to the waterside area along Hornstull Strand. It no longer houses the trendy street market, but there's always something happening along here and it's full of cafes. The website is in Swedish, but gives you an idea of what is going on. Then chill out in Tantolunden's green spaces. 🕐 *1½ hr. Hornstull Strand 4. www.hornstullstrand.se.*

8 ★★ **kids** **Lasse I Parken.** On a road leading down to the small bridge that crosses onto Långholmen, this charming restaurant is tucked away in its own garden. It's the perfect place for an alfresco coffee or casual lunch, and looks and feels more like a private house than a restaurant. *Högalidsgatan 56.* 📞 *08-658 33 95. www.lasseiparken. se. T-bana: Hornstull. Main dishes 187–245 SEK.*

9 ★★ **kids** **Långholmen.** Walk directly north to the delightful island of Långholmen, separated from Södermalm by a small stretch of water crammed with moored boats. From 1724 to 1975 the island housed a large prison, which preserved Långholmen's peace from large-scale development. It's something of a green oasis, with a walking and cycling path and places to swim on the north shore, including the small sandy Klippbadet cove. 🕐 *2 hr.*

Sandy cove on Långholmen.

⑩ ★ kids Långholmens Fangelssemuseum. The prison museum is housed inside what is now the Långholmen Hotel (see p 150). There were originally two prisons on the island, with around 700 cells, housing the usual murderers and thieves as well as journalists and politicians who had fallen foul of society. The last execution in Sweden took place here in 1910, using the guillotine that you can see, along with 300 years of Swedish prison history. ⏱ *20 min. Långholmen Hotel, Långholmsmuren 20.* ☎ *08-720 85 00. www.langholmen.com. Adults 25 SEK, children 7–14 years 10 SEK, free children 6 and under. Daily 11am–4pm. T-bana: Hornstull then walk. Bus: 4, 40 then walk.*

⑪ Bellmanmuseet. Given the fame of the 18th-century troubadour Carl Michael Bellman (1740–95), it's surprising there are so few places associated with him. So try to visit this late 17th-century house that contains a small museum devoted to him. He didn't live here, but frequently visited an opera singer friend who worked in the prison. The museum's cafe is a good place for a spot of light refreshment if you've decided to swim from the small nearby beach. ⏱ *45 min. Stora Henriksvik.* ☎ *08-669 69 69. Adults 30 SEK, free children 14 and under. May–Jun, Sept Sat, Sun noon–4pm; Jul–Aug daily noon–6pm. T-bana: Slussen. Bus: 4, 40, 66.*

A model on guard at the the old prison on Långholmen.

Östermalm

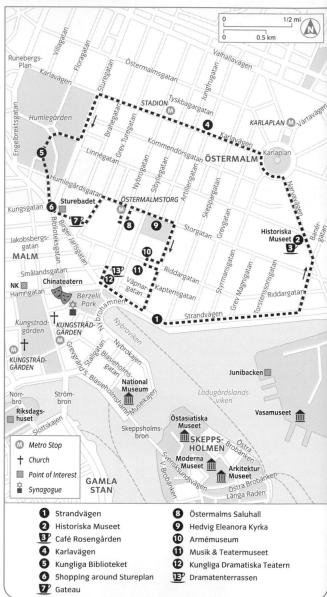

| 0 | | 1/2 mi |
| 0 | 0.5 km | |

1 Strandvägen
2 Historiska Museet
3 Café Rosengården
4 Karlavägen
5 Kungliga Biblioteket
6 Shopping around Stureplan
7 Gateau

8 Östermalms Saluhall
9 Hedvig Eleanora Kyrka
10 Armémuseum
11 Musik & Teatermuseet
12 Kungliga Dramatiska Teatern
13 Dramatenterrassen

Legend:
- Ⓜ Metro Stop
- † Church
- ▪ Point of Interest
- ✡ Synagogue

Östermalm developed in the 1870s when an expanding city pushed Stockholm north.

Östermalm developed in the 1870s when an expanding city pushed Stockholm north. Modeled on Paris, Östermalm was intended as the playground of the rich, with wide boulevards of elegant houses, squares, and avenues. Today it has the best art galleries, exclusive designer boutiques, and a lively nightlife.
START: **T-bana to Östermalmstorg.**

① ★★ Strandvägen. One of the new boulevards built between 1880 and 1910, this is posh Stockholm at its most gracious. Lime trees separate the sea from the grand Italian and French Renaissance style houses. You'll also find two of Stockholm's most famous interior design stores, **Carl Malmsten** (no. 5b) and **Svenskt Tenn** (no. 5), ideally placed for their wealthy clients. ⏱ *15 min.*

② Historiska Museet. The Museum of National Antiquities was once rather fusty and old-fashioned. Now the pre-history section is about as cutting-edge as you can get. Like the children around me, I found it fascinating, with the exhibits grouped together to tell human stories from the Stone, Bronze, and Iron Ages via a question-and-answer approach. It's done in such a way to show that our ancestors had very much the same concerns, fears, and hopes as we do today. The fearsome reputation of the Vikings (see box, p 27) is also dealt with; in fact most

were farmers and traders. The Gold Room houses a spectacular collection of Sweden's gold and silver treasures from collars to crowns—it's helped by the law that any finds made from gold, silver, or copper alloys can only be bought by the State. ⏱ *1½ hr. Narvägen 13–17. ☎ 08-519 556 00. www.historiska.se. Adults 70 SEK, free for children 17 and under. Free with Stockholm Card (see p 11). May 1–Sept 30 daily 10am–5pm; Oct 1– Apr 30 Tues–Sun 11am–5pm (Thurs to 8pm). T-bana: Karlaplan.*

③ ★ Café Rosengården. The museum cafe is welcoming and in summer you can take your coffee and sandwiches outside into the rose garden. You can eat here without going into the museum if you are passing. *Coffee and sandwiches from 90 SEK.*

④ Karlavägen. Walk up Narvägen to Karlavägen, two of the four great boulevards that, along with

The Strandvägen waterfront.

Strandvägen (see ❶) and Valkhallavägen, defined late 19th-century Östermalm. Karlavägen is one of the many parts of the city with an outdoor sculpture gallery—the north side of Humlegården has works such as *Living Iron* by Willy Gordon at Sturegatan, and *The City* by Lars Erik Husbert at Engelbrektsgatan. 🕑 *15 min.*

❺ ★ **Kungliga Biblioteket.** The Royal Library is Sweden's copyright library and has received a copy of every book printed in Sweden since 1661. With more than 3 million books and magazines, half a million posters, 300,000 maps, and portraits and pictures, it's a formidable collection. The library, originally built between 1865 and 1878 but twice expanded, stands in Humlegården, the original hop garden for the royal household created by Gustav II Adolf in 1619. 🕑 *30 min. Humlegården.* ☎ *08-463 40 00. www.kb.se. Free admission. Jan–end May, Sept–end Dec Mon–Thurs 9am–8pm, Fri 9am–7pm, Sat 10am–5pm; beginning June–mid-Aug Mon–Thurs 9am–6pm, Fri 9am–5pm, Sat 11am–3pm. T-bana: Östermalmstorg.*

❻ ★★ **Shopping around Stureplan.** Smart Stockholm comes to shop around Stureplan. Walk down Birger Jarlsgaten and then turn into Bibliotekesgatan and Grev Turegatan for antiques, designer fashion, and jewelry. This area has a concentration of top names from **Georg Jensen** to the casual denim of **Acne.** Don't forget **Sturegallerian** (p 17, ❽)— a world-class shopping mall built around the Jugendstil Sturebadet spa. 🕑 *1 hr. T-bana: Östermalmstorg.*

7 ★ **Gateau.** In Sturegallerian, make your way upstairs to the cafe where a snack adds at least a couple of inches to your waistline. *Sturegallerian, Stureplan.* ☎ *08-611*

47 57. www.gateau.se. Branches all over Stockholm. Coffee and cake around 60 SEK.

❽ ★★★ **Östermalms Saluhall.** The chic food hall is one of Stockholm's great attractions. 🕑 *30 min. See p 14,* ❸.

❾ ★ **Hedvig Eleonora Kyrka.** The church opened in 1737 for the Swedish Navy. Inside, the light interior houses the altarpiece *Jesus on the Cross*, painted in 1738 by Georg Engelhard Schröder (1684–1750), and a splendid neoclassical pulpit. Although the organ is new, its facade was designed by Carl Fredrik Adelcrantz in 1762. Today, the church is well known for its regular classical music concerts (see p 139). 🕑 *30 min. Storgatan 2.* ☎ *08-663 04 30. Daily 11am–6pm. T-bana: Östermalmstorg.*

❿ ★★ **kids Armémuseum.** The Army Museum has been located in this former arsenal since 1879. The three-story white building houses a formidable history of 1,000 years of bloody warfare that, given Sweden's reputation for neutrality, comes as a slight shock, but empires are not

Hedvig Eleonora Kyrka.

Cavalry charge in the Army Museum.

won by wimps and peaceful means. The displays start on the top floor with the Viking Age and the Thirty Years War then descend to the 20th century, much of it displayed in life-size settings. ⏱ *1 hr. Riddargatan 13.* ☎ *08-519 563 01. www.arme museum.org Adults 80 SEK, free children 17 and under. Free with Stockholm Card (see p 11). Tues 11am–8pm, Wed–Sun 11am–5pm; July, Aug Tues 10am–8pm, Mon, Wed–Sun 10am–5pm. Guided tour in English at noon, Jul & Aug. T-bana: Östermalmstorg.*

⓫ ★★ **kids Musik & Teatermuseet.** If you're at all musical this small museum with around 6,000 instruments can give you hours of fun. There are some eccentric displays of instruments, placed as if they were being played, and with enough information to satisfy without overwhelming you. The real fun comes downstairs where you can try a range of instruments from a harp to an electric guitar. ⏱ *1 hr. Sibyllegatan 2.* ☎ *08-519 554 90. www. musikmuseet.se. Adults 50 SEK, free children 18 and under. Free with Stockholm Card (see p 11). Tues–Sun noon–5pm. Closed Mon. T-bana: Kungsträdgården/ Östermalmstorg.*

⓬ ★★ **Kungliga Dramatiska Teatern.** Built between 1902 and 1908 in Jugendstil style, the theater's white marble facade and bright gilded statues make it a work of art in its own right. Carl Milles (1875–1955) created the large sculptural group in the center section; Theodor Lundberg (1852–1926) produced the golden statues of Poetry and Drama, and Carl Larsson (1853–1919) painted the ceiling in the foyer of this gorgeous landmark, popularly known just as Dramaten. See also p 140. ⏱ *1 hr. Nybrogatan 2.* ☎ *08-665 61 00. www.dramaten.se. Guided tours call for details. Free with Stockholm Card (see p 11). T-bana: Kungsträdgården/ Östermalmstorg.*

⓭ ★★ **Dramatenterrassen.** You can eat at Dramaten without attending a performance. Good Swedish dishes are the order of the day. The walls are painted by Georg Pauli (1855–1935), there's a portrait of Ingmar Bergman, and a summer terrace with views. *Nybrokajen.* ☎ *08-665 62 66. www.profilrestauranger. se/dramaten/. Club sandwich is 175 SEK.*

The flamboyant 'Dramaten' Theater.

Norrmalm & **Vasastaden**

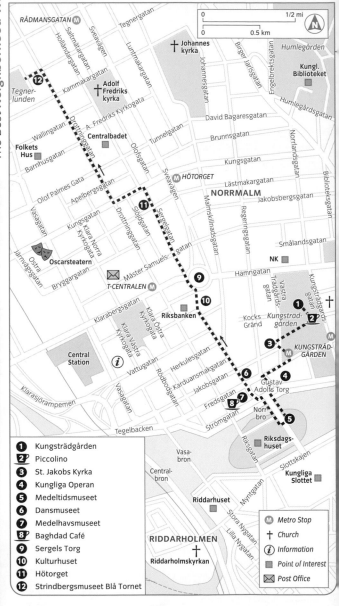

1	Kungsträdgården
2	Piccolino
3	St. Jakobs Kyrka
4	Kungliga Operan
5	Medeltidsmuseet
6	Dansmuseet
7	Medelhavsmuseet
8	Baghdad Café
9	Sergels Torg
10	Kulturhuset
11	Hötorget
12	Strindbergsmuseet Blå Tornet

M	Metro Stop
†	Church
ⓘ	Information
◼	Point of Interest
✉	Post Office

On this tour, we move away from the center and stroll north up to Vasastaden. Built at the end of the 1800s when Stockholm's population kept growing, the area is mainly residential and is bounded on the north side by large green open spaces. **START: T-bana to Kungsträdgården.**

1 ★★ **kids Kungsträdgården.** All Stockholm finds its way here, either for the public events or just to watch the world go by. Originally the Royal Kitchen Garden—the king had to grow his cabbages and carrots somewhere—Stockholm's oldest park opened to the public in 1792. ⏱ *30 min. See p 54,* **6**.

2 ★ **kids Piccolino.** Join the locals in Stockholm's first espresso bar. Piccolino is a good place to sit outside and watch the world go by or take refuge during the winter months. ☎ *08-611 78 08. T-bana: Kungsträdgården. Coffee is 25 SEK.*

3 ★ **St. Jakobs Kyrka.** The red church, dedicated to the patron saint of pilgrims, is a mix of architectural styles. Started in 1588, it was completed in 1643. The 17th century is found in the baptismal font, church plate, and some of the porches. It then went through various renovations in the 19th century,

Piccolino was Stockholm's first espresso bar.

St. Jakobs Kyrka is next to the Royal Opera.

including five stained-glass panels by the altar. Now, the church is known for its music (see p 139) ⏱ *15 min. Västra Trädgårdsgatan 2.* ☎ *08-723 30 38. www.stockholms domkyrkoforsamling.se. Free admission. Tues–Thurs noon–4pm, Fri noon–6pm, Sat, Sun 2–6pm. Closed Mon. T-bana: Kungsträdgården.*

4 ★★ **Kungliga Operan.** The Royal Opera House is a magnificent, rather bombastic-looking building of 1898. The interior is superb, with ceiling paintings above the staircase inspired by the Paris Opera. The auditorium is all gold leaf and red velvet and has its fair share of ornately decorated boxes, including the Royal Box, which is placed stage left and so almost becomes part of the action. Ingmar Bergman produced some of the operas here, and it's also the home of the Swedish Royal Ballet (p 137). ☎ *08-791 44 00, www.operan.se. Tickets 75 SEK. Guided tours summer only, Sat, Sun 1pm. T-bana: Kungsträdgården.*

Sergels Torg.

5 ★★ **kids** **Medeltidsmuseet.**
It's difficult to find the Museum of
Medieval Stockholm, but well worth
it. Located under the Norrbro bridge,
it's full of excellent displays of life-
size models, little street scenes, and
foundations. Great fun for children, it
gives a very good idea of life in the
Middle Ages, which was much the
same throughout Europe for the
peasants and townspeople. ⏱ 1½ hr.
Strömparterren, Norrbro. ☎ 08-508
31 790. www.medeltidsmuseet.stock-
holm.se. Free admission. Tues–Sun
noon–5pm (Wed to 7pm); July, Aug
also open Mon noon–5pm. T-bana:
Kungsträdgården.

6 ★★ **Dansmuseet.** This delightful museum will set your feet tapping
and make every little girl who ever

owned a pair of ballet shoes dream.
The museum was founded in 1933 in
Paris by Rolf de Maré (1888–1964),
the Swedish aristocrat and art collector who managed the Swedish Ballet
that took Paris by storm in the 1920s
with its innovative style. The Swedish
and non-European dance items were
brought here when the museum in
Paris closed in the 1940s. There's a
good cafe with a sunny terrace, and
a well-stocked shop. ⏱ 40 min. Gustav Adolfs Torg 22–24. ☎ 08-441 76
50. www.dansmuseet.se. Adults 50
SEK, free children 17 and under. Free
with Stockholm Card (see p 11). Mon–
Fri 11am–4pm, Sat, Sun noon–4pm.
Closed for public hols. T-bana:
Kungsträdgården.

7 ★★ **Medelhavsmuseet.** The
Museum of Mediterranean Antiquities has art and artifacts from
Greece, Rome, Egypt, Cyprus, and
the Near East housed in a splendid
17th-century classical building.
Musical instruments, ancient sar-
cophagi, art, terracotta figures, and
more show what the Ancient world
respected and revered. ⏱ 1 hr.
Fredsgatan 2. ☎ 08-519 553 80.
www.medelhavsmuseet.se. Adults
80 SEK, free children 19 and under.
Free with Stockholm Card (see
p 11). Tues–Fri noon–8pm, Sat,
Sun noon–5pm. Closed Mon. T-bana:
Kungsträdgården.

The Modernist Kulturhuset.

The Konserthuset looks onto Hötorget.

8 ★ **kids Baghdad Café.** I love prolonging the Near East experience in this museum cafe, which specializes in dishes from the eastern Mediterranean. It's run by the owner of Halv Grek Plus Turk (see p 116) and offers the likes of chicken and couscous salad and a set lunch on weekdays at 99 SEK. Finish with ultra-sweet, tooth-filling-defying baklava. *Fredsgatan 2.* ☎ *08-519 550 62. www.smvk.se.*

9 ★★ **Sergels Torg.** Walk along Hamngatan and be lured into NK (p 94), Stockholm's poshest department store. Then make your way to Sergels Torg. Built on two levels during the 1960s and '70s mania for the new, it's known for the glass sculpture surrounded by fountains in its center, erected in 1972 and designed by Edvin Öhrstrom (1906–94) and, bizarrely, for political demonstrations. Dramatic lighting makes this rather brutal concrete center a better sight at night. ⏱ *10 min.*

10 ★ **kids Kulturhuset.** A symbol of Swedish Modernism, the Cultural Center was designed by architect Peter Celsing (1920–74) and opened in 1974. The large glass-sided building on the southern side of the square has three galleries with changing exhibitions, a library, two stages for music, dance, and drama, and a popular Children's Room with books (some in English), plus paints and paper for drawing and storytelling. **Serieteket** is Sweden's only cartoon library and the building also houses Stockholm's **Stadsteatern** (see p 140). ⏱ *30 min. Sergels Torg.* ☎ *08-508 315 08. www.kulturhuset. stockholm.se. Free admission to building. See 'Buying Tickets,' p 136. T-bana: T-Centralen.*

11 ★ **Hötorget.** The Hay Market started as a place to trade vegetables, milk, and meat and today stalls are still piled high with sweet strawberries, bright red tomatoes, and vividly colored flowers. The square is surrounded by the indoor international food market, **Hötorgshallen** (p 37, **2**), the **PUB** department store where Greta Garbo briefly sold hats, the **Filmstaden Sergel** multiplex (p 138), and **Konserthuset** (p 137). ⏱ *15 min.*

12 ★ **Strindbergsmuseet Blå Tornet.** As you walk north up Drottninggatan, the chain stores give way to small boutiques and the Art Nouveau Centralbadet (p 17, **9**). The street becomes more residential, just the place for August Strindberg (1849–1912) who moved into Blå Tornet (the *Blue Tower*) in 1908. An old-fashioned elevator takes you up slowly to the reconstructed bedroom, dining room, and study where a permanent exhibition shows his work as author, photographer, and artist, and vividly brings the old neighborhood to life. ⏱ *45 min. Drottninggatan 85.* ☎ *08-411 53 54. www.strindbergsmuseet.se. Adults 50 SEK, free children 18 and under. Free with Stockholm Card (see p 11). Tues–Sun noon–4pm; July, Aug Tues–Sat noon–4pm, Sun 10am–4pm. T-bana: Rådmansgatan.*

Skeppsholmen

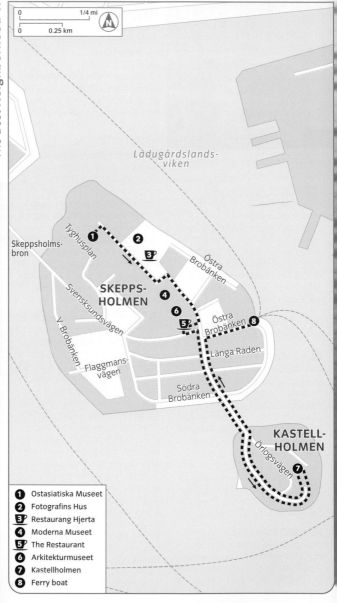

Làdugårdslands-viken

Skeppsholms-bron

Tyghusplan

Svensksundsvägen

V. Brobänken

Flaggmans-vägen

SKEPPS-HOLMEN

Östra Brobänken

Östra Brobänken

Länga Raden

Södra Brobänken

KASTELL-HOLMEN

Örlogsvägen

1. Ostasiatiska Museet
2. Fotografins Hus
3. Restaurang Hjerta
4. Moderna Museet
5. The Restaurant
6. Arkitekturmuseet
7. Kastellholmen
8. Ferry boat

I n the 17th century, Skeppsholmen provided the base for the all-conquering Swedish navy. It's a pretty island with a 1.6km (1 mile) walk around the seashore giving wonderful views of the nearby islands. Tucked away at the bottom of Skeppsholmen, the tiny island of Kastellholmen has a quaint seaside feel to it.

START: Bus 65 to the bottom of Skeppsholmen.

---

1 ★★ Ostasiatiska Museet.
The East Asian Museum is rightly popular, particularly as it holds one of the world's greatest collections of Chinese art outside Asia. More than 1,200 objects from more than 5,000 years of history are on display. Housed in a 17th-century building used to accommodate Karl XII's bodyguard, and designed by Nicodemus Tessin the Younger (1654–1728), the museum was founded by the Swedish archaeologist Johan Gunnar Andersson (1874–1960) who, in the early 1920s, came across an extraordinary collection of items from the Stone Age in China and was allowed to bring them back to Sweden. King Gustav VI Adolf (1882–1973) also left his collection of ancient Chinese arts and crafts—pottery, tools, and artifacts—to the museum. You'll also discover Buddhist sculptures and works from Japan, India, and Korea, while the shop is an excellent source for Japanese tea sets and kimonos. ⏲ *1 hr. Tyghusplan.* ☎ *08-519 5 57 50. www.ostasiatiska.se. Adults 60 SEK, free children 18 and under. Free with Stockholm Card (see p 11). Tues 11am–8pm, Wed–Sun 11am–5pm. Closed Mon. Bus: 65.*

2 ★ Fotografins Hus. On an island full of cultural landmarks, this photographic gallery is devoted to a changing program of contemporary exhibitions from international photographers. ⏲ *45 min. Slupskjulsvägen.* ☎ *08-611 69 69.*

www.fotografinshus.se. Adults 50 SEK, free children 17 and under. Wed–Fri noon–6pm, Sat, Sun noon–4pm. Closed in summer.

3 ★★ Restaurang Hjerta.
Opened in 2010, this is a favorite place for summertime dining on the outdoor terrace. In a former shipyard building, it's light, bright, and airy, just the place for a leisurely lunch or romantic dinner. *Lupskjulsvägen 28B.* ☎ *08-611 41 00. www. restauranghjerta.se. Mains are from 145–265 SEK.*

4 ★★★ Moderna Museet. The Modern Art Museum comes as a surprise to first time visitors who don't expect to find one of the world's great collections here in Stockholm. Originally opened in 1958, it brought names such as Andy Warhol, Frank Stella, and Giacometti to a Swedish audience for the first time. There's also a new and excellent photographic collection on show. The present building opened in 1998 when Stockholm was Cultural Capital of Europe, closed in 2002 due to damp problems, and then re-opened in 2004. It shows great works, some familiar, but others less so and has an active program of events as well. There's a very well-stocked shop and a restaurant shared with the Architectural Museum. ⏲ *1½ hr. See p 19,* **2***.*

The castle on the tiny island of Kastellholmen.

5 ★ **The Restaurant.** I love booking for Saturday or Sunday brunch at the Modern Museum's restaurant. It's a popular place for a family get-together with a buffet of classic Swedish salmon, herrings, cold meats, potato dishes, vegetables, and a tempting dessert selection (265 SEK per person). During the week, there's a self-service lunch and a bistro-style selection from the grill. At other times, the coffee and cakes match the splendid view. *Skeppsholmen.* ☎ *08-519 552 82. www.modernamuseet.se.*

6 ★★ **Arkitekturmuseet.** The Architectural Museum, housed in the old drill hall is a natural partner to the Moderna Museet. More than 100 architectural models are laid out like a series of superior historical dolls' houses, taking you from a 2,000-year-old Viking longhouse to 20th-century bridges. After visiting real buildings such as the Stadshuset and the Royal Palace, you can gaze down at the miniature models to spot all the details you missed. There are numerous temporary exhibitions each year and **Café Blom** is excellent for a coffee and snack. ⏲ *45 min. Exercisplan.* ☎ *08-587 270 00. www.arkitekturmuseet.se. Adults 60 SEK, free children 18 and under. Free Fri 4–6pm. Free with Stockholm Card (see p 11). Tues 10am–8pm, Wed–Sun 10am–6pm. Closed Mon. Bus: 65.*

7 ★★ **Kastellholmen.** Dominated by a rather new-looking Kastell (it was rebuilt in 1846–48 after a gun cartridge factory unfortunately blew the old castle up), the tiny island of Kastellholmen is reached via a small bridge. The island is really a very large attractive granite rock where you can clamber up to find a natural seat and join the locals with a picnic. ⏲ *1 hr.*

8 ★ **Ferry boat.** Press the button at the tiny quay and wait for a regular ferry that will take you either to Djurgården or to Slussen. ⏲ *5 min.* ●

Shopping Best Bets

Shop at Stockholm's top design shop, Svensk Tenn.

Best **Art Books & Magazines**
★★ Konst-ig, *Åsögatan 124 (p 93)*

Best **1960s' & Indie Music**
★★ Pet Sounds, *Skanegatan 53 (p 99)*

Best for **Commissioning your own Dinner Service**
★★ blås&knåda, *Hornsgatan 27 (p 93)*

Best **Old-fashioned Toys**
★ Bulleribock, Sveagen, *Sveagen 104 (p 93)*

Best **Pippi Longstocking Choice**
★ Kalikå, *Österlanggatan 18 (p 94)*; and ★ Junibacken Shop, *Galärvarvsvägen (p 53)*

Best **Posh Shopping Mall**
★★★ Sturegallerian, *Stureplan (p 94)*

Best **Alvar Aalto Classics**
★★★ Jacksons, *Sibyllegatan 53 (p 97)*

Best **1930s' Table Lamp**
★★★ Modernity, *Sibyllegatan 6 (p 98)*

Best **Traditional Swedish Craftsmanship**
★★★ Carl Malmsten, *Strandvägen 5B (p 98)*

Previous page: Ljunggrens.

Best **Design Drawing Room Look**
★★★ Svensk Tenn, *Strandvägen 5 (p 98)*

Best **Bright Bags**
★★ 10 Gruppen, *Götgatan 25 (p 98)*

Best for **Ballet Music CDs**
★★ Dansmuseet Museum Shop, *Dansmuseet (p 84, ⑥)*

Best **Clothing with a Conscience**
★★ Ekovaruhuset, *Österlanggatan 28 (p 95)*

Best **Classic Swedish Clothing**
★★ Filippa K, *Grev Turegatan 18 (p 96)*

Best **Reinvented Department Store**
★★★ PUB, *Gamla Grogatan 14 (p 94)*

Best **Kitsch for Friends Who Have Everything**
★★ Coctail, *Skanegatan 71 (p 97)*

Best **Trendy Jewelry**
★★★ Efva Attling, *Hornsgatan 45 (p 99)*

Best for **a Bargain**
★★ Stockholms Stadsmission, *Hornsgatan 58 (p 97)*

Best **Luxury Writing Books**
★★ Ljunggrens, *Köpmangatan 3 (p 100)*

Best **Superior Swedish Souvenirs**
★★ Design Torget, *Kulturhuset; (p 97)*; ★★ Skansen Shop, *Main Gate, Djurgårdsslätten (p 13)*

Best **Gourmet For Foodies**
★★★ Östermalms Saluhall, *Östermalmstorg (p 14)*

Best **Creations from the Nobel Banquet Patisserie**
★★ Xoko, *Rorstrandgatan 15 (p 39)*

North Stockholm Shopping

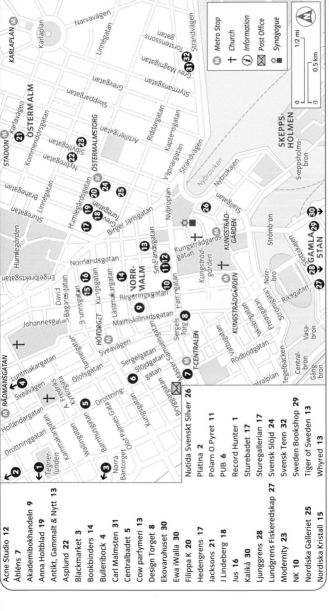

Legend:
- Ⓜ Metro Stop
- ✝ Church
- ⓘ Information
- ☒ Post Office
- ✡ Synagogue

Acne Studio **12**
Åhléns **7**
Akademibokhandeln **9**
Anna Holtblad **19**
Antikt, Gammalt & Nytt **13**
Asplund **22**
Blackmarket **3**
Bookbinders **14**
Bulleribock **4**
Carl Malmsten **31**
Centralbadet **5**
Cow parfymeri **13**
Design Torget **8**
Ekovaruhuset **30**
Ewa iWalla **30**
Filippa K **20**
Hedengrens **17**
Jacksons **21**
J Lindeberg **18**
Jus **16**
Kalikå **30**
Ljunggrens **28**
Lundgrens Fiskeredskap **27**
Modernity **23**
NK **10**
Nordiska Galleriet **25**
Nordiska Kristall **15**
Nutida Svenskt Silver **26**
Platina **2**
Polarn O.Pyret **11**
PUB **6**
Record Hunter **1**
Sturebadet **17**
Sturegallerian **17**
Svensk Slöjd **24**
Svensk Tenn **32**
Sweden Bookshop **29**
Tiger of Sweden **13**
Whyred **13**

South Stockholm Shopping

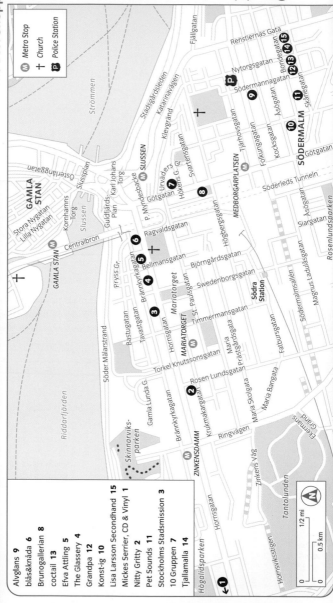

Legend:
- Ⓜ Metro Stop
- ✝ Church
- 🅿 Police Station

GAMLA STAN

SLUSSEN

SÖDERMALM

MEDBORGARPLATSEN

MARIATORGET

ZINKENSDAMM

Mariatorget

Södra Station

Strömmen

Riddarfjärden

Söder Mälarstrand

Rosenlundsparken

Tantolunden

Högalidsparken

Skinnarviks-parken

Map labels (streets/places):
Renstiernas Gata, Fjällgatan, Nytorgsgatan, Södermannagatan, Åsögatan, Skånegatan, Bondegatan, Götgatan, Tjärhovsgatan, Folkungagatan, Kocksgatan, Åsögatan, Söderleds Tunneln, Siargatan, Magnus Ladulåsgatan, Södermalmsallén, Fatburgsgatan, Maria Bangata, Maria Skolgata, Maria Prästgårdsgata, St. Paulsgatan, Timmermansgatan, Swedenborgsgatan, Björngårdsgatan, Högbergsgatan, Svartensgatan, Hökens G. Gr., Urväders Gr., Katarinavägen, Stadsgårdsleden, Klevgränd, P. Myndesbacke, Karl Johans Torg, Guldfjärds-Plan, Götgatan, Ragvaldsgatan, Bellmansgatan, Brännkyrkagatan, Tavastgatan, Bastugatan, Pryss. Gr., Hornsgatan, Torkel Knutssonsgatan, Rosen Lundsgatan, Krukmakargatan, Ringvägen, Brännkyrkagatan, Gamla Lunda G., Zinkens Väg, Hornsgatan, Hornsviksstigen, Ekermans Gränd, Östlänggatan, Stora Nygatan, Lilla Nygatan, Kornhamns Torg, Slussplan, Slussen, Centralbron

⊕ N

0   1/2 mi
0   0.5 km

Listing:
- Alvglans **9**
- blåsknåda **6**
- Brunogallerian **8**
- coctail **13**
- Efva Atling **5**
- The Glassery **4**
- Grandpa **12**
- Konst-ig **10**
- Lisa Larsson Secondhand **15**
- Mickes Serrier, CD & Vinyl **1**
- Nitty Gritty **2**
- Pet Sounds **11**
- Stockholms Stadsmission **3**
- 10 Gruppen **7**
- Tjallamalla **14**

Stockholm **Shopping A to Z**

Bookshops

★ **Akademibokhandeln** NORRMALM The Academy bookstore has a particularly good selection of books in English, maps, and travel books. *Master Samuelsgatan 28.* ☎ *08-744 11 00. www.akademi bokhandeln.se. AE, DC, MC, V. T-bana: T-Centralen/Hötorget. Map p 91.*

★ **kids Alvglans** SÖDERMALM From the Belgian Spirou to Modesty Blaise, X-Men, and Spiderman, this specialist comic shop stocks all the greats and collectors' items. *Folkungagatan 84.* ☎ *08-642 69 98. www. alvglans.se. AE, DC, MC, V. T-bana: Slussen. Map p 92.*

★★★ **Hedengrens** ÖSTERMALM Since 1898 Hedengrens has been Stockholm's smartest bookstore, stocking 80,000 titles in nine languages from the arts to gardening; also holds exhibitions and regular book readings. *Sturegallerian, Stureplan 4.* ☎ *08-611 51 38. www.hedengrens.se. AE, DC, MC, V. T-bana: Östermalmstorg. Map p 91.*

★★ **Konst-ig** SÖDERMALM This leading art bookshop stocks a formidably wide range of international titles and top international magazines. *Åsögatan 124.* ☎ *08-20 45 20. www.konstig.se. AE, MC, V. T-bana: Medborgarplatsen. Map p 92.*

★★ **Sweden Bookshop** GAMLA STAN The Swedish Institute's popular bookshop is the best place to find books about Sweden, from literature to architecture, in 47 languages. *Slottsbacken 10.* ☎ *08-453 78 00. www.swedenbookshop.com. AE, DC, MC, V. T-bana: Gamla Stan. Map p 91.*

Ceramics & Glass

★★ **blås&knåda** SÖDERMALM Loosely and jokingly translated as 'blow and throw', this light and airy shop is run by a cooperative of around 50 glass and ceramic artists. It has a wide stock plus it sells members' works from functional to collectable. *Hornsgatan 26A.* ☎ *08-642 77 67. www. blasknada.com. AE, DC, MC, V. T-bana: Slussen. Map p 92.*

★★ **The Glassery** SÖDERMALM This exciting gallery showcases up-and-coming names. If you're a collector or an aspiring one, come here for art glass by names such as Simon Klenell and Frederik Neilsen. *Hornsgatan 38.* ☎ *08-25 11 95. www.theglassery. se. AE, DC, MC, V. T-bana: Slussen. Map p 92.*

★★ **Nordiska Kristall** NORRMALM Swedish glass is rightly famous and here you'll find stunning examples of the art from names such as Kosta Boda and Orrefors (founded 1742). *Kungsgatan 9.* ☎ *08-10 43 72. AE, DC, MC, V. T-bana: T-Centralen. Map p 91.*

Children's Clothes & Toys

★★ **kids Bulleribock** VASASTADEN It started in the 1960s stocking only toys made of wood and natural materials, eschewing all things plastic. Now Bulleribock is wildly fashionable again. No computer games, just traditional playthings, mostly for children up to age 10. *Sveagen 104.* ☎ *08-673 61 21. www.bulleribock.nu. AE, MC, V. T-bana: Rådmansgatan. Map p 91.*

★★ **kids** **Kalikå** GAMLA STAN Great for a wide collection of striped tops, stuffed toys, and Pippi Long-stocking items, furniture, and bags in the shapes of houses and buses that grown-up girls will also covet. *Österlånggatan 18.* ☎ *08-20 52 19. www.kalika.se. AE, DC, MC, V. T-bana: Gamla Stan. Map p 91.*

★ **kids** **Polarn O.Pyret** NOR-RMALM The 'Pal and the Tot' made its name in 1976 for comfort-able, casual children's designs, and its signature stripes. The stripes are still around for children up to age 12. *Hamnagatan 10.* ☎ *08-411 41 40. www.polarnopyret.se. AE, DC, MC, V. T-bana: Östermalmstorg. Map p 91.*

Cosmetics

★★ **Cow Parfymeri** ÖSTER-MALM All the top cosmetics from Laura Mercier to L'Artisan Parfume-rie with knowledgeable staff and professional make-up artists; expen-sive, but the best. *Master Samuels-gatan 9.* ☎ *08-611 15 04. www. cowparfymeri.se. AE, MC, V. T-bana: Mariatorget. Map p 91.*

Pippi Longstocking rag dolls at Kalikå.

Department Stores/Shopping Malls

★ **Åhléns** NORRMALM This huge chain started in 1899 with mail order, and opened the first Stockholm store in 1932. It's a mid-range store, good for fashion, beauty, home interiors, and electronics; also has a day spa. *Klarabergsgatan 50.* ☎ *08-676 60 00. www.ahlens.se. AE, DC, MC, V. T-bana: T-Centralen. Map p 91.*

★ **Brunogallerian** SÖDERMALM Also known as Galleria Bruno, this small mall has a mix of international names (Miss Sixty) and Swedish (Whyred). The chic gather at Ljungg-rens bar/restaurant. *Götgatan 36.* ☎ *08-757 76 00. www.brunogallerian. se. Credit cards vary from shop to shop. T-bana: Slussen/Medborgar-platsen. Map p 92.*

★★★ **NK** NORRMALM The elegant Nordiska Kompaniet is the last name in Swedish high-class style. It's a favorite of Princess Victoria, is strong on clothes and beauty, and known for gourmet food and Swedish crafts. Café Entrée caters to weary shop-pers. *Hamnagatan 18–20.* ☎ *08-762 80 00. www.nk.se. AE, DC, MC, V. T-bana: Kungsträdgården/ Öster-malmstorg. Map p 91.*

★★★ **PUB** ÖSTERMALM Founded in 1852 and named after the founder, Paul Urbanus Bergström, the former old-fashioned depart-ment store has transformed itself into the young and trendy choice for top and funky boutiques. It also offers vintage clothing, accessories, cosmetics, art and design, and a lot more for the fashion-conscious with an edge. *Gamla Grogatan 14.* ☎ *08-508 28 508. www.pub.se. AE, DC, MC, V. T-bana: Hötorget. Map p 91.*

★★★ **Sturegallerian** ÖSTER-MALM Chic Stockholm residents shop here when they've done with NK. It's a good mix of Swedish and international names for clothes and

NK is Stockholm's top department store.

accessories, plus revered bookshop Hedengrens (p 93). *Stureplan. www.sturegallerian.se. Credit cards vary from shop to shop. T-bana: Östermalmstorg. Map p 91.*

Fashion

★★ Blackmarket VASASTADEN   Go down the steps into this store for flamboyant labels from Henrik Vibskov, Minimarket, Jeremy Scott, and also Comme des Garçons and Peter Jensen; exhibition space plus seats for partners to wait. *St Eriksgatan 79.* ☎ *08-30 26 60. www.blackmarketsthlm.se. AE, MC, V. T-bana: St. Eriksplan. Map p 91.*

★ Ekovaruhuset GAMLA STAN   This boutique takes organic and eco to where it should be: chic and fashionable using Fair Trade practices. Handmade designer prototypes from names such as Anja Hynynen and Modiga Barn. *Österlanggatan 28.* ☎ *08-22 98 45. www.ekovaruhuset.se. MC, V. T-bana: Gamla Stan. Map p 91.*

★★ Grandpa SÖDERMALM   Where the young and increasingly hip residents of Söder come for their denims, shirts, and knitwear.

And while you're here, check out the designer items and vintage furniture to take you back to your '70s' student days. *Södermannagatan 21.* ☎ *08-643 60 800. www.grandpa.se. AE, DC, MC, V. T-bana: Medborgarplatsen. Map p 92.*

★★ Jus NORRMALM   One of the first of the new boutiques to encourage new talent in the late 1990s, both local and international, this chic venue stocks the likes of Ann-Sofi Back and the casual Burfitt. *Brunnsgatan 7.* ☎ *08-20 67 77. www.jus.se. AE, DC, MC, V. T-bana: Hötorget. Map p 91.*

★★ Nitty Gritty SÖDERMALM   One of the shops making Söder a shopping destination, Nitty Gritty has seven adjoining shops for clothes, shoes, and accessories from names such as Dries Van Noten and Fred Perry; also has CDs, books, a children's store, and a cafe. *Krukmakargatan 26.* ☎ *08-658 24 40. www.nittygritty.se. AE, DC, MC, V. T-bana: Slussen. Map p 92.*

Fashion—Swedish Designers

★★ Acne Studio ÖSTERMALM   Famous in Sweden and expanding (now in New York, Paris, London, and Oslo), Acne began as an advertising agency before turning to jeans in 1997. It's an all-round design store with casual chic as its inspiration. Several shops in Stockholm. *Norrmalmstorg 2.* ☎ *08-611 64 11. www.acnestudios.com. AE, DC, MC, V. T-bana: Östermalmstorg. Map p 91.*

★★ Anna Holtblad ÖSTERMALM   The calm and cool interior of Anna Holtblad's store is a great setting for her strong shapes and colors, particularly in her signature knitwear, which has become the last name in Scandinavian chic. *Grev Turegatan 13.* ☎ *08-545 02 220. www.annaholtblad.se. AE, DC, MC, V. T-bana: Östermalmstorg. Map p 91.*

★ **Ewa iWalla** GAMLA STAN For the romantic look, visit Ewa iWalla's original small, crowded boutique. Her clothes float, are made of natural fabrics, and make you feel as if you're in a Bergman film; but definitely for the young. *Österlånggatan 23C.* ☎ *08-245 887. www. ewaiwalla.se. AE, MC, V. T-bana: Gamla Stan. Map p 91.*

★★ **Filippa K** ÖSTERMALM This label is favored by Princess Victoria for its clean lines, simple shapes, and good quality. This is classic dressing for men and women. Founded in 1993 by Filippa Knutsson, it's now one of the leading Swedish brands, with stores in Stockholm and throughout northern Europe. *Grev Turegatan 18.* ☎ *08-545 88 8 88. www.filippa-k.com. AE, DC, MC, V. T-bana: Östermalmstorg. Map p 91.*

★★ **J Lindeberg** ÖSTERMALM Originally the progressive name in Swedish fashion, John Lindeberg is known for casual fashion and formal wear. He made his reputation with sporting styles favored by golfers. The label is now more mainstream and is sold in 20 countries. *Grev Turegatan 9.* ☎ *08-678 61 65. www. jlindeberg.com. AE, DC, MC, V. T-bana: Östermalmstorg. Map p 91.*

★★ **Tiger of Sweden** NORRMALM Started by tailors Markus Schwamann and Hjalmar Nördstrom in 1903, Tiger has seen fashions come and go and emerged as one of the strongest Swedish labels with an emphasis on good cutting. Also has clothes for women, shoes, and accessories. *Jakobsbergsgatan 8.* ☎ *08-440 30 60. www.tigerof sweden.com. AE, DC, MC, V. T-bana: Östermalmstorg. Map p 91.*

★ **Tjallamalla** SÖDERMALM Small boutique with big ideas stocking new names for the young. *Bondegatan 46.* ☎ *08-640 78 47. www.* *tjallamalla.com. AE, MC, V. T-bana: Medborgarplatsen. Map p 92.*

★★ **Whyred** ÖSTERMALM Three former H&M employees set up Whyred in 1999, and it's now a name for cool style for men and women. Two stores in Stockholm, Whyred North and Whyred South (in Brunogallerian, p 94 in Södermalm). *Whyred North, Master Samuelsgatan 3.* ☎ *08-660 01 70. www. whyred.com. AE, DC, MC, V. T-bana: Kungsträdgården. Map p 91.*

Fashion—Vintage & Secondhand

★★ **Lisa Larsson Secondhand** SÖDERMALM Stockholm's best-known secondhand store stocks most styles and eras, from 1950s' leather jackets to '80s' party dresses. Designers such as Pucci stand next to names that sank without trace until turning up here; also stocks suits, shoes, and hats. *Bondegatan 48.* ☎ *08-643 61 53. www. lisalarssonsecondhand.com. No credit cards. Bus 2, 53, 59, 76. Map p 92.*

Fab secondhand and vintage at Lisa Larsson.

Get those dancing shoes at coctail.

★★ Stockholms Stadsmission

SÖDERMALM Five secondhand shops run by a homeless charity set up in the 1800s offer a wide range of just about everything. There are clothes and bric-a-brac in the Kungsholmen shop; the biggest range is at Gröndal, south of Lilla Essingen. *Hornsgatan 58.* ☎ *08-642 93 35. www.stadsmissionen.se. AE, MC, V. T-bana: Slussen. Map p 92.*

Fishing

★★★ Lundgrens Fiskeredskap

GAMLA STAN Founded in 1892, this old-fashioned specialist shop sells all the equipment that fishermen need. Expert staff help you make the right choices. *Storkyrkobriken 12.* ☎ *08-10 21 22. www. lundgrensfiske.com. AE, DC, MC, V. T-bana: Gamla Stan. Map p 91.*

Gifts & Souvenirs

★★ kids coctail SÖDERMALM

Plastic duck? Pink cuckoo clock? Improbable chandelier? Coctail de luxe and coctail supply all necessities of kitsch life and a few more you'd be hard put to imagine. They have furniture, too, in case you want to go all the way. Also coctail de luxe at Bondesgatan 34. *Skånegatan 71.* ☎ *08-642 07 40. www. coctail.nu. AE, DC, MC, V. Bus 2, 53, 59, 76. Map p 92.*

★★ kids Design Torget NOR-

RMALM It began in 1993 in an empty shop in Kulturhuset where one of the founders of Design Torget worked as an architect. It has expanded and has other stores but keeps the core philosophies of seeking out young designers and working with design schools in Sweden. The stock is fresh, new, and varied. *Sergelgangen 29.* ☎ *08-21 91 50. www.designtorget.se. AE, MC, V. T-bana: T-Centralen. Map p 91.*

★★ kids Svensk Slöjd ÖSTER-

MALM If you're after good souvenirs, come here for reindeer, textiles, wooden toys, and one of those famous Dala horses. *Nybrogatan 23.* ☎ *08-640 97 77. www. svenskslojd.se. AE, MC, V. T-bana: Östermalmstorg. Map p 91.*

Interiors—Antiques & Secondhand

★★★ Jacksons ÖSTERMALM For

nearly 30 years, Jacksons has supplied top quality furniture, ceramics, glass, and textiles to the discerning. Specializing in the 20th century, they deal in the big Scandinavian and Nordic designers (Alvar Aalto to Carl Westman), and international names such as Mies van der Rohe. *Sibyllegatan 53.* ☎ *08-665 33 50. www.jacksons.se. AE, DC, MC, V. T-bana: Östermalmstorg. Map p 91.*

Modernity.

★★★ **Modernity** ÖSTERMALM Scotsman Andrew Duncanson stocks a wide range of 20th-century Scandinavian design, mainly post World War II, from the Egg Chair of Arne Jacobsen to jewelry by Swedish designers. Like Jacksons, Modernity is a familiar name at international arts, design, and antiques fairs. *Sibyllegatan 6.* ☎ *08-20 80 25. www.modernity.se. AE, DC, MC, V. T-bana: Östermalmstorg. Map p 91.*

Interiors—Contemporary Design & Furnishings
★ **Asplund** ÖSTERMALM The Asplund brothers fill their store with new Swedish and international designs of candlesticks, furniture, and carpets, and their own brand by Thomas Sandell. *Sibyllegatan 31.* ☎ *08-662 52 84. www.asplund.org. AE, MC, V. T-bana: Östermalmstorg. Bus 56, 62. Map p 91.*

★★★ **Carl Malmsten** ÖSTERMALM Carl Malmsten (1888–1972) was one of the Swedish modern masters of furniture design, championing traditional craftsmanship when it seemed under threat. His imaginative designs, light wood, and consummate craftsmanship worked and his designs and techniques—he founded two schools—still grace

the homes of the design conscious. *Strandvägen 5.* ☎ *08-23 33 80. www.c.malmsten.se. MC, V. T-bana: Östermalmstorg. Map p 91.*

★★★ **Nordiska Galleriet** ÖSTERMALM This treasure trove mixes design classics of the past still being produced from names such as Arne Jacobsen with the eccentric creations of Philippe Starck and Swedish designer Johan Bohlin. *Nybrogatan 11.* ☎ *08-442 83 60. www.nordiska galleriet.se. AE, DC, MC, V. T-bana: Östermalmstorg. Map p 91.*

★★★ **Svensk Tenn** ÖSTERMALM This classic store, founded by pewter designer Estrid Ericson in 1924, was expanded with Functionalist furniture from Gunnar Asplund. Known for furniture and textiles by Josef Frank, whose designs still brighten the store today, the newly renovated store also stocks contemporary designers and supplies the Royal Family, so you're in good company. *Strandvägen 5.* ☎ *08-670 16 0. www.svenskttenn.se. AE, DC, MC, V. T-bana: Östermalmstorg. Map p 91.*

★★ **10 Gruppen** SÖDERMALM Ten young textile designers set up this store back in 1970, producing geometric designs in bright primary colors. All 10 are no longer in charge, but their fabrics, bags, cushions, and oven gloves are still there. *Götgatan 25.* ☎ *08-643 25 04. www.tiogruppen.com. MC, V. T-bana: Slussen. Map p 92.*

Jewelry

★★ Antikt, Gammalt & Nytt NORRMALM A real gem of a shop for fashionistas and stylists after that outlandish piece of rhinestone or something designed in the 1940s and lying undiscovered. *Master Samuelsgatan 11.* ☎ *08-678 35 30. AE, DC, MC, V. T-bana: Östermalmstorg. Map p 91.*

★★★ Efva Attling SÖDERMALM The famous jeweler has had a varied career: from playing in the 1980s' X Models band to designing clothes for Levi's and H&M. But she's best known for her jewelry in gold, silver, and precious stones. The wide range attracts clients such as Madonna; also in Birger Jarlsgatan. *Hornsgatan 44.* ☎ *08-642 99 49. www.efvaattlingstockholm.com. AE, DC, MC, V. T-bana: Slussen. Map p 92.*

★★ Nutida Svenskt Silver ÖSTERMALM Sixty silver- and goldsmiths belong to the

10 Gruppen in Södermalm.

cooperative running this gallery. From silverware to the most delicate of silver enamel, the bold to the subtle. *Arsenalsgatan 3.* ☎ *08-611 67 18. www.nutida.nu. AE, MC, V. T-bana: Kungsträdgården. Map p 91.*

★★ Platina VASASTADEN Specializing in contemporary jewelry, you'll find Swedish and international names, skull rings, brooches, pendants, and items like gold price labels to fix to your lapel. Prices from 20 SEK to the skies make this a must for jewelry fans of every persuasion. *Odengatan 68.* ☎ *08-30 02 80. www.platina.se. AE, MC, V. T-bana: Odenplan. Map p 91.*

Music

★ Mickes Serrier, CD & Vinyl SÖDERMALM Wide selection of vinyl and offerings from the likes of the Rolling Stones plus a good jazz section and everything from garage to soul on CD. *Långholmsgatan 20.* ☎ *08-668 10 23. www.mickescdvinyl.se. MC, V. T-bana: Hornstull. Map p 92.*

★★ Pet Sounds SÖDERMALM The oldest and still known for the best indie music, although all the main names and music styles are also here. *Skånegatan 53.* ☎ *08-702 97 98. www.petsounds.se. AE, MC, V. T-bana: Medborgarplatsen. Map p 92.*

★★ Record Hunter VASASTADEN Go for retro vinyl, pop, hard rock, soul, reggae, and hip hop and fill all those holes in your collection. Also sells tickets to major gigs. *St. Eriksgatan 70.* ☎ *08-32 20 23. www. recordhunter.se (Swedish only). MC, V. T-bana: St. Eriksplan. Map p 91.*

Spas

★★★ Centralbadet NORRMALM One of the most beautiful spas you'll ever visit and newly renovated. Take

Prime Shopping Areas

High-end fashion shopping doesn't come much posher than in Norrmalm, around Stureplan, and in nearby streets such as Birger Jarlsgatan, Grev Turegatan, Sibyllegatan, and Biblioteksgatan. Hamngatan has NK, Stockholm's best department store, and the Gallerian, good for everyday items. For **antiques,** good hunting grounds include Vasastaden and the streets of Upplandsgatan and Odengatan, and Gamla Stan. Serious antique hunters should look for shops that are members of Sveriges Konst och Antikhandlareforening (SKAF). Södermalm has good **vintage stores** in and around Bondegatan and a host of small **boutiques** around Götgatan in SoFo which has become the place to shop for new fashion (p 73).

a treatment or just chill out in their pool and thermal pools, get fit in the gym, and sunbathe on the roof terrace in summer. *See p 17. Drottninggatan 88. ☎ 08-545 213 00. www. centralbadet.se. Entrance 180–220 SEK. AE, DC, MC, V. T-bana: Hötorget. Map p 91.*

★★ Sturebadet ÖSTERMALM
This posh spa dates from 1885 and offers all major treatments, though it's pricier than Centralbadet. Admission gives you all the usual goodies such as pool, gym, and group exercise classes. *See p 17,* **⑧**. *Sturegallerian 36. ☎ 08-545 015 00. www. sturebadet.se. Daily guest fee 495–595 SEK. AE, DC, MC, V. T-bana: Östermalmstorg. Map p 91.*

Stationery
★ Bookbinders NORRMALM   Get your life organized here with coordinated boxes, ranges of paper, photo albums, bound notebooks, and more. Founded in 1927, the company still designs and produces all its stock. *Sturegallerian, Grev Turegatan 13A–C. ☎ 08-611 57 70. www.bookbindersdesign.com. AE, DC, MC, V. T-bana: Östermalmstorg. Map p 91.*

★★ Ljunggrens GAMLA STAN
There's an international fan club for the shop's exquisite ranges of paper and paper products, handmade books, and specially designed rubber stamps. Opened in 1913, the store was bought in 1989 by Barbara Bunke who trained as a graphic designer then bookbinder, and only stocks what she herself loves to use. *Köpmangatan 3. ☎ 08-676 03 83. www.ljunggrenspapper.com. AE, DC, MC, V. T-bana: Gamla Stan. Map p 91.* ●

Postcards at Ljunggrens.

5

Stockholm
Outdoors

Skansen

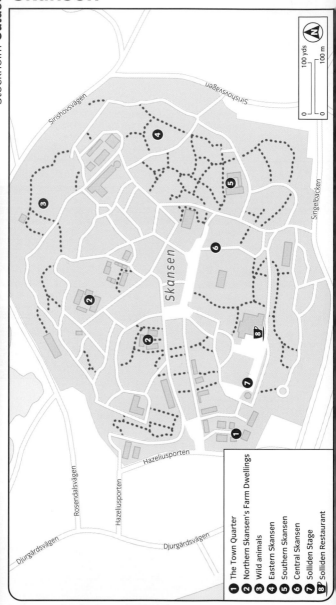

100 yds
100 m

Sirishovsvägen

Sirishovsvägen

Singelbacken

Skansen

Rosendalsvägen

Hazeliusporten

Hazeliusporten

Hazeliusporten

Djurgårdsvägen

Djurgårdsvägen

1 The Town Quarter
2 Northern Skansen's Farm Dwellings
3 Wild animals
4 Eastern Skansen
5 Southern Skansen
6 Central Skansen
7 Solliden Stage
8 Solliden Restaurant

Previous page: Crossing the canal to Långholmen.

In 1891, Artur Hazelius founded Skansen, the world's first open-air museum. It's a huge living history park, with more than 150 buildings and a zoo. It was opened at a time when industrialization was threatening the rural way of life and the idea was to preserve some of the buildings and culture of old Sweden. START: Bus 47, tram 7 or summer ferry to Djurgården from Nybroplan.

① The Town Quarter. Ten old houses, bought up by the municipality of Stockholm to clear the way for modern properties in Södermalm, were brought to Skansen between 1926 and 1933 to start the delightful Town Quarter. Here you find the **Glassworks,** established in 1936, where you can watch glass being blown, and then buy the delicate results in the shop. The **Furniture Factory, Engineering Works, Pottery,** and **Shoemaker's House** stand cheek-by-jowl with the **Bookbindery** and a **worker's home.** Skansen also has a serious purpose—endangered species, especially the common plants once found in the gutters and alleyways of old Stockholm, are planted outside the **Shoemaker's House.** Step into **Charles Tottie's Residence,** built by Sweden's richest merchant in the 18th century, to see how the other half lived. The dining room has sweet-smelling cedar paneling while the drawing room is in Cuban mahogany. Skansen naturally has the **Hazelius Mansion,** the birthplace of the founder. The house was built around 1720 as a silk factory, and only converted into a house in 1803. Next door, the **Pharmacy** is full of old equipment for weighing chemicals and distilling liquids to make medicines. If you're flagging, go into **Petissan,** a little cafe that once served coffee to engineering students in Södermalm in the late 19th century.

The Old Shop in the Town Quarter.

The Sami camp with the Nordiska museet in the background.

❷ Northern Skansen's Farm Dwellings. The early 19th-century **Älvros Farmstead** comes from north Sweden where farmers lived by rearing animals and tending the land, or from forestry, hunting, and fishing. It was a hard life with everyone sleeping in one room beside an open fire, though not as primitive as the **Sami Camp.** The Sami (indigenous Laplanders) built turf and wood huts as they followed the herds of reindeer. In contrast, the **Delsbo Farmstead** shows a well-to-do farm of 1850, with a splendidly decorated doorway, all frills and furbelows. Don't miss the beautifully carved wooden 14th-century **Vastveit Storehouse,** one of the oldest buildings at Skansen.

❸ Wild animals. You can see elk, horses, lynx, foxes, polecats, wild boars, and European bison in one section, though by far the most popular animals here are the brown bears. They may be Sweden's largest predator, but they look remarkably cute. There are also rare breeds such as fluffy goats, southern Swedish country cows that were believed to have died out in 1993, and the Gotland pony. The **Children's Zoo,** open May to September, has small animals; children can ride on horses and ponies at the stables.

❹ Eastern Skansen. The **Finn Settlement** buildings came from Varmland where Finnish farmers settled in the 16th century to escape oppression and raids from Russia. The Finns were given land where they built farms and lived off the slash-and-burn style of cultivation. The settlement has a wooden building for drying and threshing corn, a smoke cabin, storehouse, and barn. In the early 19th century excessive alcohol consumption encouraged the temperance movement, led by people such as Peter Sieselgren, a Swedish priest who, in 1855, persuaded parliament to prohibit distilling spirits at home. The small **Temperance Hall** was just one of hundreds of such places, which both educated and entertained the locals.

❺ Southern Skansen. A lot of the fun of this outdoor museum is in the details. In the small house in the **Oktorp Farmstead,** you can imagine the farmer sitting in his 'high seat' warming his feet at the open fire, while beggars lurked in the kitchen behind a special beam to keep them, literally, in their place.

❻ Central Skansen. Seglora Church dates from 1730. It was shut up, abandoned in 1903, and transported here in 1916. The simple wooden church with its wooden floors and old-fashioned box pews is now one of Sweden's most popular wedding venues. Market Street leads you past the country market stalls to **Bolinastorget,** popular for both Midsummer celebrations and the Christmas market that is one of Stockholm's winter highlights (see p 45, ❷). Finally, **Skogaholm Manor** makes me want to decorate my own house in Scandinavian fashion. It's gracious without being too grand, furnished in Swedish rococo style, and has a wonderful collection

of blue-and-white china in the pantry. There's a Chinese drawing room, a nursery, bedchamber, and parlor. Well, I can always dream.

❼ Solliden Stage. When the stage was built here in 1938, its broadcasting equipment made it the most modern in the country and every major name came to perform here, such as the Swedish tenor Jussi Björling who gave an annual concert until his death in 1960. Today there are events throughout the year, from concerts to folk-dance displays.

🍴 Solliden Restaurant. You get a good view of Stockholm from the main restaurant, Solliden. It's a lovely building with decorations by well-known artists and serves a tempting smorgasbord. The Tre byttor occupies three small rooms and is a replica of an 18th-century tavern. It serves dishes such as fish casserole (165 SEK) and Caesar salad (165 SEK). The Terrace, open all year, is self-service and has a summer outdoor eating area. ☎ 08-566 370 00. www. profilrestauranger.se.

Practical Matters—Skansen

Tickets range from 70 SEK for adults and 30 SEK for children aged 6 to 15 years old, depending on the time of year. Free with Stockholm Card (see p 11). Open daily May to June 23 and September 10am to 8pm; June 24 to August 31 10am to 10pm; October, March, April 10am to 4pm; November to February Monday to Friday 10am to 3pm, Saturday, Sunday 10am to 4pm. For other dates, telephone or check on the website. They have folk music and dancing in the summer months and during the year on public holidays, including Christmas (see p 45, ❷). Bus 47, tram 7, ferry to Djurgården (summer). **Djurgårdsslätten 49–51.** ☎ 08-442 80 00. www.skansen.se.

Hagaparken

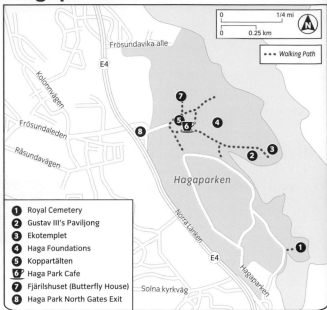

0	1/4 mi
0	0.25 km

N

● ● ● Walking Path

Frösundavika alle

E4

Kolonnvägen

Frösundaleden

Råsundavägen

Hagaparken

Norra Länken

E4

Hagaparken

Solna kyrkväg

① Royal Cemetery
② Gustav III's Paviljong
③ Ekotemplet
④ Haga Foundations
⑤ Koppartälten
⑥ Haga Park Cafe
⑦ Fjärilshuset (Butterfly House)
⑧ Haga Park North Gates Exit

Hagaparken was created by architect Fredrik Magnus
Piper (1746–1824) as part of King Gustav III's grand design
to build a new castle and the kind of romantic park that the English
excelled in. Surprisingly few visitors come out here, but make
the effort—it's easy and quick to reach from central Stockholm.
START: **T-bana to Odenplan then bus 515 to Haga Norra, or bus 59
to Haga Norra from central Stockholm.**

① ★ **Royal Cemetery.** Watch
out on the bus for the sign for Haga
Norra. Get off here by the Haga
Forum building and walk into the
park with the restaurant and tennis
courts to your right. It's all well signposted with maps every few hundred meters. The park was designed
in the mid-18th century when
Europe was having a full-blown love
affair with all things Oriental, hence
the small Turkish Pavilion and Chinese Pagoda. Just beyond, a tiny

island contains the Royal Cemetery.
Recent monarchs buried here,
rather than in Riddarholmskyrkan
(p 61), include Gustav VI Adolf
(1882–1973), and his second wife,
the former Lady Louise Mountbat-
ten (1889–1965), who was the current Duke of Edinburgh's aunt.
🕐 *30 min. May–Aug Thurs 1–3pm.*

② ★★ **kids Gustav III's Paviljong.** The path meanders beside
the water to this neoclassical palace, plain outside but glorious

Relax in Hagaparken.

within, with a magnificent hall of mirrors and classical Italian-style rooms. In March 1792, King Gustav III left here to go to the opera in Stockholm and never returned. He was assassinated that night and his ambitious plans for the park died with him. 🕐 *45 min.* 📞 *08-402 61 30. www.royalcourt.se. Admission: Adults 70 SEK, children 7–18 years 35 SEK. Free with Stockholm Card (see p 11). Jun and Aug Tues–Sun guided tours only noon, 1pm, 2pm, & 3pm.*

❸ ★ kids **Ekotemplet.** The odd round structure behind the pavilion was designed in the 1790s as a summer dining room for the Royal Family. The gracious pale building, Haga Slott was built from 1802 to 1804 for Gustav IV Adolf. The present King of Sweden, Karl XVI and his sisters were born and brought up here. Today it's the home of Princess Victoria and her husband and is not open to the public. 🕐 *25 min.*

Ekoparken National Park

Ekoparken, the world's first National City Park, was established in 1995. It stretches from Ulriksdal in the north out into the archipelago with the inclusion of the Fjäderholmarna islands. The park—the equivalent in area of Stockholm's inner city—covers an astonishing 27sq km (10.4sq miles): 19sq km (9.4sq miles) are land and 8sq km (3sq miles) are water. This urban National Park includes Haga Park and Djurgården and so is home to some of Stockholm's great museums, making it a unique mix of both natural wonders and human cultural achievements. The biodiversity is impressive; certain plants and insects are only found here, and it has the densest concentration of oak trees in Europe.

A Historical Bike Ride

The Royal National City Park, part of Ekoparken, is a wonderful place for a bike ride. The Stockholm authorities have made a 36km (14-mile) long bike route, fully signposted, from Ulriksdal in the north to Blockhusudden (the tip of Djurgården that juts out into the Baltic Sea) in the south. Pick up a map in the Haga Park Museum or at the Tourist Office, hire a bike (see p 63, ❶ and p 170) and take a ride past many of Stockholm's most beautiful buildings. You can do just one part of it as it's conveniently divided into three parts.

❹ **Haga Foundations.** Follow the signs to the Koppartälten (see below) but branch off to the right for the only evidence left of Gustav III's grandest design, the magnificent Versailles-inspired palace. The king's death stopped the project in its tracks and all that is here are the foundations. ⏱ *15 min.*

❺ ★ **kids Koppartälten.** You can see the vivid blues and golds of the Copper Tents from way off as they glint in the sunshine. Like the Drottningholmen Guards' Tent (see p 43, ❻), these delightful constructions, completed in 1790, were built as stables. The horses have long gone, replaced by the **Haga Park Museum** and a cafe/restaurant. The small museum shows the buildings of the park and has a model of the palace as it was intended to be. ⏱ *30 min. Museum:* ☎ *08- 27 42 52. www.sfv.se. Free Admission. Oct 1– May 14 Thurs–Sun 10am–3pm; May 15–Sept 31 Thurs–Sun 11am–5pm. Cafe:* ☎ *08-27 70 02. www. koppartalten.se. May–Sept 10am– 5pm; Oct–Apr 11am–4pm. Bus: 515.*

☕ **Haga Park Cafe.** Stop for a coffee or sandwich, and eat in the shelter of the Koppartälten (see above) or on the grass outside. *Coffee and sandwich 60 SEK.*

❼ ★★ **kids Fjärilshuset (Butterfly House).** The glass structures were the original greenhouse of the palace but plants have been replaced by exotic butterflies and birds that fly around you as you wander through the equivalent of a tropical rainforest. There are new exhibits with lake and river environments, plus African and South American exhibits with different varieties of fish. It's a great place for families, with a good cafe/restaurant and a decent-sized play area. ⏱ *1 hr. Haga Trädgård.* ☎ *08-730 39 81. www.fjarilshuset. se (in Swedish only). Adults 95 SEK, children 4–15 years 50 SEK. Free with Stockholm Card (see p 11). Apr–Sept Mon–Fri 10am–5pm, Sat, Sun, public hols 11am–6pm; Oct–Mar, closes one hour earlier. Bus: 515.*

❽ ★★ **kids Haga Park North Gates Exit.** From the Butterfly House, turn right along a path out of the park through the ornate official gates. Walk over the bridge and down to the road for bus 59 or 70 back to central Stockholm. ●

Dining Best Bets

Best **Old-School Swedish**
★★ Restaurangen Prinsen, *Master Samuelsgatan* (p 120)

Best **New Gastropub**
★★★ Pubologi, *Stora Nygatan 20* (p 119)

Best for **that Sublime Meal**
★★★ Mathias Dahlgren, *Grand Hotel* (p 118)

Best **Up-and-Coming Chefs**
★★★ Frantzén/Lindeberg, *Lilla Nygatan 21* (p 115)

Best **Seaside Experience**
★★★ Pontus by the Sea, *Tullhus 2* (p 119)

Best **Desserts**
★★ Xoko, *Rörstrandgatan 15* (p 39)

Best for **Eating in the Garden**
★★ Blå Porten, *Djurgardsvägen 64* (p 63); and ★★ Rosendals Trädgårdard, *Rosendalsterrassen 12* (p 65)

Best **Vegetarian**
★ Hermans Trädgårdarscafé, *Fjällgatan 23* (p 72)

Previous page: Grill Ruby. Below: Restaurangen Prinsen.

Best for **Historic Surroundings**
★★ Den Gyldene Freden, *Österlånggatan 51* (p 114)

Best for **Top Cooking with Drama**
★★★ Operakällaren, *Operahuset* (p 118); and ★★★ Teater Grillen, *Nybrogatan 3* (p 121)

Best **Moules**
★★ Brasserie Bobonne, *Storgatan 12* (p 114)

Best **Steak & Fries**
★★ Grill Ruby, *Österlånggatan 14* (p 113)

Best **Local Bistro**
★★ PA & Co, *Riddargatan 8* (p 118); and ★★ Bistrot Paname, *Hagagatan 5* (p 114)

Best **New Hotel Dining**
★★★ Lydmar Restaurant, *Södra Blasieholmen 2* (p 117)

Best for **Meatballs & Schnapps**
★★ Pelikan, *Blekingegatan 40* (p 118)

Best for **Surfing the World's Cuisines**
★★ Kungsholmen, *Norr Mälarstrand* (p 117)

Best for **Top Italian in Down-to-Earth Surroundings**
★★ Lo Scudetto, *Åsögatan 163* (p 117)

Best for **Södermalm Trend- Setters**
★★★ Nytorget Urban Deli, *Nytorget 4* (p 118)

Best for **Fish Lovers**
★★★ Lisa Elmquist/Lisa på Torget, *Östermalms Saluhall* (p 117)

Best **Snack on the Go**
★ Nystekt Strömming, *Södermalmstorg* (p 122)

North Stockholm Dining

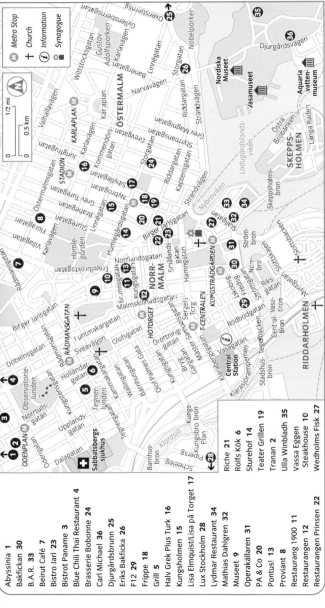

Legend:
- Ⓜ Metro Stop
- ✝ Church
- ⓘ Information
- ✡■ Synagogue

Abyssinia **1**
Bakfickan **30**
B.A.R. **33**
Beirut Café **7**
Bistro Jarl **23**
Bistrot Paname **3**
Blue Chili Thai Restaurant **4**
Brasserie Bobonne **24**
Carl Michael **36**
Djurgårdsbrunn **25**
Eriks Bakficka **26**
F12 **29**
Frippe **18**
Grill **5**
Halv Grek Plus Turk **16**
Kungsholmen **15**
Lisa Elmquist/Lisa på Torget **17**
Lux Stockholm **28**
Lydmar Restaurant **34**
Mathias Dahlgren **32**
Museet **9**
Operakällaren **31**
PA & Co **20**
Pontus! **13**
Proviant **8**
Restaurang 1900 **11**
Restaurangen **12**
Restaurangen Prinsen **22**
Riche **21**
Rolfs Kök **6**
Sturehof **14**
Teater Grillen **19**
Tranan **2**
Ulla Winbladh **35**
Vassa Eggen Steakhouse **10**
Wedholms Fisk **27**

Gamla Stan Dining

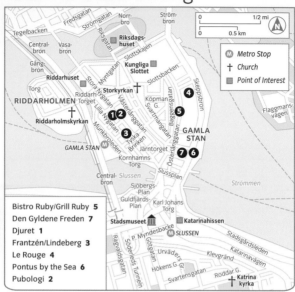

M Metro Stop
† Church
■ Point of Interest

Bistro Ruby/Grill Ruby **5**
Den Gyldene Freden **7**
Djuret **1**
Frantzén/Lindeberg **3**
Le Rouge **4**
Pontus by the Sea **6**
Pubologi **2**

Södermalm Dining

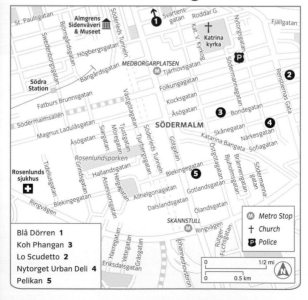

M Metro Stop
† Church
P Police

Blå Dörren **1**
Koh Phangan **3**
Lo Scudetto **2**
Nytorget Urban Deli **4**
Pelikan **5**

Stockholm Dining A to Z

★ **Abyssinia** VASASTADEN *ETHIOPIAN* Eat with your fingers and try *injera*, the thin pancake-like bread of Ethiopia for a genuine experience. For the full effect order the Abyssinia Special meal and don't forget to try the Ethiopian coffee. *Vanadisvägen 20.* ☎ *08-33 08 40. www. abyssinia.se. Mains 85–165 SEK. AE, DC, MC, V. Mon–Fri lunch & dinner, Sat 4pm–midnight. T-bana: Odenplan. Map p 111.*

★★ **Bakfickan** NORRMALM *SWEDISH/BRASSERIE* I like eating at the bar of the 'Hip Pocket' where it's more relaxed than Operakällaren (p 118). It shares the same kitchen as its posher sister so expect superb tournedos Rossini, or go Swedish with smoked Baltic herring with potatoes, caviar, and chives. *Kungliga Operan, Karl XII's Torg.* ☎ *08 676 58 08. www. operakallaren.se. Mains 160–298 SEK. AE, DC, MC, V. Mon–Fri 11:30am–11pm, Sat noon–10pm. T bana: Kungsträdgården. Map p 111.*

★★ **B.A.R.** ÖSTERMALM *SWEDISH/FRENCH* At Blasieholmens Akvarium o Restaurant (B.A.R.) Ocean Grill, you can choose from the fish tank or the meat and veg counter and decide on the cooking. Or, for ease, go for set dishes, which range from sandwiches and seafood pastas to excellent grills. Fun and affordable. *Blasieholmsgatan 4A.* ☎ *08-611 53 35. www.restaurangbar.se. Mains 98–235 SEK. AE, MC, V. Mon–Fri 10am–1am, Sat 4pm–1am, Sun 5–11pm. T-bana: Kungsträdgården. Map p 111.*

★★ **Beirut Café** NORRMALM *LEBANESE* This Lebanese restaurant with a warm, low-lit interior takes you straight to the Middle East. Cooking is excellent; for a good mix of dishes, I recommend ordering the wide *meze* selection at 330 SEK per person. *Engelbrektsgatan 37.* ☎ *08-21 20 25. www. beirutcafe.se. Mains 240–290 SEK. Set meze menus 33–450 SEK. AE, DC, MC, V. Dinner daily. T-bana: Tekniska högskolan. Map p 111.*

★★ **Bistro Jarl** ÖSTERMALM *SWEDISH/FRENCH* In a top shopping area, this is not as bistro-like as it sounds. In fact, it's high-end Stockholm having fun on French-inspired cooking. The restaurant is elaborate with gold and green decor and chandeliers; the bar buzzes. *Birger Jarlsgatan 7.* ☎ *08-611 76 30. www.bistrojarl.se. Mains 135–265 SEK. AE, DC, MC, V. Mon–Fri 11:30am–1am, Sat 1pm–2am. T-bana: Östermalmstorg. Map p 111.*

★★ kids **Bistro Ruby/Grill Ruby** GAMLA STAN *FRENCH/AMERICAN* This is Paris/Texas side by side. Bistro Ruby is traditional French given a Swedish twist; the Grill serves large well-cooked portions of steak and fries. The Bistro is more intimate;

Grill Ruby.

the Grill noisy and jumping. *Österlånggatan 14. Bistro:* ☎ *08-20 57 76. www.bistroruby.com. Mains 169–325 SEK. Grill:* ☎ *08-20 60 15. www.grillruby.com. Mains 179–499 SEK. AE, DC, MC, V. Both: dinner daily, Sat, Sun brunch. T-bana: Gamla Stan. Map p 112.*

★★ **kids** **Bistrot Paname** VASASTADEN *FRENCH* Rabbit with mustard on Monday; bouillabaisse on Friday. The locals who flock to this French place are rewarded with simple decor, an open fire in winter, and French classics. Eat outdoors in summer. *Hagagatan 5.* ☎ *08-31 43 38. www.bistrotpaname.se. Mains 102–245 SEK. AE, MC, V. Tues–Thurs 5pm–midnight; Fri, Sat 5pm–1am. T-bana: Östermalmstorg. Map p 111.*

★ **kids** **Blå Dörren** SÖDERMALM *SWEDISH* On the main square at Slussen, this old-style Swedish restaurant delivers simple classics. Good value, friendly and well-located. *Södermalmstorg 6.* ☎ *08-743 07 40. www.bla-dorren.se. Mains 124–224 SEK. AE, MC, V. Mon 10:30am–11pm; Tues–Thurs 10:30am–midnight; Fri 10:30am–1am; Sat 1pm–1am; Sun 1–11pm. T-bana: Östermalmstorg. Map p 112.*

★ **kids** **Blue Chili Thai Restaurant** VASASTADEN *THAI* Strong flavors are on offer in this small, pretty Thai restaurant which serves all the classics from traditional spicy soup to red curry with beef. Drink beer or a soft drink. *Surbrunnsgatan 38.* ☎ *08-673 69 69. www.bluechili. se. Mains 149–169 SEK. AE, MC, V. Mon–Fri lunch & dinner; Sat noon– 10pm; Sun noon–9pm. T-bana: Odenplan. Map p 111.*

★★ **kids** **Brasserie Bobonne** ÖSTERMALM *BRASSERIE* I love this small friendly restaurant for its local feel and classic brasserie dishes from the chalkboard, cooked in an open kitchen. If you're longing for a plate of moules marinières or a boeuf Bourguignon, this is the place. *Storgatan 12.* ☎ *08-660 03 18. www.brasseriebobonne.se. Mains 185–295 SEK. Prix fixe menu 498 SEK. AE, MC, V. Mon–Sat 5–11pm. T-bana: Östermalmstorg. Map p 111.*

★★ **Carl Michael** DJURGÅRDEN *MODERN SWEDISH* A favorite with Stockholmers—locals come for the elegant 18th-century feel, and a sophisticated kitchen which produces a mix of traditional and modern. Try dishes like grilled char with roe, crème fraiche, fennel, snap peas, and steamed potatoes. *Allmänna Gränd 6.* ☎ *08-667 45 96. www.carlmichael.se. Mains 165–295 SEK. AE, DC, MC, V. Lunch Mon– Tues; Wed–Sat noon–10pm; Sun noon–6pm. Bus 47. Map p 111.*

★★ **Den Gyldene Freden** GAMLA STAN *SWEDISH* This is a real oldtimer (since 1772) with three floors of snug corners and old-fashioned decor. But it's not stuck in a time warp; try adventurous dishes such as baked Arctic char with fennel relish, smoked potatoes and wild garlic sauce. Yes, it's full of tourists, but it's also a Stockholm stalwart. *Österlånggatan 51.* ☎ *08-24 97 60. www. gyldenefreden.se. Mains 185–365 SEK. Set menu (whole table only) 3 courses 620 SEK. AE, DC, MC, V. Lunch Mon–Fri; dinner Mon–Sat. T-bana: Gamla Stan. Map p 112.*

★★ **Djuret** GAMLA STAN *SWEDISH* Translated as 'animal', Djuret is a carnivore's delight. Each month they feature a different animal, and use all the cuts and cooking methods possible for main dishes: roast, stuffed, grilled, casseroled. The small dining room in the Collector's Victory Hotel is closed in summer, but their courtyard restaurant (Svinet) opens for barbecues. *Lilla Nygatan 5.* ☎ *08-506 400 84. www.djuret.se. Mains 195–325 SEK. Mon–Sat*

5pm–midnight. Closed end June–end Aug. T-bana: Gamla Stan. Map p 112.

★★ kids Djurgårdsbrunn

DJURGÅRDEN *SWEDISH* The canalside setting is magical and the terrace fills up fast in summer. The menu covers everything from moules frites to beef tartar and does it very well. *Djurgårdsbrunnsvägen 68.* ☎ *08-624 44 00. www. djurgardsbrunn.com. Mains 195–295 SEK. Jan–mid-Apr & mid-Sep–Nov Sat & Sun lunch; Mid-Apr–May 23 Sat, Sun lunch, Wed–Sun dinner; May 24– mid-Sep daily lunch & dinner; Dec daily lunch & dinner. AE, DC, MC, V. Bus: 69. Map p 111.*

★★ kids Eriks Bakficka ÖSTER-

MALM *SWEDISH* I always take friends to Eriks Gondolen for a drink but for a casual meal, I prefer Eriks's little sister. This small local restaurant has home comfort dishes such as Eriks's cheeseburger and seabass in Niçoise sauce with potato and anchovy croquette. *Fredrikshovsgatan 4.* ☎ *08-660 15 99. www. eriks.se. Mains 175–325 SEK. Set menus 495–585 SEK. AE, DC, MC, V. Lunch Mon–Fri; dinner Mon–Sat. T-bana: Karlaplan. Map p 111.*

★★★ F12 NORRMALM *MODERN*

SWEDISH F12 is thoroughly

The sleek and fashionable F12.

Beside the canal at Djurgårdsbrunn.

fashionable and very Swedish high society. The cooking is innovative and seasonally led and the menu is positively poetic. 'Fishing the Open Water' is langoustine lightly smoked with hemp and pepper shoots; 'Slow Cooked – Late Winter' arrives as brisket of Wagyu beef with sunflower roots, licorice, and consommé. *Fredsgatan 12.* ☎ *08-24 80 52. www.fredsgatan12.com. Mains 320–420 SEK. Set menu (whole table) 1,195 SEK. AE, DC, MC, V. Lunch Mon–Fri; dinner Mon–Sat. T-bana: T-Centralen. Map p 111.*

★★★ Frantzén/Lindeberg

GAMLA STAN *CONTEMPORARY*

Labeled as 'the ones to watch,' chefs Björn Frantzén and Daniel Lindeberg are rising international culinary stars. The restaurant is tiny with only 19 covers. With a menu dictated by what is bought daily and from their own gardens, you hand yourself over to the master chefs. This is sophisticated, experimental cooking. *Lilla Nyagatan 21.* ☎ *08-20 85 80. www.frantzen-lindeberg.se. Set menus 1,395 SEK and 1,595 SEK. AE, DC, MC, V. Dinner Tues–Sat. T-bana: Gamla Stan. Map p 112.*

★ **kids** **Frippe** NORRMALM *SWEDISH* With its moody black-and-white photos, long bar with seats, large windows, and proximity to the smaller stage of the Dramaten Theater, this is the perfect pre- or post-theater dining spot. It's good value, too, offering a menu of favorites. *Nybrogatan 6.* ☎ *08-665 61 42. www.frippe. gastrogate.com. Mains 189–265 SEK. AE, DC, MC, V. Mon 11:30am–2:30pm; Tues–Wed 11:30am–11pm; Thurs, Fri 11:30am–midnight; Sat 1:30pm– midnight; Sun 4–10pm. T-bana: Kungsträdgården. Map p 111.*

★★ **kids** **Grill** NORRMALM *CONTEMPORARY* It's best to decide on

your mood and style before booking here. Swedish traditional? American steaks? French courtesan? Grill is a huge old furniture store converted into different areas. Choose your cuisine from Asian to Mediterranean. *Drottninggatan 89.* ☎ *08-31 45 30. www.grill.se. Mains 190–695 SEK. AE, DC, MC, V. Lunch Mon–Fri, Sat 4pm–1am, Sun 3–11pm. T-bana: Rådmansgatan. Map p 111.*

★ **kids** **Halv Grek Plus Turk** ÖSTERMALM *GREEK/ TURKISH* Bright colors, Turkish cushions, and blue tiles. The menu is *meze*-based, with the classics alongside more unusual concoctions such as seared tuna with sorbet of fried tomato. *Jungfrugatan 33.* ☎ *08-665 94 22. www.halvgrekplusturk.se. Meze 57–99 SEK. AE, DC, MC, V. Mon–Fri lunch & dinner; Sat, Sun 6pm–midnight. T-bana: Stadion. Map p 111.*

★★ **kids** **Koh Phangan** SÖDERMALM *THAI* This brightly decorated, buzzing restaurant stretching back into small spaces of bamboo booths and huts among pools of water also serves some of the best Thai food outside Thailand. Be prepared to queue with a drink until

Black and white photographs at Frippe.

French bordello style at Grill.

your name is called. *Skånegatan 57.* ☎ *08-642 68 65. www.kohphangan. se. Mains 189–291 SEK. AE, DC, MC, V. Mon, Tues 11am–midnight; Wed– Fri 11am–1am; Sat, Sun 1pm–1am. T-bana: Medborgarplatsen. Map p 112.*

★★ **Kungsholmen** KUNGSHOLMEN *CONTEMPORARY* The restaurant has a lovely waterfront, complete with summer pontoon. It's based around seven open kitchens— choose from Sushi, Swedish, Fast Food, Spiced Grills, Slow Food, Luxury and Fruit. It's large (seats 200), loud, crowded, open late, and fun. *Norr Mälarstrand.* ☎ *08-50 52 44 50. www.kungsholmen.com. Mains 140–485 SEK. AE, DC, MC, V. Summer: dinner daily; winter: dinner Mon–Sat. Closed June 24–26. T-bana: Radiuses. Map p 111.*

★★ **Le Rouge** GAMLA STAN *CONTEMPORARY* There's more than a touch of the Moulin Rouge in this dramatic restaurant with its red velvet seating, drapes, and old master style art. There's a large dining room, bar for lunch and small dishes in the evening, an outside terrace, and two entrances. *Brunnsgrand 2–4.* ☎ *08-505 244 30. www. lerouge.se. Mains 295–455 SEK. AE, DC, MC, V. Dinner Mon–Sat. Bar Mon-Thurs lunch & dinner; Fri 11:30am–1am; Sat 5pm–1am. T-bana: Gamla Stan. Map p 112.*

★★ **kids Lisa Elmquist/Lisa på Torget** ÖSTERMALM *SWEDISH/ FISH* Based in the fabulous food emporium of Östermalms Saluhall, every Stockholmer will have eaten at Lisa Elmqvist at least once in their lives. Along with Lisa på Torget outside, this is the place for classic fish dishes. *Östermalms Saluhall.* ☎ *08-55 34 04 00. www.lisa elmqvist.se. Mains 150–289 SEK. AE, DC, MC, V. Mon–Thurs 9:30am–6pm; Fri 9:30am–7pm; Sat 9:30am–4pm. T-bana: Östermalmstorg. Map p 111.*

★★ **kids Lo Scudetto** SÖDERMALM *ITALIAN* It took a while to find Lo Scudetto the first time, but it was worth the effort—the restaurant serves great Italian food and is far better than you'd imagine from the simple candlelit decor. Relaxed and always crowded, so book. *Klimmendörsgatan 46.* ☎ *08-640 42 15. www.loscudetto.se. Mains 157–297 SEK. Set menus 59–797 SEK. AE, DC, V. Dinner Mon–Sat. T-bana: Medborgarplatsen. Map p 112.*

★★★ **Lux Stockholm** KUNGSHOLMEN *SWEDISH* Henrik Nordström is the genius behind this experimental, starred restaurant in the former Electrolux canteen. Expect Swedish ingredients cooked with a contemporary concern for the unexpected. *Primusgatan 116.* ☎ *08-619 01 90. www.luxstockholm.com. Mains 370– 390 SEK. Set menus 950–1,175 SEK. AE, DC, MC, V. Tues–Fri lunch & dinner; Sat 5–11pm. T-bana: Rådhuset. Map p 111.*

★★ **kids Lydmar Restaurant** BLASIEHOLMEN *SWEDISH* The dining room of the trendiest hotel in

Stockholm is remarkably at ease, decorated like a large living room with bookshelves and casual tables. The feel is carried through with a friendly waiting staff and a menu of comforting bistro classics—duck breast, tuna, and mussels. *Södra Blasieholmshamnen 2.* ☎ *08-22 31 60. www.lydmar.com. Mains 195–345 SEK. AE, DC, MC, V. Breakfast, lunch & dinner daily. T-bana: Kungsträdgården. Map p 111.*

★★★ **Mathias Dahlgren** NORRMALM *FRENCH* What can be said about this Michelin-starred grand restaurant where sublime dishes are ordered by the wealthy gourmet? Only that you should go if you want the best and can afford it. But there is the chance to eat the master's food at a more reasonable price by booking at the smaller Matbaren. This may be less a temple of gastronomy, but it is still top notch. *Grand Hotel, Södra Blasieholmshamnen 6.* ☎ *08-679 35 84. www. mdghs.com. Matsalen menus 1,250– 1,500 SEK. Matbaren mains 135–315 SEK. AE, DC, MC, V. Dinner Tues–Sat. Matbaren lunch Mon–Fri, dinner Mon–Sat. T-bana: Kungsträdgården. Map p 111.*

★★ **Museet** ÖSTERMALM *FRENCH/ SWEDISH* Big cocktail bar with serious mixers behind it, wooden floors, and crisply set tables plus the odd quirky artifact; the new bistro in town is proving popular. Add to that classic French dishes like mussels, chips, and aioli and honest prices (steak frites at 195 SEK). *Birger Jarlsgatan 41.* ☎ *08-20 10 08. www. restaurantmuseet.se. Mains 155–295 SEK. AE, DC, MC, V. Mon–Thurs 11am–1am; Fri 11am–2am; Sat 5pm–2am; Sun 5pm–1am. T-bana: Östermalmstorg. Map p 111.*

★★ kids **Nytorget Urban Deli** SÖDERMALM *SWEDISH* The fittingly hip N.U.D. is a well-stocked deli, food hall, and restaurant/bar. Weekly themes like 'French Invasion,' excellent charcuterie, oysters, seafood, dishes such as côte de boeuf, lobster, and steaks plus children's menus mean the former post office buzzes every night. *Nytorget 4.* ☎ *08-599 091 80. www.urban deli.org. Mains 189–360 SEK. AE, MC, V. Sun–Tues 8am–11pm; Wed, Thurs 8am–midnight; Fri, Sat 8am– 1am. Bus 2. Map p 112.*

★★★ **Operakällaren** NORRMALM *SWEDISH/FRENCH* All gilded walls, mirrors, and chandeliers, it's a suitably theatrical setting for some dramatic cooking. Dishes such as steak tartare with duck liver terrine, mushrooms in champagne jelly, and caviar are complex and skillfully prepared. *Operahuset, Karl XII's Torg.* ☎ *08-676 58 00. www. operakallaren.se. Mains 310–495 SEK. Set menu 1,050 SEK; tasting menu (whole table, before 9pm) 1,400 SEK. AE, DC, MC, V. Dinner Tues–Sat. Closed Jul. T-bana: Kungsträdgården. Map p 111.*

★★ kids **P.A. & Co.** ÖSTERMALM *BISTRO* It looks like a bistro in a small French town and delivers the goods. Classics are the order of the day here—veal burgers and traditional sausages chalked up on a blackboard. *Riddargatan 8.* ☎ *08- 611 08 45. Mains 155–345 SEK. AE, DC, MC, V. Dinner daily. T-bana: Östermalmstorg. Map p 111.*

★ **Pelikan** SÖDERMALM *SWEDISH* Go to this beer hall for a feel of old Stockholm. Wood-paneled, with painted walls, and very popular, this is the place for traditional meatballs, ice-cold schnapps, and beer. *Blekingegatan 40.* ☎ *08-55 60 90 92. www.pelikan.se. Mains 154–244 SEK. AE, MC, V. Mon–Thurs 4pm– midnight; Fri, Sat 1pm–1am; Sun 1pm–midnight. T-bana: Skanstull. Map p 112.*

P.A. & Co. is a friendly local bistro.

★★ **Pontus!** NORRMALM *MODERN SWEDISH* Pontus Frithiof is something of a local hero and this restaurant, with its new entrance and Seafood Bar, is great fun. The menu is a free-for-all where you can mix different concepts and tailor your orders to a budget or just go all out for it. Nettle soup or foie gras? Or how about Grandma's organic meatballs? It's all very good. *Brunnsgatan 1.* ☎ *08-545 27 300. www.pontusfrithiof.com. Mains 185–325 SEK. AE, DC, MC, V. Lunch Mon–Fri; dinner Mon–Sat. T-bana: Hötorget. Map p 111.*

★★ **kids Pontus by the Sea** GAMLA STAN *SEAFOOD* On the waterfront, this relaxed venue of star chef Pontus Frithiof looks out onto the water and is the place to go for fresh seafood. I recommend a glass of wine in the outdoor bar looking at the sea for a real summer experience. *Tullhus 2, Skeppsbron.* ☎ *08-20 20 95. www.pontusfrithiof.com. Mains 230–445 SEK. Seafood platters 375–1,395 SEK. AE, DC, MC, V. Jan 10–Apr 30 lunch Mon–Fri, dinner Wed–Sat; from 1st May lunch Mon–Fri, dinner Mon–Sat. Closed early Jan. T-bana: Gamla Stan. Map p 112.*

★★ **Proviant** ÖSTERMALM *BRASSERIE* Mattias Edlund and Håkan Thor moved from Sweden's top restaurant, Edsbacka Korg, to open this brasserie and bar looking onto the park. It's a local restaurant, good value, and has a menu that concentrates on Scandinavian seasonal produce such as pike, Swedish veal, and homemade sausage. *Sturegatan 19.* ☎ *08-22 60 50. www.proviant.se. Mains 235–295 SEK. AE, DC, MC, V. Lunch Mon–Fri; dinner daily. T-bana: Östermalmstorg. Map p 111.*

★★ **kids Pubologi** GAMLA STAN *GASTROPUB* You sit on high barstool-type chairs at a long table or at tables down the side; cutlery is in a drawer in front of you. Dishes or plates come in half sizes, from top charcuterie (two people should order the selection of six at 295 SEK) to three sausages of veal, beef and lamb with unusual spicing. It's very well done, and popular; you must book. *Stora Nygatan 20.* ☎ *08-506 400 86. www.pubologi.se. Plates 100–180 SEK. AE, DC, MC, V. Mon–Fri 5pm–midnight; Sat noon–midnight. T-bana: Gamla Stan. Map p 112.*

★★ **Restaurang 1900** NORRMALM *SWEDISH* Known for his TV appearances, chef Niklas Ekstedt moved to central Stockholm to open his latest restaurant. It's a simple room with light wood furniture; the menu is divided into classic and modern and the cooking concentrates on Swedish ingredients, as well as using Oriental spicing. *Regeringsgatan 66.* ☎ *08-20 60 10. www.r1900.se. Mains 215–355 SEK. AE, DC, MC, V. Lunch Mon–Fri; dinner Mon–Sat. T-bana: Kungsträdgården. Map p 111.*

★★ **Restaurangen** NORRMALM *SWEDISH* Opened in 1999, this is the place to try the 'grazing' concept. Circle your choice from a menu which classifies dishes by the predominant flavor. So 'garlic' is tortellini of snails; 'miso' means glazed lamb cutlet with Japanese radish and sesame; 'saffron' is ossobucco with toast and citrus. Portions are small so order at least five dishes. *Oxtorgsgatan 14.* ☎ *08-22 09 52. www.restaurangentm.com. 3 dishes 350 SEK, 5 dishes 450 SEK, 7 dishes 550 SEK. AE, DC, MC, V. Lunch Mon–Fri; dinner Mon–Sat. T-bana: Hötorget. Map p 111.*

★★ **Restaurangen Prinsen** ÖSTERMALM *BRASSERIE* The charming old-fashioned decor in this busy brasserie has a real French feel to it. The menu of classics like salmon pie, pork belly, and braised veal has been satisfying a wide range of customers since 1897. *Master Samuelsgatan 4.* ☎ *08-611 13 11. www.restaurangprinsen.se. Mains 179–375 SEK. AE, DC, MC, V. Mon–Fri 11:30am–11:30pm; Sat 1–11:30pm; Sun 1–10:30pm. T-bana: Östermalmstorg. Map p 111.*

★★ **Riche** ÖSTERMALM *SWEDISH/ EUROPEAN* Bustling, beautiful, and full of beautiful people, Riche is fun with its modern decor and buzzing atmosphere. The cooking is fine, but it's the scene you're here for. *Birger Jarlsgatan 4.* ☎ *08-545 035 60. www.*

Rich pleasures at Riche.

riche.se. Mains 120–335 SEK. AE, DC, MC, V. Mon 11:30am–midnight; Tues–Fri 11:30am–2am; Sat noon–2am. T-bana: Östermalmstorg. Map p 111.

★★ **Rolfs Kök** NORRMALM *INTERNATIONAL/BRASSERIE* Famous for its wall-hung chairs, this trendy, minimalist-designed bar/restaurant has a great atmosphere and modern cooking, done with a flourish in the open kitchen. It's a favorite for lunch. *Tegnérgatan 41.* ☎ *08-10 16 96. www.rolfskok.se. Mains 195–355 SEK. AE, DC, MC, V. Mon–Fri 11:30am–1am; Sat, Sun 5pm–1am. T-bana: Rådmansgatan. Map p 111.*

★ **Sturehof** NORRMALM *SWEDISH/ FRENCH* Despite the thoroughly modern clientele, the menu majors in fish and sticks to the classics, both Swedish and French, from herrings with cheese to turbot with sugar snap peas. Meat eaters get a good choice as well. *Stureplan 2.* ☎ *08-440 57 30. www.sturehof.*

RESTAURANG PRINSEN

Cafe Society

With the Swedes among the biggest coffee drinkers in the world, Stockholm's cafes are all-important. **Petite France,** John Ericssonsgatan 6, ☎ 08-618 28 00, www.petitefrance.se, is an archetypal French cafe on Kungsholmen. **Per Olsson Choklad & Konditori (POCK)** sells great cakes in a bright pink and white cafe in west Södermalm (Heleneborgsgatan 19, ☎ 08-668 10 11, www. pock.nu). Get your cupcakes at **Cupcake Sthlm,** Sankt Eriksgatan 83, ☎ 08-83 80 83, www.cupcakesthlm.se. Östermalm's **Saturnus,** Eriksbergsgatan 6, ☎ 08-611 77 00, www.cafesaturnus.se, has a great breakfast to start the day.

com. Mains 125–485 SEK. AE, DC, MC, V. Mon–Fri 11am–2am; Sat noon–2am; Sun 1pm–2am. T-bana: Östermalmstorg. Map p 111.

★★ **Teater Grillen** ÖSTERMALM SWEDISH/FRENCH Beside the Dramaten Theater, this restaurant just has to be theatrical. And it is, with a silver trolley doing the rounds when the famous salt-baked entrecote steak is ordered. Otherwise go for the classics. Expensive but a good evening's entertainment. Nybrogatan 3. ☎ 08-545 035 60. www. teatergrillen.se. Mains 165–495 SEK. AE, DC, MC, V. Lunch Mon–Fri;

dinner Mon–Sat. T-bana: Kungsträdgården. Map p 111.

★★ **kids** **Tranan** VASASTADEN SWEDISH With its red-and-white check tablecloths, and honest dishes from moules to classic Biff Rydberg, this deservedly popular restaurant gets very crowded. There's also a heaving cellar bar with DJs pumping out late-night music. Karlbergsvägen 14. ☎ 08-527 2 81 00. www.tranan.se. Mains 145–295 SEK. AE, DC, MC, V. Mon–Fri 11:30am–1am; Sat, Sun 5pm–1am. T-bana: Odenplan. Map p 111.

Stylish Vassa Eggen Steakhouse.

Cheap Eats

Eating in Stockholm is expensive, with alcohol upping the bill. But you *can* eat cheaply. Most restaurants offer special *dagens lunch* or lunch of the day deals, anything from 80 to 125 SEK at the top end. One of the best deals in town is a herring plate or sandwich (around 45 to 75 SEK) at the kiosk **Nystekt Strömming,** on Södermalmstorg just outside the Slussen T-bana station. Several restaurants in **Hötorgshallen** offer good-value meals. Try **Izmir Kebab** for a good Turkish kebab, or the excellent **Kajsas Fish.** You'll get great lunchtime dumplings and salad or grilled chicken plus sea views at **Jin & Peeters Dumpling and Chicken Deli,** Kungsholms Strand 157, ☎ 08-654 03 00, www.jinandpeeters.se. In Södermalm, go for great crepes at **Creperie Fyra Knop,** Svartensgatan 4, ☎ 08-640 77 27, and lovely juicy kebabs at all hours at **Jerusalem Kebab,** Götgatan 59, ☎ 08-644 39 82.

★★ **Ulla Winbladh** DJURGÅRDEN *SWEDISH* Romantic and old-fashioned is just what you expect—and get—in this pretty venue named after a friend of the famous composer Carl Michael Bellman. The menu is Swedish classics with French flourishes. Eat outside in summer. *Rosendalsvägen 8.* ☎ *08-534 897 01. www.ullawinbladh.se. Mains 145–315 SEK. AE, DC, MC, V. Mon 11:30am–10pm; Tues–Fri 11:30am–11pm; Sat 12:30–11pm; Sun 12:30–10pm. Bus 47. Map p 111.*

★★ **Vassa Eggen Steakhouse** ÖSTERMALM *FRENCH* The 'Sharp Edge' is just that—chic, stylish, and elegant, attracting the movers and shakers of Stockholm. The menu majors in steaks and the charcoal grill. In the evening the bar gets seriously full of late-night clubbers,

albeit of an extremely elegant kind. *Birger Jarlsgatan 29.* ☎ *08-21 61 69. www.vassaeggen.com. Mains 190–495 SEK. AE, DC, MC, V. Lunch Mon–Fri; dinner Mon–Sat. Closed July. T-bana: Hötorget. Map p 111.*

★★★ **Wedholms Fisk** ÖSTER-MALM *SEAFOOD* This elegant well-established institution started by the revered Bengt Wedholm in 1985 is now under the care of Nils Molinder and the approach has lightened. But you still get some of the best fish and seafood cooking in Sweden. In summer book a table outside. *Nybrokahen 17.* ☎ *08-611 78 74. www.wedholmsfisk.se. Mains 265–595 SEK. AE, DC, MC, V. Lunch Mon–Fri; dinner Mon–Sat. T-bana: Kungsträdgården/Österlmalmstorg. Map p 111.* ●

Nightlife Best Bets

Best for Beer Fiends
★★ Akkurat, *Hornsgatan 18 (p 127)*

Best for Design Freaks and Foodies
★★ Brasserie Godot, *Grev Turegatan 36 (p 127)*

Best New Place to be Seen
★★★ Guldbaren, *Norrmalmstorg 2–4 (p 128)*

Best for a Drink with a View
★★★ Eriks Gondolen, *Stadsgården 6 (p 127)*; and ★★ Och Himlen Dartill, *Götgatan 78 (p 128)*

Best New Nightclub
★★★ Kåken, *Regeringsgatan 66 (p 129)*

Best for a Voodoo Moment
★★ Marie Laveau, *Hornsgatan 66 (p 129)*

Best Friday Night Gay Club
★★ Kolingsborg, *Gula Gängen (p 130)*

Best for Jazz Legends
★★★ Fasching, *Kungsgatan 63 (p 131)*

Best for Rocking the Night Away
★★ Debaser Medis, *Medborgarplatsen 8 (p 132)*

Best for Jazz Brunch
★★★ Mosebacke, *Mosebacke Torg 3 (p 132)*

Best for a Cool Moment
★★★ Ice Bar, *Vasaplan 4 (p 128)*

Beer heaven at Akkurat.

How to Get In

Stockholm has one of Europe's liveliest nightlife scenes but some of the clubs are members only (which can be quite flexible so don't be put off when you hear that). Also you're often faced with long queues and an undefined dress code that you can only pick up on by looking at the beautiful people in the queue—and by then it's too late to change. So if you're going out, dress carefully, and turn up before 10pm to avoid the late-night crowds and get past the doormen. The most challenging clubs are around Stureplan, which is Stockholm nightlife central. Many of them charge for the cloakroom—which can be up to 150 SEK per person, so be prepared for unexpected extras.

Previous page: The Anglais bar.

North Stockholm Nightlife

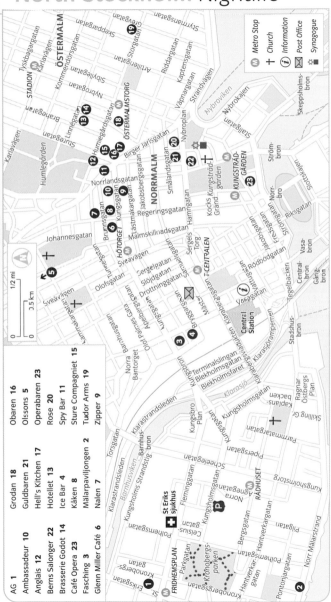

Legend

- Ⓜ Metro Stop
- + Church
- ⓘ Information
- ⊠ Post Office
- ✡ Synagogue

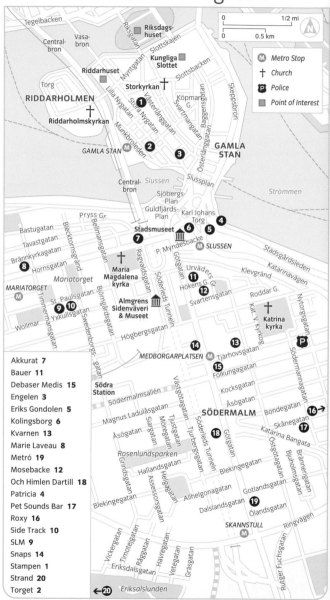

Bars & Pubs

★★ AG KUNGSHOLMEN AG is a bar/restaurant/lounge housed in an old silver workshop. It's difficult to find and is industrial in feel inside so it's bound to be a hit. *Kronobergsgatan 37.* ☎ *08-410 681 00. www.restaurangag.se. T-bana: Fridhemsplan. Map p 125.*

★★ Akkurat SÖDERMALM For an impressive beer list, drink at this wooden-floored and -paneled pub (which also has a good whisky bar) with 28 beers on tap, more than 600 bottles, and 44 whiskies. Sunday evening live music helps the Leffes go down. *Hornsgatan 18.* ☎ *08-644 00 15. www.akkurat.se. T-bana: Marlatorget/Slussen. Map p 126.*

★★ Anglais NORRMALM One of Stockholm's chicest hotel bars is a great place for a relaxing drink with a view out to the street. The separate top floor Terrace Bar has extensive views. *Humlegårdsgatan 23.*

☎ *08-517 340 00. www.scandic hotels.com/anglais. T-bana: Östermalmstorg. Map p 125.*

★ Bauer SÖDERMALM This big space with a large bar area is decorated like a child's manic dream— huge cartoons cover the walls and the color scheme is primary. Good tapas to accompany beers and wines and great atmosphere. *Götgatan 15.* ☎ *08-640 08 20. T-bana: Slussen. Map p 126.*

★★ Brasserie Godot ÖSTERMALM The startling white brasserie serves great food and offers one of Stockholm's chicest cocktail bars for the young and/or fashionable. *Grev Turegatan 36.* ☎ *08-660 06 14. www.godot.se. T-bana. Östermalmstorg. Map p 125.*

★★★ Eriks Gondolen SÖDERMALM Sipping a drink and looking at the view should be on everybody's list. But you'll have to work hard to get your drink at this hugely

Chic drinking at Grodan.

popular venue. *Stadsgården 6.*
☎ *08-641 70 90. www.eriks.se.*
T-bana: Slussen. Map p 126.

★★★ **Grodan** ÖSTERMALM
Despite heavy competition from
newer venues, Grodan stays top of
the nightlife league. The restaurant/
bar and small downstairs club offer
different decors while bar staff are
pleased to mix you your own particular cocktail. *Grev Turegatan 16.*
☎ *08-679 61 00. www.grodan.se.*
T-bana: Östermalmstorg. Map p 125.

★★★ **Guldbaren** ÖSTERMALM
The Nobis hotel's Gold Bar is gorgeous. All decked out in deep colors, and gold of course, it's become
the magnet for smart office after-
hours drinkers. Great cocktails help,
as does the soaring atrium which
takes the considerable overflow.
The outdoor terrace is perfect for
people-watching. *Norrmalmstorg
2–4.* ☎ *08-614 10 00. www.nobis
hotel.se. T-bana: T-Centralen. Map
p 125.*

★★ **Hotellet** ÖSTERMALM This
chic venue was a success the
moment it opened in 2003. It's a bar
where the cocktails are as beautiful

*The traditional beer hall exterior of
Kvarnen.*

as the bar staff and customers.
Dress up, not down. *Linnégatan 18.*
☎ *08-442 89 00. www.hotellet.info.*
T-bana: Östermalmstorg. Map p 125.

★★ **Ice Bar** NORRMALM In the
Nordic Sea Hotel, this is, literally,
the coolest place in town to drink.
Don a fur-lined coat and boots
before sampling vodka, served in
ice glasses. Be warned, it's expensive. *Vasaplan 4.* ☎ *08-50 56 30 00.*
www.nordicseahotel.se. T-bana:
T-Centralen. Map p 125.

★ **Kvarnen** SÖDERMALM It looks
traditional from the outside—just
like the former beer hall it was
before its present life. Today it's a
popular late-night pub with a couple
of bars and DJs spinning the music
most nights. Fun and friendly.
Tjarhovsgatan 4. ☎ *08-643 03 80.*
*www.kvarnen.com. Entrance around
130 SEK for shows only. T-bana:
Medborgarplatsen. Map p 126.*

★★ **Och Himlen Dartill** SÖDER-
MALM The view from the 26th-
floor Skybar gives Gondolen a run
for its money. The decor is so cool it
almost hurts. And the cocktails?
Very good. Also a jaw-droppingly
expensive restaurant. *Götgatan 78.*
☎ *08-660 60 68. www.restaurang
himlen.se. T-bana: Medborgarplatsen. Map p 126.*

★★★ **Operabaren** NORRMALM
This is an unusually peaceful place
for a drink in splendid Jugendstil surroundings. The old-fashioned wait-
ers are charming; the atmosphere
club-like. *Operahuset, Karl XII's Torg.*
☎ *08-676 58 00. www.operakallaren.
se. T-bana: Kungsträdgården. Map
p 125.*

★ **Snaps** SÖDERMALM Huge bar
with summer outdoor terrace and
dining area for all-day eating and
drinking. There's also a dance club

and basement bar that get going after 11pm. *Götgatan 48.* ☎ *08-640 28 68. www.snapsbar.se. Entrance 100 SEK after 11pm. T-bana: Medborgarplatsen. Map p 126.*

★ **Tudor Arms** ÖSTERMALM Stockholm's oldest British pub, founded in 1969, is the place where homesick Brits gather in the wood-beamed room for fish 'n' chips, a pint of bitter, and a game on the huge TV screen. In 2011, it was voted the best pub outside Britain. *Grevgatan 31.* ☎ *08-660 27 12. www.tudorarms.com. T-bana: Östermalmstorg. Map p 125.*

Dance & Nightclubs

★★ **Ambassadeur** NORRMALM This nightclub has three different rooms, Ambassadeur White (great vocals), Black (for R&B and Soul), and Gold (go for the '70s' retro music). It's very trendy; dress the part to get in and feel at home. *Kungsgatan 18.* ☎ *08-545 076 02. www.stureplansgruppen.se. Prices vary. T-bana: Kungsträdgården. Map p 125.*

★★ **Berns Salonger** NORRMALM One of Stockholm's institutions since it first opened in 1863, this elegant club is in two rooms (more relaxed upstairs, garage downstairs). In theory, it's members only (and hotel guests), so turn up early looking good. *Berzelii Park 9.* ☎ *08-566 322 00. www.berns.se. Tickets from 160 SEK. T-bana: Kungsträdgården. Map p 125.*

★★ **Café Opera** NORRMALM You're in, quite simply, one of the smartest nightclubs in town, which fills up with beautiful young things. If you have the money, the best thing to do is dine at Operakällaren (see p 118) then party on here until 3am. *Operahuset, Kungsträdgården.*

Berns Salonger opened in 1863.

☎ *08-676 58 07. www.cafeopera. se. Admission 300 SEK. Map p 125.*

★★ **Hell's Kitchen** ÖSTERMALM Under Sturecompagniet, this is the place for over-the-top, hellish decor (skulls are all the rage here) and a young, beautiful, and rich crowd. Tables have waitress service; go with a full wallet. *Sturegatan 4.* ☎ *08-545 076 75. www.stureplansgruppen. se. Entrance 200 SEK. T-bana: Östermalmstorg. Map p 125.*

★★★ **Kåken** NORRMALM Both bar and club, the space under Restaurant 1900 is turning into the place where young media and arty types mix. Great cocktails and modish food like mussels and chorizo, and blackened pork chops keep them going for the live acts and music regularly held here. *Regeringsgatan 66.* ☎ *08-20 60 10. www.kaken. r1900.se. T-bana: Kungsträdgården. Map p 125.*

★★ **Marie Laveau** SÖDERMALM This trendy nightspot, named after the New Orleans voodoo Queen, is a bar and club with great DJs. Also has a good restaurant if you want to spin out the evening yourself. *Hornsgatan 66.* ☎ *08-66 88 500. www. marielaveau.se. Entrance fee varies for different shows. T-bana: Slussen. Map p 126.*

★★ Metró SÖDERMALM The black-and-red decor and a slick Södermalm crowd who come for the DJs spinning in two bars guarantee its success. Minimum age of 23 is strictly applied. *Götgatan 93.* ☎ *08-673 38 00. T-bana: Medborgarplatsen. Map p 126.*

★★ Obaren ÖSTERMALM Above the restaurant Sturehof, DJs and live acts (at least two a week) mix just about everything to an equally mixed crowd, who come here for the music as much as the vibe, and keep going to 2am. *Stureplan 2.* ☎ *08-440 57 30. www.sturehof.com. No cover. T-bana: Östermalmstorg. Map p 125.*

★★ Olssons VASASTADEN What do you do with an old shoe shop? In Stockholm, you turn it into a party venue. It's small and very crowded, the decor dominated by a fish tank, and the clientele dance informally to the bar's music mix on Wednesday and to club nights on Saturday. The cocktails are legendary. *Odengatan 41.* ☎ *08-673 38 00. www.storstad. se. Entrance varies. T-bana: Odenplan. Map p 125.*

Spy Bar for funk and soul.

★ Rose NORRMALM Attracting a slightly older crowd who appreciate the red plush and crystal chandeliers, Rose is a restaurant and club. Small dance floor but big on atmosphere with funky sounds. *Hamngatan 2.* ☎ *08-440 56 30. www.villagesthlm. com. No cover. T-bana: Östermalmstorg. Map p. 125.*

★★ Spy Bar NORRMALM Stockholm's best-known bar and club still packs them in. You're with a mixed bunch—media and clubbers. Expensive once you're past the velvet rope and bouncers. Music ranges from funk to soul. *Birger Jarlsgatan 20.* ☎ *08-545 07 655. www.sture plansgruppen.se. No cover. T-bana: Östermalmstorg. Map p 125.*

★★ Strand SÖDERMALM Large and very popular restaurant, concert venue, and club open every day and evening to late (except Sunday) with international names. Great for brunch and great for late-evening clubbing. *Hornstull Strand 4.* ☎ *08-658 63 50. www.hornstullstrand.se. Various prices for concerts. T-bana: Hornstull. Map p 126.*

★★★ Sture Compagniet ÖSTERMALM One of Stockholm's top clubs and difficult to get into, it's the capital's biggest, brash, vibrant, and full of a thoroughly cool crowd of 20-somethings. Only go if you're dressed right and feeling brash yourself. *Sturegatan 4.* ☎ *08-545 076 01. www.sturecompagniet.se. Entry: Fri, Sat 120 SEK. T-bana: Östermalmstorg. Map p 125.*

Gay & Lesbian Bars/Clubs
★★ Kolingsborg SÖDERMALM Paradise on Fridays claims to be Stockholm's biggest gay club (disco, party, house, and club, 20 plus) while Garage on Saturdays is great for good hip hop (23 plus). *Gula*

Gången, Södermalmstorg 2. ☎ *08-643 39 46. www.clubkak.se. Prices vary. T-bana: Slussen. Map p 126.*

★★ Mälarpaviljongen

KUNGSHOLMEN   An outdoor bar/ restaurant on the waterfront with a new jetty and great view. During the day it's mixed, at night it's gay. Summer only. *Norr Mälarstrand 64.* ☎ *08-650 87 01. www.malarpaviljongen. se. T-bana: Rådhuset/ Fridhemsplan. Map p 125.*

★★ Patricia SÖDERMALM

Winston Churchill spent time on his boat (hence an eponymous room), built in Middlesbrough, England in 1938, and it became the British royals' private yacht. Now, it has restaurants, live music, and DJs. But it's best known for Sunday gay nights, famous throughout the international gay community. *Stadsgårdskajen 152.* ☎ *08-743 05 70. www.patricia. st. T-bana: Slussen. Map p 126.*

★ Roxy SÖDERMALM

Run by three women, this enjoyably casual restaurant and bar attracts mainly a female crowd of all ages and is known as a lesbian favorite. It's right in the heart of trendy SoFo, the menu is reasonably priced and the atmosphere fun. *Nytorget 6.* ☎ *08-640 96 55. www.roxysofo.se. T-bana: Skanstul/Medborgarplatsen. Map p 126.*

★ Side Track SÖDERMALM

Good food and great atmosphere at this casual basement venue. It's popular, informal, and fun for the mainly male crowd. *Wollmar Yxkulls-gatan 7.* ☎ *08-641 16 88. www. sidetrack.nu. No cover. T-bana: Mariatorget. Map p 126.*

★★ SLM SÖDERMALM

This male-only venue is a warren of small dark rooms. The website lays it out: this is the place for leather, rubber, uniform, and fetishes. Dress as you feel. *Wollmar Yxkullsgatan 18.* ☎ *08 643 31 00. www.slm stockholm.se. Membership cards 1 year 400 SEK; 1 month 150 SEK; Sat after 11pm 50 SEK or valid ECMC membership. T-bana: Mariatorget. Map p 126.*

★★ Torget GAMLA STAN

The gay bar most visitors have heard of hasn't been spoilt by its popularity. This is an excellent venue with good food, DJs Thursdays to Saturdays, and an international audience. *Mälartorget 13.* ☎ *08-20 55 60. www.torgetbaren.com. T-bana: Gamla Stan. Map p 126.*

★★ Zipper ÖSTERMALM

Popular Saturday night large club for gays and lesbians with a variety of different bars and dance floors for pop, R'n'B, and more. *Lästmakargatan 8.* ☎ *08-20 62 90. www.zippersthlm. com. Entrance 120 SEK. T bana: Östermalmstorg. Map p 125.*

Jazz Clubs

★★★ Fasching NORRMALM

This is a jazz club that does deserve the 'legendary' label—the photographs on the walls show you the great names that have performed here. Concerts and jazz sessions every night and a knowledgeable crowd of all ages come for the mix of music from funk to mainstream jazz, Friday Latin Club, and Soul on Saturdays. *Kungsgatan 63.* ☎ *08-21 62 67. www.fasching.se. Tickets* ☎ *08-534 82 960. Tickets 60–300 SEK. T-bana: T-Centralen. Map p 125.*

★ Glenn Miller Café NORRMALM

Tiny and cramped, this friendly pub hosts a variety of jazz acts. It's decorated with black-and-white photos on tobacco-colored walls and has simple wooden chairs and tables. Free admission but you're asked to contribute something. *Brunnsgatan 21a.* ☎ *08-10 03 22. www.glenn millercafe.com. T-bana: Hötorget. Map p 125.*

★★★ Stampen GAMLA STAN

This jazz club, founded in 1968, is so small you really get up close to the musicians. Two floors: trad jazz and R&B upstairs (and an older audience); rockabilly and country for the younger downstairs. Cluttered interior and grainy old photos. *Stora Nygatan 5.* ☎ *08-20 57 93. www.stampen.se. Some nights free; otherwise prices from 120 SEK. T-bana: Gamla Stan. Map p 126.*

Music Clubs

★★ Debaser Medis SÖDERMALM

Tops for live rock, Debaser and its other venue Debaser Slussen (Karl Johns Torg 1, ☎ 08-30 56 20) attract a young crowd for nightly concerts of country, rock, pop, hip-hop, and reggae. Debaser Medis is huge with bars, dance floors, cinema, gallery, and restaurant on three floors. *Medborgarplatsen 8.* ☎ *08-694 79 00. www.debaser.se. Admission varies. T-bana: Medborgarplatsen. Map p 126.*

Engelen rocks in Gamla Stan.

★★ Engelen GAMLA STAN The

old-fashioned look fits in well to Gamla Stan. But push open the door and you're met with up-to-date bands playing nightly. The downstairs cellar takes up where the upstairs leaves off, with old favorites and new music providing the atmosphere. *Kornhamnstorg 59.*

☎ *08-50 55 60 90. www.engelen.se. Entrance after 8pm: Mon–Thurs 70 SEK; Fri, Sat 100 SEK. T-bana: Gamla Stan. Map p 126.*

★★★ Mosebacke SÖDERMALM

Right at the heart of Stockholm's historic entertainment center, many of Sweden's best have played here. There's a wide variety at the main stage, at Kägelbanan and in Södra Bar which turns into a nightclub at around 9pm with DJs or live bands. There's a jazz brunch at weekends. *Mosebacke Torg 1–3.* ☎ *08-531 99 490. www.mosebacke.se. Some evenings free, or tickets 50–250 SEK. T-bana: Slussen. Map p 126.*

★★ Nalen NORRMALM Renova-

tion turned Stockholm's original top jazz venue into a place with a range of music, from American folk singers like Elliott Murphy to the latest Swedish rock group, soul and swing. The large venue has three stages, a restaurant, rock club, and studio. *Regeringsgatan 74.* ☎ *08-505 292 00. www.nalen. com. Tickets* 60–265 SEK. T-bana: Hötorget. Map p 125.*

★★ Pet Sounds Bar SÖDERMALM

It started in the rock store opposite; now you can get indie-rock and DJs spinning the evening out in the bar and basement below the restaurant. Good restaurant also. *Skånegatan 80.* ☎ *08-643 82 25. www.pet soundsbar.se. Admission prices vary. T-bana: Medborgarplatsen. Map p 126.* ●

Stockholm Arts & Entertainment

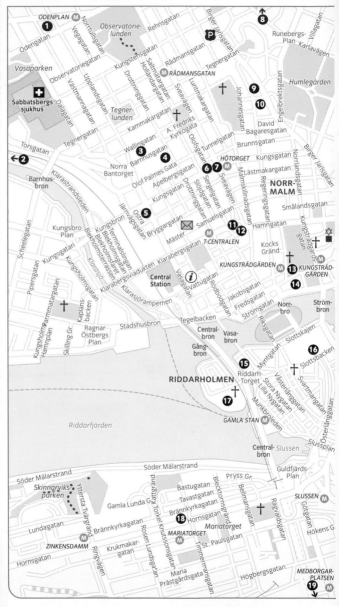

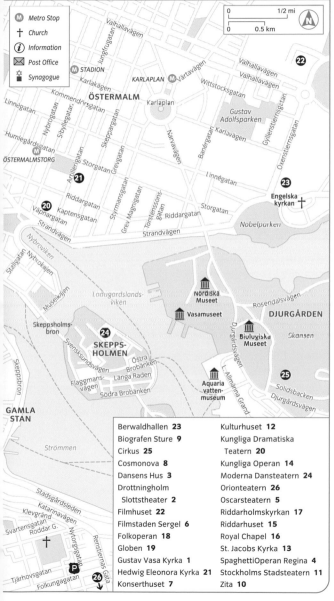

Legend:
- Ⓜ Metro Stop
- † Church
- ⓘ Information
- ✉ Post Office
- ✡ Synagogue

Arts & Entertainment Best Bets

The fabulous Kungliga Opera house.

Best **Modern Music Premieres**
★★ Berwaldhallen, *Dag Hammarskjoldsväg 3 (p 137)*

Best **Classical Music in an Architectural Masterpiece**
★★ Konserthuset, *Hötorget (p 137)*; and ★★ Riddarhuset, *Riddarhustorget 10 (p 137)*

Best **Contemporary Dance**
★★ Dansens Hus, *Barnhusgatan 12–14 (p 137)*

Best **Opera in a Regal Setting**
★★★ Kungliga Operan, *Gustav Adolfs Torg (p 137)*

Best for **an Ingmar Bergman Moment**
★★ Filmhuset, *Borvagen (p 138)*

Best **Baroque Stage Design**
★★★ Drottningholm Slottstheater, *Drottningholm Palace (p 139)*

Best **Complete Evening's Entertainment**
★★ SpaghettiOperan Regina, *Drottninggatan 71A (p 139)*

Best for **Romeo & Juliet**
★★ Kungliga Operan, *Gustav Adolfs Torg (p 137)*

Best for **Ice Hockey Frenzy**
★★ Globen, *Globentorget 2 (p 140)*

Buying Tickets

You'll find information on special events in the official *What's On Stockholm* guide, free at most hotels and tourist information centers. For the latest concert, theater, and event listings pick up a copy of the ***På stan,*** the Thursday supplement of newspaper *Dagens Nyheter,* at newsstands (Swedish only). Useful websites include www.alltom stockholm.se and www.stockholmtown.com. Buy tickets at the venues themselves, via their websites, or at the Stockholm Tourist Office. Or book via **Ticnet,** ☎ 077-170 70 70, www.ticnet.se.

The season runs mainly from September to May or June, so if you come expecting theater, music, and dance in the summer, you'll probably be disappointed.

Chapter opener image: Orpheus sculpture group by Carl Milles outside Konserthuset.

Arts & Entertainment **A to Z**

Classical Music & Concert Venues

★★ Berwaldhallen ÖSTERMALM This modernist concert hall is the home of the Swedish Radio Symphony Orchestra and the Radio Choir, founded in 1967. The Orchestra is known for commissioning new Swedish music. *Dag Hammarskjoldsväg 3.* ☎ *08-784 18 00. www. berwaldhallen.se. Tickets 55–1,250 SEK. T-bana: Karlaplan. Map p 135.*

★★ Konserthuset NORRMALM Konserthuset, an architectural masterpiece, was built in 1926 for the Royal Philharmonic Orchestra, which commissions modern works as well as playing the major classical works, under the principal conductor, Sakari Oramo. The Konserthuset also hosts international orchestras, dance companies, and jazz. *Hötorget.* ☎ *08 506 677 00. www. konserthuset.se. Tickets 70–340 SEK. T-bana: Hötorget. Map p 134.*

★★★ Riddarhuset. GAMLA STAN The magnificent House of the Nobility hosts concerts every autumn and spring, including jazz. You get first-class music in a magnificent setting. See p 61, ❾. *Riddarhustorget 10.* ☎ *08-723 39 90 .www.riddarhuset. se. Tickets 220–290 SEK. T-bana: Gamla Stan. Map p 135.*

Dance & Opera

★★★ Dansens Hus NORRMALM The major venue for Swedish contemporary dance and performance artists offers an exciting program on its two stages. Companies performing here range from the Helsinki Dance Company to small groups and individuals. *Barnhusgatan 12–14.* ☎ *08-508 990 90. www. dansenshus.se. Tickets 230–280 SEK. T-bana: Hötorget/T-Centralen. Map p 134.*

★★★ Kungliga Operan NORRMALM 'The dancers are not disagreeable and perform accurately; they promise to become quite good in time.' King Gustav III was modestly proud of the Swedish Royal Ballet Company he formed, along with the Royal Opera, in 1773. The company today, one of the four oldest in the world, performs classical and contemporary dance. *Gustav Adolfs Torg. Box office* ☎ *08-791 44 00. www.operan.se. Tickets 60–790 SEK. T-bana: Kungsträdgården. Map p 134.*

★ Moderna Dansteatern SKEPPSHOLMEN The former torpedo factory on Skeppsholmen island is a fitting setting for the innovative contemporary and performance art this exciting company stages from Swedish and international companies. *Slupskjulsvägen 30, Telefonplan.* ☎ *08-611 14 56. www.mdtsthlm.se. Tickets 180 SEK. T-bana: Kungsträdgården, bus 65. Map p 134.*

★★ kids Orionteatern SÖDERMALM Founded in 1983 in an old factory, this outstanding avant-garde theater works with international companies from the Peking Opera in Shanghai to Théâtre de Complicité in London and Le Cirque Invisible from Paris. *Katarina Bangata 77. Info:* ☎ *08-649 29 70. Tickets* ☎ *08-43 88 80. www. orionteatern.se. Tickets 80–250 SEK. T-bana: Skanstull. Map p 135.*

Film

★★ **Biografen Sture** ÖSTERMALM Opened in 1915, the delightful, old-fashioned Sture shows arthouse films from Sweden and the rest of Europe in the original language with subtitles in Swedish. *Birger Jarlsgatan 41.* ☎ *08-562 948 80. www.biosture.se. Tickets 95–100 SEK. T-bana: Östermalmstorg. Map p 135.*

★★ **kids Cosmonova** FRESCATI Sweden's only IMAX cinema in the Natural History Museum (p 55, ⑪) shows movies on a 760sq m (8,180sq ft.) dome-shaped screen. 3-D options include getting up close to Egyptian mummies. *Naturhistoriska Riksmuseet. Frescativägen 40.* ☎ *08-519 540 00. www.nrm.se. Tickets included in museum admission. Separate tickets adults 90 SEK, children 5–18 years 50 SEK. T-bana: Universitetet; bus: 40, 540. Map p 134.*

★★ **Filmhuset** GÄRDET Housing the Swedish Film Institute, the Film House screens arthouse films, often English with Swedish subtitles, all week. A ticket for one show costs 65 SEK; for more, buy an annual membership for 180 SEK. *Borvägen 1–5.* ☎ *08-665 11 00. www.sfi.se. T-bana: Karlaplan. Map p 135.*

★ **kids Filmstaden Sergel** GÄRDET Foreign subtitled films are shown in some of the 14 screens in this huge complex. *Hötorget.* ☎ *08-56 26 00 00. www.sf.se. Tickets 95 SEK. T-bana: Hötorget. Map p 134.*

★★ **Zita** ÖSTERMALM You're likely to find a film by Ken Loach, a Japanese cartoon, or the latest Swedish art film in this movie theater where you can quench your thirst at the bar. *Birger Jarlsgatan 37.* ☎ *08-23 20 20. www.zita.se. Tickets 90 SEK. T-bana: Östermalmstorg. Map p 135.*

Music in Churches

★ **Gustav Vasa Kyrka** VASASTADEN Stop by for lunchtime organ concerts on Thursdays at noon and regular summer concerts on Wednesdays. *Odenplan.* ☎ *08-508 886 00. www.gustafvasa.nu. Tickets 50–150 SEK. T-bana: Odenplan. Map p 134.*

Gustav Vasa Kyrka's painted dome.

★ Hedvig Eleonora Kyrka

ÖSTERMALM   Organ music Monday, Wednesday, and Friday at 12:15pm. From May to November the church bells play a psalm tune, daily 9am, noon, 3pm, 6pm, and 9pm. *Storgatan 7.* ☎ *08-545 675 70. www.hedvigeleonora.se. Lunchtime music tickets 40 SEK. T-bana: Östermalmstorg. Map p 135.*

★★ Riddarholmskyrkan GAMLA

STAN   Enjoy summer concerts of classic and Gregorian music, from chamber ensembles to instrumental solos and voice. No advance booking. *Birger Jarls Torg.* ☎ *08-402 61 30. Adults 30 SEK; children 7–15 & students 15 SEK. Jun–mid-Aug, Sat, Sun at 1pm. www.kungahuset.se. T-bana: Gamla Stan. Map p 135.*

★★ Royal Chapel GAMLA

STAN   Organ concerts are held on Fridays by the Court and the City Hall Organists. From mid-August to mid-September, the *Royal Music Festival* fills the Royal Chapel and the great Hall of State with the best classical music. *Kungliga Slottet Gamla Stan.* ☎ *08-402 61 30. www. royalcourt.se. Royal Music Festival: www.royalfestivals.se. Tickets 240– 360 SEK. T-bana: Gamla Stan. Map p 135.*

★ St. Jakobs Kyrka ÖSTER-

MALM   Every Friday at 5pm the church has a free organ recital. Also Saturday concerts at 3pm. *Jakobs Torg 5.* ☎ *08-723 30 38. www. stockholmsdomkyrkoforsamling.se. T-bana: Kungsträdgården. Map p 134.*

Opera

★★★ Drottningholm Slottsthe-

ater DROTTNINGHOLM PALACE   This is one of Stockholm's most exclusive opera festivals, offering Monteverdi, Haydn, and more in the baroque 18th-century theater of the Royal Family's country home, May to September. All music is performed on period instruments and the original stage equipment is used. A special theater bus provides transport from central Stockholm. *Drottningholm Palace.* ☎ *08-660 82 25. www.royalcourt.se. Tickets* ☎ *077-170 70 70;* ☎ *08-660 82 25. www.dtm.se. Tickets 275–795 SEK. For Drottningholm see p 40. Map p 134.*

★★ Folkoperan SÖDERMALM

The unconventional Folk Opera is internationally known for its cutting-edge approach. The theater offers both classic and modern works in an intimate setting. Very popular, so book well ahead. *Hornsgatan 72.* ☎ *08-616 07 50. www.folkoperan. se. Tickets 260–450 SEK. T-bana: Mariatorget. Map p 134.*

★★★ kids SpaghettiOperan

Regina NORRMALM   Great entertainment here where the guests become part of the performance as the singers perform on the stage and between the tables (in *Cosi fan Tutte* you're guests at a wedding party). Performances are either specially adapted full operas or *Spaghettiopera* nights with highlights. *Drottninggatan 71A.* ☎ *08-411 63 20. www.regina-operamathus.com. Tickets 745 SEK for performance, 3-course meal, coffee. No drinks included in price. Luxury package 1,290 SEK performance, Champagne aperitif, wine, and special 3-course dinner. T-bana: T-Centralen. Map p 134.*

Rock & Performance Venues
★★ kids Cirkus DJURGÅRDEN

Built in 1892 for circus troupes, this round building seats 1,650 and puts on a wide variety of shows. There's also a restaurant, so packages of show and dinner are available. *Djurgårdsslätten 43–45. Box office* ☎ *08-660 10 20. www.cirkus.se. Tickets from 400 SEK. Special* packages from 965 SEK. Bus: 47. Tram: 7. Map p 135.

★★ **kids** **Globen** JOHANNESHOV Stockholm's huge, globe-shaped indoor arena is visible from all over Stockholm. It's the venue for big rock concerts (REM, Coldplay, Bruce Springsteen), one-person shows (Leonard Cohen), and sports such as ice hockey. *See p 47. Globentorget 2. Box office* ☎ *077-131 00 00. www. globearenas.se. Tickets 200–1,695 SEK. T-bana: Globen. Map p 134.*

Theater

★★ **Kulturhuset** KUNGSHOLMEN This huge complex has two stages, Kilen and Horsalen, and the Klara movie theater. The annual International Writers' Stage hosts international guests. *Sergels Torg. Box office* ☎ *08-508 31 509. www. kulturhuset.stockholm.se. Tickets 90–360 SEK. T-bana: T-Centralen. Map p 134.*

★★★ **Kungliga Dramatiska Teatern** ÖSTERMALM The Royal Dramatic Theater is splendidly housed in a flamboyant building. It's the major theater in Stockholm, with the country's best actors performing Shakespeare and Strindberg and more unconventional theater. The second stage (Elverket, Linnégatan 69) shows modern performance art. *Nybroplan. Box Office* ☎ *08-667 06 80. www.dramaten.se. Tickets 100– 380 SEK. T-bana: Östermalmstorg/ Kungsträdgården. Map p 134.*

★★ **kids** **Oscarsteatern** NOR-RMALM Large venue putting on musicals such as *Monty Python's Spamalot. Kungsgatan 63. Box office* ☎ *08-20 50 00. www.oscarsteatern. se. Tickets 90–615 SEK. T-bana: T-Centralen. Map p 134.*

★★ **Stockholms Stadsteatern** NORRMALM Scandinavia's large theater umbrella organization has six stages and the outdoor Parkteatern program in different venues. Wide range from classics to avant-garde. *Sergels Torg.* ☎ *08-506 202 00. www.stadsteatern.stockholm.se. Tickets 230–380 SEK. T-bana: T-Centralen. Map p 134.* ●

Ingmar Bergman

Ernst Ingmar Bergman, born in Östermalm in 1918, was one of the most influential film-makers of modern cinema. But the nine-times Academy-nominated playwright, director, and producer was also important in the theater and the opera, which was his first love. His first unpaid job was at the opera and in 1991 he returned for a last opera production of *Bacchanalia*. From 1963 to 1966 he was Director of the Dramatiska Teatern, creating more than 100 theatrical productions. But he is best known for the great cinematic classics *Smiles of the Summer Night* (1955), *The Seventh Seal* (1957), *Wild Strawberries* (1957), and, near the end of his career, the magnificent *Fanny and Alexander* (1982). He died in 2007 and is buried on the island of Fårö, off Sweden's southeastern coast.

Stockholm Lodging

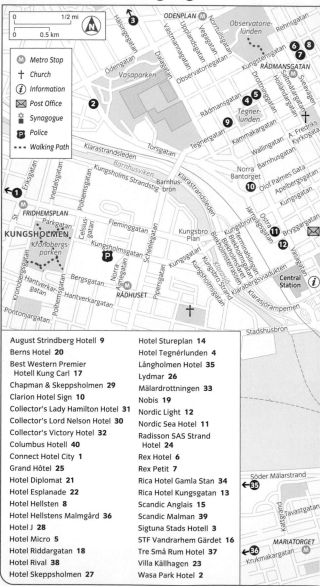

August Strindberg Hotell **9**

Berns Hotel **20**

Best Western Premier
  Hotell Kung Carl **17**

Chapman & Skeppsholmen **29**

Clarion Hotel Sign **10**

Collector's Lady Hamilton Hotel **31**

Collector's Lord Nelson Hotel **30**

Collector's Victory Hotel **32**

Columbus Hotell **40**

Connect Hotel City **1**

Grand Hôtel **25**

Hotel Diplomat **21**

Hotel Esplanade **22**

Hotel Hellsten **8**

Hotel Hellstens Malmgård **36**

Hotel Micro **5**

Hotel Riddargatan **18**

Hotel Rival **38**

Hotel Skeppsholmen **27**

Hotel Stureplan **14**

Hotel Tegnérlunden **4**

Långholmen Hotel **35**

Lydmar **26**

Mälardrottningen **33**

Nobis **19**

Nordic Light **12**

Nordic Sea Hotel **11**

Radisson SAS Strand
  Hotel **24**

Rex Hotel **6**

Rex Petit **7**

Rica Hotel Gamla Stan **34**

Rica Hotel Kungsgatan **13**

Scandic Anglais **15**

Scandic Malman **39**

Sigtuna Stads Hotell **3**

STF Vandrarhem Gärdet **16**

Tre Små Rum Hotel **37**

Villa Källhagen **23**

Wasa Park Hotel **2**

Previous page: Waterside views at the Radisson SAS Strand.

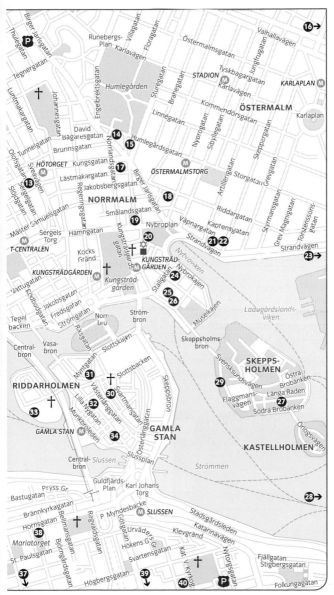

Lodging Best Bets

Best for **Star Quality**
★★★ Nobis, *Norrmalmstorg 2–4* (p 150)

Best for **Winners & Would-Be Award Winners**
★★★ Grand Hôtel *Södra Blasiehol-mshamnen 8 (p 147)*

Best **Fabulous New Boutique Hotel**
★★★ Lydmar, *Södra Blasieholmsh-amnen 2 (p 150)*

Best **Budget Hotels**
★ Rex Petit, *Luntmakargatan 73 (p 151);* and ★ Connect Hotel City, *Alströmergatan 41 (p 147)*

Best for **That Away-From-It-All Feel**
★★★ Hotel Skeppsholmen, *Gröna gången 1 (p 149)*

Best for **Cutting-Edge Design**
★★★ Clarion Hotel Sign, *Östra Järnvagsgatan 35 (p 146);* and ★★★ Nordic Light, *Vasaplan 7 (p 151)*

The Entrance to Berns Hotel.

Best for **Late-Night City Revelers**
★★★ Berns Hotel, *Berzelli Park (p 145)*

Best **Medieval Location**
★★★ Collector'sVictory Hotel, *Lilla Nygatan 5 (p 147)*

Best **Business Hotel**
★★ Best Western Premier Hotell Kung Carl, *Birger Jarlsgatan 21 (p 145)*

Best for **Antiques**
★★ Collector's Lady Hamilton Hotel, *Storkyrkobrinken 5 (p 146)*

Best **Floating Option**
★ Chapman & Skeppsholmen, *Flaggmansvägen 8 (p 145)*

Best **Ecclesiastical View**
★★ Columbus Hotell, *Tjärhovs-gatan 11 (p 147)*

Best **Sea Views**
★★★ Radisson SAS Strand Hotel, *Nybrokajen (p 151)*

Best for **Nautical Types**
★★★ Hotel J, *Ellensbiksvägen 1 (p 148);* and ★★ Mälardrottningen, *Vasaplan 7 (p 150)*

Best for **Families**
★★ Långholmen Hotel, *Långholms-muren 20 (p 150)*

Best for **Lovers**
★★★ Hotel Hellsten, *Luntmakar-gatan 68 (p 148)*

Best for **Posh Shoppers**
★★ Hotel Stureplan, *Birger Jarls-gatan 24 (p 149)*

★ August Strindberg Hotell

NORRMALM   Just around the corner from playwright August Strindberg's former home, the eponymous hotel has small rooms prettily decorated in pale pastels. The open fire is welcoming in the dining room in winter, and there's a garden for summer breakfasts. *Tegnérgatan 38.* ☎ *08-35 50 06. www.hotellstrindberg.se. 27 units. Doubles 1,395–1,595 SEK w/ breakfast. AE, MC, V. T-bana: Rådmansgatan. Map p 142.*

★★★ Berns Hotel NORRMALM

Berns is chic and elegant with a star following. All rooms are very well appointed; rates follow room size and the more expensive ones have balconies. If you can, go for the Clock Suite that looks out over Berzelli Park. *Nåckströmsgatan 8.* ☎ *08-56 63 22 00. www.berns.se. 82 units. Doubles 1,600–5,500 SEK w/breakfast. Clock Suite 6,500– 10,500 SEK. AE, DC, MC, V. T-bana: Kungsträdgården/Östermalmstorg Map p 143.*

★★ Best Western Premier Hotell Kung Carl NORRMALM

This may be a conference hotel, although old tiled stoves and balconies in the conference rooms are a big hit, but it's just as good for holiday guests, with individually decorated rooms in bold colors, a great location, and a warm welcome. *Birger Jarlsgatan 21.* ☎ *08-463 50 00. www.kungcarl.se. 134 units. Doubles 1,690–2,640 SEK w/breakfast. AE, DC, MC, V. T-bana: Hötorget/Östermalmstorg. Map p 143.*

★ kids Chapman & Skeppsholmen SKEPPSHOLMEN

This hostel must have one of the best locations anywhere. It's on a fully rigged ship moored off Skeppsholmen, so you'll be rocked quietly to sleep—although there is a land hostel as well. The boat's bar serves breakfast plus drinks and snacks. *Flaggmansvägen 8.* ☎ *08-463 22 66. www.slf chapman.com. 175 units. Twin room land: 700 SEK, ship 810 SEK. (Join Hostelling International and get 50*

Dining room at the Best Western Premier Hotell Kung Carl.

Columbus Hotell.

SEK per room discount per night.) AE, MC, V. T-bana: Kungsträdgården. Map p 143.

★★★ Clarion Hotel Sign NOR-RMALM
Stockholm's largest hotel is a striking granite-and-glass structure. Each floor celebrates a different iconic Scandinavian or Nordic designer, so if you fancy a room furnished with Arne Jacobson's Egg, you can book it. The Aquavit Grill and Raw Bar adds a touch of Manhattan and the rooftop spa keeps

Chapman & Skeppsholmen

you fit. *Östra Järnvägsgatan 35.* ☎ *08-676 98 00. www.clarionsign. com. 558 units. Doubles 1,500–2,500 SEK w/breakfast. AE, DC, MC, V. T-bana: T-Centralen. Map p 143.*

★★ Collector's Lady Hamilton Hotel GAMLA STAN
The Lady Hamilton is stuffed full of antiques and has traditional paintings from the Dalarna region on the walls. Bistro Emma is open all day. It's ideal for single women—who find special lady kits in their rooms—as well as families. *Storkyrkobrinken 5.* ☎ *08-506 401 00. www.ladyhamiltonhotel. se. 34 units. Doubles 1,690–3,090 SEK w/breakfast. AE, DC, MC, V. T-bana: Gamla Stan. Map p 143.*

★★ kids Collector's Lord Nelson Hotel GAMLA STAN
This 17th-century building is long and narrow (6m/ 20 ft wide). You're greeted by assorted naval artifacts and a portrait of Nelson. Each floor is named after a deck and each room after a ship (a model of which adds to the room's decor). A small rooftop terrace gives a bird's eye view of Gamla Stan. *Västerlång-gatan 22.* ☎ *08-506 401 20. www. lordnelsonhotel.se. 29 units. Doubles 1,490–2,190 SEK w/breakfast. AE, DC, MC, V. T-bana: Gamla Stan. Map p 143.*

★★★ Collector's Victory Hotel

GAMLA STAN   This is the top hotel in the small Berglssen family-owned group. Like the others, nautical decoration makes seafaring Brits feel at home. There's a good restaurant, Djuret (see p 114), a gay-friendly bar, and a summer terrace to keep guests returning. *Lilla Nygatan 5. ☎ 08-506 400 00. www.victory hotel.se. 45 units. Doubles 1,690–5,090 SEK w/breakfast. AE, DC, MC, V. T-bana: Gamla Stan. Map p 143.*

★★ kids Columbus Hotell

SÖDERMALM   The entrance through a courtyard and small lobby doesn't prepare you for the delightful rooms, classically decorated, in this series of town houses built in 1780. The two-roomed Lorenz Sifvert Suite comes with its own lobby and looks directly at Katarina Kyrka (p 71). In summer, take breakfast out to the courtyard. *Tjärhovsgatan 11. ☎ 08-503 112 00. www. columbus.se. 40 units. Doubles 1,295–2,295 SEK w/breakfast. AE, DC, MC, V. T-bana: Medborgarplatsen. Map p 143.*

★ kids Connect Hotel City

KUNGSHOLMEN   For the budget conscious, choose from a small cabin room to an extra large one.

All come with good bathrooms. On mainly residential Kungsholmen but only a short metro ride into T-Centralen or up to Vasastaden. *Alströmergatan 41. ☎ 08-441 02 30. www.connecthotel.se. 86 units. Doubles 695–1,295 SEK w/breakfast. AE, DC, MC, V. T-bana: Fridemsplan. Map p 142.*

★★★ Grand Hôtel

BLASIEHOLMEN   The Grand is in a superb location with gorgeous decorations, an award-winning spa, plus northern Europe's largest suite, the Princess Lilian (from 70,000 SEK), with its own movie theater, gym, and sauna. Nobel Laureates are traditionally guests here after the main awards ceremony. Chef Matthias Dahlgren produces first-class dining (p 118). *Södra Blasieholmshamnen 8. ☎ 08-679 35 00. www.grandhotel.se. 368 units. Doubles 1,750–7,200 SEK. AE, DC, MC, V. T-bana: Kungsträdgården. Map p 143.*

★★★ Hotel Diplomat

ÖSTERMALM   Still owned by the Malmström family, the 1914 Art Nouveau building is decorated in classic style and manages to be both comfortable and comforting. The outdoor terrace of T/Bar is a local meeting place and great for people-watching

Hotel Hellsten.

in the summer. *Strandvägen 7C.* ☎ *08-459 68 00. www.diplomat hotel.com. 130 units. Doubles 1,995–4,500 SEK. AE, DC, MC, V. T-bana: Östermalmstorg. Map p 143.*

★★ **Hotel Esplanade** ÖSTER-MALM   In an Art Nouveau building, this rather faded hotel is the place to go if cutting-edge fills you with dread. Old-fashioned furnishings and gentle renovations are comfortable and reassuring. *Strandvägen 7A.* ☎ *08-663 07 40. www.hotel esplanade.se. Doubles 1,795–2,595 SEK w/breakfast. AE, DC, MC, V. T-bana: Östermalmstorg. Map p 143.*

★★ **Hotel Hellsten** VASASTADEN This is a dramatic hotel in an 1898 building—the dark-colored walls, velvet drapes, original tiled stove, and chandeliers in my large room resembled a stage set. Bathrooms are superb with slate-lined walls and heated floors. The bar, with jazz evening every Thursday (not in summer), is full of colonial artifacts. *Luntmakargatan 68.* ☎ *08-661 86 00. www.hellsten.se. 78 units. Doubles 1,290–2,490 SEK w/breakfast. AE, DC, MC, V. T-bana: Rådmansgatan. Map p 142.*

★★ **Hotel Hellstens Malmgård** SÖDERMALM   Per Hellsten, who

introduced boutique hotels to Stockholm, has just opened another of his sexy hotels. The latest is again in a restored old building of 1770 and has all the Hellsten touches—modern four-poster beds, stripped wooden floors, old tiled stoves in the rooms, and very well-equipped bathrooms. *Brännkyrkagatan 110.* ☎ *08-465 058 00. www.hellstens malmgard.se. 50 units. Doubles 890–2,290 SEK w/breakfast. AE, DC, MC, V. T-bana: Mariatorget. Map p 142.*

★★★ **Hotel J** NACKA STRAND You could pitch up here in your boat, moor in the hotel's private harbor, and swap your bunk for a fabulously designed bedroom. You'll still feel nautical with the blue-and-white furnishings and scrubbed wooden floors. The J stands for the America's Cup J boats; it's all very Newport, Rhode Island. The delightful restaurant is on the pier. *Ellensbiksvägen 1.* ☎ *08-601 30 00. www. hotelj.com. 158 units. Doubles 1,545–4,095 SEK w/breakfast. AE, DC, MC, V. Taxi. Map p 143.*

★ **Hotel Micro** VASASTADEN   It's advertised as an alternative to a hostel with small cabins decorated in blues and reds, bunk beds, male and female bathrooms, but no windows. You check in at the Hotel

The boutique Hotel Stureplan.

Långholmen Hotel was once a prison.

Tegnérlunden (p 150, it's in their basement). No breakfast, no frills, just good value. *Tegnérlunden 8.* ☎ *08-545 455 69. www.hotelmicro. se. 33 units. Single rooms 545 SEK, + supplement per person of 100 SEK. AE, DC, MC, V. T bana: Rådmansgatan. Map p 142.*

★ Hotel Riddargatan ÖSTER-
MALM   Rooms are pleasantly decorated at this centrally located hotel, which prides itself on its warm welcome and service. Four themed suites offer a larger alternative. The breakfast room has an open fireplace for cold winter days. Good bar. *Riddargatan 14.* ☎ *08-555 730 00. www.profilhotels.se. 78 units. Doubles 1,250–2,495 SEK. AE, DC, MC, V. T-bana: Östermalmstorg. Map p 143.*

★★ Hotel Rival SÖDERMALM
You can't get trendier than this boutique hotel, opened in 2003 by Benny Andersson of Abba fame. Good-sized rooms come in a variety of decors, from the distinctly jazzy colored to the svelte and sexy de luxe style. Some have balconies. There's a striking foyer with bar and bistro, separate cafe, and bakery (p 20). *Mariatorget 3.* ☎ *08-545 789 00. www.rival.se. 99 units. Doubles 1,595–2,995 SEK. Breakfast inc weekends, but not weekdays. AE, DC, MC, V. T-bana: Mariatorget. Map p 143.*

★★★ Hotel Skeppsholmen
SKEPPSHOLMEN   On an island with a peaceful country feel, this hotel is housed in two old buildings of 1699. Floors are stripped wood; furniture is modern Scandinavian. Relatively small rooms are designed for maximum effect and style; bathrooms follow suit (check out the stone basins). Rooms at the front look over the water to Södermalm. *Grona Gången 1.* ☎ *08 407 23 19. www.hotelskeppsholmen.se. 79 units. Doubles 1,595–2,195 SEK w/ breakfast. AE, DC, MC, V. Bus 65. Ferry to Djurgården and Slussen. Map p 143.*

★★ Hotel Stureplan ÖSTER-
MALM   Just above Stureplan shopping mall, this very central boutique hotel has spacious, high-ceilinged rooms, classically and elegantly decorated; pretty loft rooms have skylights. The modern rooms are decorated in pale colors, are good sized, and have large bathrooms. An excellent breakfast is served in the dining room. *Birger Jarlsgatan 24.* ☎ *08-440 66 00. www.hotel stureplan.se. 101 units. Doubles 1,375–5,100 SEK w/breakfast. AE, DC, MC, V. T-bana: Östermalmstorg. Map p 143.*

★ **Hotel Tegnérlunden** NORRMALM This hotel looks out onto the green Tegnérlunden park and has comfortable rooms simply designed. Breakfast is served in a rooftop dining room. The two suites on the fifth and sixth floors are spacious with wooden floors and bright furnishings. *Tegnérlunden 8.* ☎ *08-545 455 50. www.hoteltegnerlunden. se. 102 units. Doubles 1,090–2,690 SEK w/breakfast. AE, DC, MC, V. T-bana: Rådmansgatan. Map p 142.*

★ **Långholmen Hotel** LÅNGHOLMEN Former prisons make good hotels (especially to kids), if you don't mind small rooms with windows high up in the walls; but thick walls and doors keep the noise down. The cells here have been well renovated with comfortable bunk beds and good bathrooms (some are doubles). The restaurant serves ambitious food and there's a friendly bar and an outside terrace. *Långholmsmuren 20.* ☎ *08-720 85 00. www.langholmen.com. 102 units. Doubles 1,070–1,590 SEK. AE, DC, MC, V. T-bana: Hornstull. Map p 142.*

★★★ **Lydmar** BLASIEHOLMEN This is just spectacular and currently Stockholm's most sought-after hotel. In a building of 1829 that once housed the National Museum's archives, it's decorated in chic boutique style, with furniture sourced from around the world's design and antique shops. *Södra Blasieholmshamnen 2.* ☎ *08-22 31 60. www. lydmar.com. Doubles 3,800–12,500 SEK w/breakfast. AE, DC, MC, V. T-bana: Kungsträdgården. Map p 143.*

★★ **Mälardrottningen** GAMLA STAN Landlubbers should steer clear of this hotel on a luxury motor yacht (built for American socialite, Barbara Hutton's 18th birthday) on Riddarholmen. Cabins are very well appointed, with en-suite bathrooms, and some have a lake view. *Riddarholmen.* ☎ *08-545 187 80. www. malardrottningen.se. 61 units. Doubles 800–2,350 SEK w/breakfast. AE, MC, V. T-bana: Gamla Stan/T-Centralen. Map p 143.*

★★★ **Nobis** NORRMALM The ground floor has the 'wow' factor— a soaring atrium, the destination restaurant, Caina, with luxurious deep colors, a bar that fills to bursting each night, a 24-hour bistro for guests, and rooms in soothing shades of light browns, grays, and whites. Some bedrooms are

Welcoming breakfast room at the Radisson SAS Strand.

relatively small, so go for the most you can afford to get the best experience. *Norrmalmstorg 2–4.* ☎ *08-614 10 11. www.nobishotel. com. 201 units. Doubles 1,990–2,290 SEK. AE, DC, MC, V. T-bana: Östermalmstorg. Map p 143.*

★★★ **Nordic Light** VASASTADEN Light is this lifestyle hotel's striking feature, with a lobby that changes color according to the time of day and individual lighting systems in the 'Mood' bedrooms. You can call a light therapist and masseuse to your room to combat the winter darkness. With a chic bar and lounge, I recommend you dress appropriately; the staff look as if they've stepped out of a magazine, but are delightful with it. *Vasaplan 7.* ☎ *08-50 56 30 00. www.nordic lighthotel.se/en. 175 units. Doubles 1,570–4,370 SEK. AE, DC, MC, V. T-bana: T-Centralen. Map p 143.*

★★ **Nordic Sea Hotel** NORRMALM Less trendy than its smart cousin, Nordic Light, it nonetheless boasts the ultra-chic Icebar (see p 46). Bedrooms are blue and white; bathrooms are good sized and it's as central as you can get, right next to the Arlanda Express from the airport. *Vasaplan 4.* ☎ *08-50 56 30 00. www. nordicseahotel.se/en. 367 units. Doubles 970–3,670 SEK w/breakfast. AE, DC, MC, V. T-bana: T-Centralen. Map p 143.*

★★★ **Radisson SAS Strand Hotel** BLASIEHOLMEN This large hotel has a wonderful position looking straight onto boats and the sea. The open, airy lobby, comfortable lounge, and boldly colored dining room and bar act as a welcoming meeting place. Rooms are relatively small but suites have good lounges. *Nybrokajen 9.* ☎ *08-506 640 00. www.strand.stockholm.radissonsas. com. 152 units. Doubles 2,075–2,595*
SEK w/breakfast. AE, DC, MC, V. T-bana: Östermalmstorg. Map p 143.*

★★ **kids Rex Hotel** VASASTADEN The Rex, in a building of 1866, is the sister to the Hotel Hellsten (p 148) right opposite. It's less flamboyant, but has lovely rooms, all with old pine floors and tastefully decorated in good colors, around a splendid grand staircase. Rex Petit (see below) is in the basement. *Luntmakargatan 73.* ☎ *08-16 00 40. www.rexhotel.se. 55 units. Doubles 1,090–2,290 SEK w/breakfast. AE, DC, MC, V. T-bana: Rådmansgatan. Map p 142.*

★ **Rex Petit** VASASTDEN The basement of the Rex Hotel was converted in 2008 into 20 cabin-style rooms, making small and windowless but attractive rooms at a very attractive price. Breakfast is in the Hotel Rex's dining room upstairs. *Luntmakargatan 73.* ☎ *08-16 00 40. www.rexhotel.se. 22 units. Doubles (with private bathroom) 595–1,295 SEK; (with shared bathroom) 495–1,095 SEK, all w/breakfast. AE, DC, MC, V. T-bana: Rådmansgatan. Map p 142.*

★★ **Rica Hotel Gamla Stan** GAMLA STAN Located in the oldest part of the city, this 17th-century building is decorated in classic style, with antiques in the small but cozy bedrooms. *Lilla Nygatan 5.* ☎ *08-723 72 59. www.rica.se. 51 units. Doubles 1,245–2,575 SEK. AE, DC, MC, V. T-bana: Gamla Stan. Map p 143.*

★★ **Rica Hotel Kungsgatan** NORRMALM Located above the PUB department store, and looking onto the outdoor market in Hötorget square, the hotel has large, high-ceilinged rooms. A perfect location for those needing retail therapy. *Kungsgatan 47.* ☎ *08-723 72 20. www.rica.se. 269 units. Doubles 995–2,475 SEK. AE, DC, MC, V. T-bana: Hötorget. Map p 143.*

★★★ **Scandic Anglais** NORMALM The Anglais is cool and chic and you step into a white lobby complete with a red wire moose sculpture. Rooms are equally contemporary, some with good views. The bar is the place to see and be seen (see p 127). The Anglais is particularly environmentally friendly and, as with all Scandic hotels, kids go free. *Humlegårdsgatan 23.* ☎ *08-517 340 00. www.scandic hotels.com. 230 units. Doubles 1,290–3,690 w/breakfast. AE, DC, MC, V. T-bana: Östermalmstorg. Map p 143.*

★★ **Scandic Malman** SÖDERMALM All Scandic hotels are good value, and this one is no exception. It has well-decorated, light and airy rooms, and a very popular bar that fills up most evenings. Breakfast sets you up for the day and kids go free in the rooms. *Götgatan 49–51.* ☎ *08-51 73 47 00. www.scandic hotels.com. 332 units. Doubles 1,190–3,090 SEK w/breakfast. AE, DC, MC, V. T-bana: Medborgarplatsen. Map p 143.*

★★★ kids **Sigtuna Stads Hotell** SIGTUNA This is where Stockholmers come to escape the city; it's decorated in pretty pale shades and natural materials. The elegant dining room looks out over the sea. The restaurant is well known for top dining, and breakfast was one of the best I've ever had. A sauna keeps you warm on chilly days. *Stora Nygatan 3, Sigtuna.* ☎ *08-592 501 00. www.sigtunastadshotell.se. 26 units. Doubles 2,190–2,590 SEK w/ breakfast. AE, DC, MC, V. Directions see p 142.*

★ **STF Vandrarhem Gärdet** GÄRDET The hostel opened in July 2008 and is part of the centrally run hostel association. Rooms are brightly decorated, have showers and TVs, and it's only a short hop into central Stockholm. Some have no windows, so check when you book. Join Hostelling International and get 50 SEK per person discount per night. *Sandhamnsgatan 65.* ☎ *08-463 22 99. www.svenskaturist foreningen.se. 53 units. Doubles from 815 SEK. AE, MC, V. T-bana: Gärdet. Map p 143.*

★ **Tre Små Rum Hotel** SÖDERMALM The three rooms have been increased to seven, sharing shower rooms. Rooms are small, but it's friendly and welcoming and the owner Jakob von Arndt is never far away. *Högbergsgatan 81.* ☎ *08-641 23 71. www.tresmarum.se. 7 units. Doubles 795 SEK w/breakfast. MC, V. T-bana: Mariatorget. Map p 143.*

★★★ **Villa Källhagen** DJURGÅRDEN Perfectly positioned beside the Djurgården canal, rooms have views over the water or onto green spaces. The freshly decorated rooms come in different color schemes, echoing the seasons. There's a good restaurant and you can take your breakfast on the terrace. *Djurgårdsbrunnsvägen 10.* ☎ *08-665 03 00. www.kallhagen.se. 36 units. Doubles 1,190–4,000 SEK w/breakfast. AE, DC, MC, V. Bus: 69. Map p 143.*

★ **Wasa Park Hotel** VASASTADEN This old-fashioned hotel in an early 19th-century house keeps prices down by locating bathrooms just outside the rooms, which are decorated in blue and white. There's a simple continental breakfast. *St. Eriksplan 1.* ☎ *08-545 453 00. www. wasaparkhotel.se. 15 units. Doubles 850–1,050 SEK w/breakfast. MC, V. T-bana: St. Eriksplan. Map p 142.* ●

Sigtuna

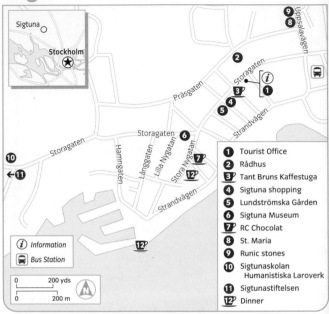

1 Tourist Office
2 Rådhus
3 Tant Bruns Kaffestuga
4 Sigtuna shopping
5 Lundströmska Gården
6 Sigtuna Museum
7 RC Chocolat
8 St. Maria
9 Runic stones
10 Sigtunaskolan Humanistiska Laroverk
11 Sigtunastiftelsen
12 Dinner

(i) Information
🚌 Bus Station

0   200 yds
0   200 m

ew visitors make it to Sigtuna, which is a great shame because this former Viking settlement is Sweden's oldest existing town. It's only one hour from Stockholm and just 30 minutes from the airport, so I recommend you plan to stay a night either at the beginning or end of your holiday. START: **Sigtuna Tourist Office.**

1 ★★★ kids **Tourist Office.** It all began when Eric the Victorious settled here in A.D. 980 to fulfill his ambition of building a Christian center in what was a Viking-led country. Pick up information at the well-stocked tourist office housed in the 18th-century house known as the Dragon. Then start along the main street that follows Eric's original city plan of 8-sq m (86-sq ft.) plots for each of Eric's followers—and a much larger one for Eric himself at the end of the street. *Tourist Office,*

Previous page: Fjäderholmarna.

Stora Gatan 33. 📞 *08-594 806 52. www.sigtunaturism.se. June–Aug Mon–Sat 10am–6pm, Sun 11am–5pm; Sept Mon–Fri 10am–5pm, Sat, Sun 11am–4pm; Oct–May Mon–Fri 10am–5pm, Sat 11am–4pm, Sun noon–4pm.*

2 ★ **Rådhus.** Is Sigtuna's Town Hall the smallest in Europe? It's a compact, wooden building in a spacious square, and was built in 1744. Inside, the main Council Chamber is a gem with portraits of kings, old

chairs, and a gleaming crystal chandelier. Outside, open shutters conceal a hook for a key, left there over the centuries for any drunken citizen who was fearful of the wrath of his family. He could take the key, open a cell, lock himself in, and sleep it off to return home sober in the morning. It's a delightful story, though it's hard to imagine how that fooled anyone. 🕐 *20 min. June–Aug noon–4pm.*

3🅿★★ **kids** **Tant Bruns Kaffestuga.** 16th-century Aunt Brown's Cafe is in the oldest wooden house in town. Inside it's cozy, and the open fire in winter makes it the place for a cup of hot chocolate. In summer, grab a bench in the small garden and sit back under the old trees. They serve coffee, snacks, and not-to-be-missed homemade pies; I recommend the blueberry version. *Laurentii Gränd 3.* ☎ *08-592 509 34. www.tantbrunsigtuna.se.*

4 ★★ **Sigtuna shopping.** The main street and the little streets running off it are lined with stores

The Lundström's drawing room.

Sigtuna's main street.

selling books, crafts, gifts, and design items. Look out for a range of goods made of leather using traditional methods at **Lottas Garfveri** (Långgatan 9) and the range of items making good presents at the Tourist Office. 🕐 *45 min.*

5 ★★ **kids** **Lundströmska Gården.** In 1873, Carl August Lundström bought this house, enlarged it, and added a store at the front. Opened as a museum in 1958, it shows the life of a middle-class family—and life was clearly good to the Lundströms. Past the shop, full of tempting items that are sadly not on sale, you step straight into the heart of the house, the kitchen with its large fireplace and oven. The family was wealthy enough to have a separate drawing and living room and an upper floor, reached by a narrow staircase, of small bedrooms. The house is full of period furniture, but you can't help wondering, where's the bathroom? 🕐 *30 min. Stora Gatan 39. Adults 10 SEK; children 17 and under 5 SEK. Daily June–Aug noon–4pm.*

Sigtuna's Annual Events

The annual Viking Fair (end June–end July) takes place in the town's very own Viking camp. Jewelers, bakers, fighters, and weavers live and work here for a month, just as their ancestors did. At the annual **Market Fair,** held over the last weekend in August, you meet Sigtuna's three best-known residents. Aunt Green, Aunt Brown, and Aunt Lavender first appeared in a children's book in 1918, written by Elsa Maartman Beskow (1874–1953), one of the founders of children's literature in Sweden. Buy the English version (*Aunt Green, Aunt Brown and Aunt Lavender*) here if you have children; it'll keep them occupied all day. Sigtuna's **Christmas Market** takes place on the four Sundays before Christmas Eve, filling the streets with stalls selling traditional handicrafts. Copious glasses of grogg help the dancing, singing, and general merriment.

❻ ★ Sigtuna Museum. The king had his plot at the end of the main street where you now find the museum. Sigtuna might have been small but it was important, as revealed by the gold rings, coins (Sigtuna was the first place to mint coins, produced by English workers brought over by King Ulaf in 995), runic inscriptions, and a superb, tiny Viking head. 🕑 *30 min. Stora Gatan 55. ☎ 08-597 838 70. www.sigtuna museum.se. Adults 20 SEK; free for 18 and under. Daily June–Aug noon–4pm; Sept–May Tues–Sun noon–4pm.*

❼ ★★ RC Chocolat. Customers flock here for its baguettes which you can eat in or take away for a picnic; but its real purpose is as an excellent chocolate shop, so stock up on gifts to take home. *Stora Gatan 49. ☎ 08-594 803 85. www.rcchocolat.se. Filled baguettes 60 SEK.*

❽ ★ St. Maria. The 13th-century church of St. Maria was built by the Dominicans who brought the art of brick-making here and made this

Vikings limbering up for a fight in the town square.

Runic stone.

Sweden's first brick building. It was a large abbey with separate buildings for the monks but, in 1540, the country's conversion to Lutheranism brought destruction to the abbey and the church is all that is left. Nearby the atmospheric ruins of the churches of St. Lars, St. Per, and St. Olof are reminders of the time when Sigtuna produced most of Sweden's bishops and archbishops. ⏱ *30 min.*

9 ★★ Runic stones. Sigtuna may be small but it has more runic stones than anywhere else in the world: more than 150 have been found. Carved with crosses and fantastic beasts, these huge stones are memorials to worthy dead men (although some were put up by the living) as a sure ticket into the next world. ⏱ *30 min.*

10 ★ Sigtunaskolan Humanistiska Laroverk. Sweden's top private school stands on the hills above Sigtuna. The present king was educated at this boarding school, the largest in Sweden, where the teaching is based on humanist principles.

11 ★ Sigtunastiftelsen. The Sigtunastiftelsen is a private cultural institution with its origins in Christian humanistic ethics, founded in 1917 when education and temperance were strong principles in

Sweden. It's a peaceful place to walk around, offering a real retreat from life. ⏱ *30 min.*

12 ★★★ Dinner. Sigtuna is home to two restaurants that attract diners from all over Sweden. You can eat excellent seafood on the small boathouse, **Båthuset Krog & Bar** (☎ 08-592 567 80, www.bathuset. com Main courses from 235 SEK), or push another boat out at the critically acclaimed 1909 **Sigtuna Stads Hotell** (p 152) where superbly cooked food, particularly fish (such as the zander with clam jus at 325 SEK), is served in very pleasant surroundings (Stora Nygatan 3, ☎ 08-592 501 00, www. sigtunastadshotell.se. Closed Sun).

Practical Matters—Sigtuna

Take the Pendeltåg train (www.sl.se) or the Uppsala train (www.tim-trafik.se) from T-Centralen to Märsta (about 30 min). From Märsta, take bus no. 570 to Hällsboskolan to Sigtuna bus station (about 30 min), and then it's a 3-minute walk to the main street. From/to Arlanda, book a taxi or get the no. 803 bus that leaves hourly and takes about 30 minutes to the airport.

Stay at the Sigtuna Stads Hotell (p 152), or at 32 Rum o Kök, Stora Gatan 79 ☎ 08-592 566 95, www.32rok.se.

Fjäderholmarna

To Stockholm

Fjäderholmarnas Hamn

5 Fjäderholmarnas Krog

Fjäderholmarna
Island

Stockholm

(i)

1 Rökeriet

2

3

Allmogebåtar

Krogviken

4

2

Saltsjon

To Vaxholm

(i) Information

1 Rökeriet
2 Island Walk
3 Mackmyra Svensk Whisky
4 Swimming
5 Fjäderholmarnas Krog

| 0 | 50 yds |
| 0 | 50 m |

Four islands make up Fjäderholmarna, although Stora Fjäderholmen is the one visitors go to. It's a pretty island, with enough to keep you there for a half or whole day. As it's a mere 25 minutes by boat from Stockholm, it can be busy on summer weekends. Half the fun is, of course, taking the boat out there. START: **Nybroplan for the boat to the island.**

1 ★ kids **Rökeriet.** With fish dishes from its own smokery (mussels, gravadlax, and, of course, herrings 150–255 SEK) and a perfect position out on the waterside, this restaurant is open end of April to September. There's also a cafe serving sandwiches and coffee (around 100 SEK) before taking the less-than-arduous circular island stroll. ☎ *08-716 50 88. www.rokeriet.nu.*

2 ★★ kids **Island Walk.** A path takes you right around the island, but it's worth taking the path to the west and south to avoid the crowds. The stroll goes past **Workshop Row** and **Handicrafts Terrace,** where woodturners and ceramicists work and sell their goods. Attractions are few and so you may find yourself taking an inordinate amount of interest in the charming small **Allmogebåtar** (**Boat Museum** ☎ 070-573 69 97, www. allmogebatar.nu)—a couple of boathouses where they restore historic sailing boats. ⏱ *45 min.*

❸ ★★ Mackmyra Svensk Whisky. No, this is not a mistake; since 2001 this distillery has been producing Swedish whisky with Swedish ingredients and stored in Swedish oak barrels. The main distillery is in Gastrikland but you can see the museum and warehouse with the old equipment and barrels and taste and buy it here—and believe me, Swedish whisky makes a great talking point. It's also very good. ⌚ *1 hr guided tour and warehouse; 2 hr tasting.* ☎ *08-556 025 80. www.mackmyra.com. Museum free; guided tour museum and warehouse if requested in advance.*

❹ ★★ Swimming. Take your swimming gear and spend a sunny afternoon diving off the rocks into the clear waters of the Baltic. It's sheer bliss—and surprisingly not too cold.

❺ ★★ Fjäderholmarnas Krog. As you will see, a lot of eating and drinking is done on the island and many people come from Stockholm

Catch the steam ferry boat to Fjäderholmarna.

just for a meal at this lovely waterside location in the summer season. Go for the Baltic herring, or halibut with horseradish, and if you can, get a seat on the seaside terrace. *Stora Fjäderholmen.* ☎ *08-718 33 55. www.fjaderholmarnaskrog.se. Main courses from 195 SEK.*

Practical Matters—Fjäderholmarna

From Slussen, Fjäderholmslinjen ferries (www.fjaderholmslinjen. se) run daily from the end of April to the beginning of September on the hour from 10am with the last departure from Fjäderholmarna at half past midnight; return fare is 110 SEK for adults, 55 SEK for children. From Nybroplan, **Strömma Kanalbolaget** (www.stromma kanalbolaget.se) ferries run mid-May to mid-August every half hour from 10am until 8:30pm, then 9:30pm, 10:30pm and 11:30pm; from the end of April to mid-May and then mid-August to the beginning of September ferries run every hour from 10am to 8pm, then 9:30pm and 11:30pm. Return times for both ferries are a half hour later than the outward journey. One way 80 SEK; return 110 SEK (half price children accompanied by adults aged 6–11; free 5 and under) or free with Stockholm Card (p 11). Information on the island: www.fjaderholmarna.se.

Vaxholm

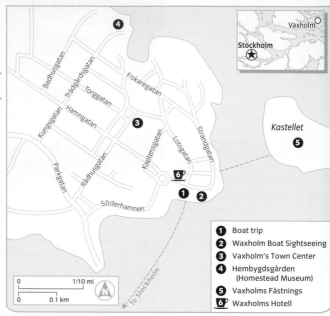

1 Boat trip
2 Waxholm Boat Sightseeing
3 Vaxholm's Town Center
4 Hembygdsgården (Homestead Museum)
5 Vaxholms Fästnings
6 Waxholms Hotell

This small island, known as the Gateway to the Archipelago, is a popular half- or full-day trip. Vaxholm is 17km (10½ miles) from Stockholm by road. But it's more fun to arrive in traditional style—by boat. It can be busy in summer, so avoid weekends if you can. If you want to stay, book ahead and take waterproofs because it can rain heavily. START: **Strömkajen or Strandvägen for the boat trip.**

1 ★★ kids **Boat trip.** The best way to get to Vaxholm is by a short 1-hour boat journey. The trip takes you past the southern end of Djurgården, and then past Fjäderholmarna (see p 158) and on to this island, which is the capital of the archipelago. For information, see Practical Matters box p 159. ⏱ *1 hr.*

2 ★ **Waxholm Boat Sightseeing.** A 50-minute tour around Vaxholm on a small sightseeing boat gives you the sea view of the island

and its castle. ⏱ *50 min. Waxholm Sightseeing.* ☎ *0708-74 75 85. www.waxholmsightseeing.se. Tickets: adults 110 SEK; children 6–11 years 55 SEK; free 5 and under. Tours run daily 8th July–8th Aug at 11am–5:20pm from two different departures. Check website for details and other times.*

3 ★ **Vaxholm's Town Center.** The island has been inhabited since the 16th century when King Gustav Vasa, victorious against Denmark in the 1540s, founded a defensive city

Herrings & History

Vaxholm was known for Baltic herrings, which its workforce caught in their spare time when not building Gustav Vasa's castle in the 16th century. On the first Saturday in August, locals row old boats carrying 1kg (½ lb) of herrings all around Vaxholm, commemorating the days when the first fisherman landed his catch and sold all his herrings. There's little left today of the herring tradition except for the Baltic herring sandwiches sold in boxes on Thursdays to Sundays at Trädgården. Take them away for a picnic on a headland looking out to sea.

here. The fortress (see below), built between 1548 and the 1560s, needed a civilian population to serve as watchmen. Gustav Vasa had to coerce the poor and beggars here and then offered farmers free fishing rights, tax-free status, and land. Today's crowds come more voluntarily to this little town, where galleries and shops sell souvenirs and nautical what-nots. **Vaxholm Kyrka,** designed in the 1760s by Carl Fredrik Adelcrantz, has models of boats to placate God and the sea. The church holds summer concerts. 🕐 *30 min.*

❹ ★★ Hembygdsgården (Homestead Museum). Only open on summer weekends, the museum is tiny and easy to miss because it's part of the cafe/restaurant at Norrhamnen. Go inside for a very real idea of the simple life of 100 years ago. 🕐 *15 min. Tradgårdsgatan 19.* ☎ *08-541 319 80.*

❺ ★★ kids Vaxholms Fästnings. In the early days, the strategically built fortress provided an effective defense against the Poles in 1598, the Danes in 1612, and the Russians in 1719, all trying to reach the rich city of Stockholm. After Sweden lost Finland to the Russians in 1809, the country was dragged into the Napoleonic Wars and conflict with England. Once again, Vaxholm Fortress became important,

A local shop sells nautical themed goods.

Inside the fortress.

spooky, with models suddenly moving as you approach, but children love it. Today you reach the island citadel by a ferry that goes every 20 minutes, but if the ferry is on a leisurely timetable, the cafe provides refreshment. ⏱ *1 hr.* ☎ *08-541 718 90. www.vaxholmsfastning.se. Admission: Adults 50 SEK; under-19s free. Free with Stockholm Card. Ferry: Adults 50 SEK round-trip, one way 30 SEK; children 7–12 years and pensioners 30 SEK. Daily June noon–4pm; Jul, Aug 11am–5pm; Sept first two weekends 11am–5pm.*

and was rebuilt between 1833 and 1863. But during those 30 years, defenses changed and, when a Swedish naval ship fired three cannonballs directly at the citadel as a test, all of them embarrassingly went straight through the walls. Luckily the fortress was not needed after that. The museum shows how fighting has changed from the 16th century to today. It can be a bit

6 Waxholms Hotell. Built in 1901, this vaguely Art Nouveau hotel was designed in 1899 by Erik Lallerstedt, a well-known Swedish architect (1864–1955). It's the best place on the island to eat, specializing in freshly caught fish. Try the local fried perch with dill (249 SEK) or the famous Baltic herring buffet (198 SEK). *For details see below, Practical Matters.* ●

Practical Matters—Vaxholm

Waxholmsbolaget runs boats from Strömkajen (☎ 08-679 58 30, www.waxholmsbolaget.se), and operates throughout the archipelago, offering special island-hopping fares valid for several days. **Strömma Kanalbolaget** leaves from Strandvägen (☎ 08-587 140 00, www.strommakanalbolaget.com), operating the steamship *S/S Stockholm*, built in 1931. Ferries from **Cinderellabåtarna** (☎ 08-587 140 00, www.cinderellabatarna.com) run between the islands. Prices are around 140 SEK single to 220 SEK return, depending on the company. Or take the T-bana to Tekniska Högskolan, and then bus no. 670 to Vaxholm (about 1 hr). The **Tourist Office** is in the old Rådhuset (Town Hall) (☎ 08-541 314 80, www.vaxholm.se). There are B&Bs on the island (book via the tourist office) and one hotel, Waxholms Hotell, Hamngatan 2 (see above ☎ 08-541 301 50. www.waxholmshotell.se).

The **Savvy Traveler**

Before You Go

Government Tourist Offices

In the U.S.: (Not open to the public) Visit Sweden, 655 Third Ave., New York, NY 10017 (☎ 212/885-9700). **In the U.K.:** Sweden House, 5 Upper Montagu St, London W1H 2AG (☎ 020-7870 5600). www.visit sweden.com or www.goscandinavia. com.

The Best Times to Go

May to September is the most popular time to visit Stockholm because the weather is glorious. You'll find that the city gets very crowded with tourists in late June to August, while the Stockholmers themselves generally leave town for their summer cottages. Most of the theaters and concert halls shut in July and August and some restaurants also close. However, many other attractions, particularly those with outdoor features, only open fully during this time and operate restricted opening times during the rest of the year. Due to the country's high latitude, it stays light long into the summer nights, with the skies only getting dusky from around midnight to 3am in June. At **Midsummer,** hotels are often full in Stockholm, so book in advance. The low season is from **November to March.** During the coldest times in winter, the sea can freeze over. Conversely, cultural life is very lively at this time. **December** is a magical month in Stockholm, with Christmas markets, beautifully decorated shop windows, clear light, and the whiteness of snow and ice providing a wonderful reflective quality.

Festivals & Special Events

SPRING. One of the high points of the artistic calendar is **Market** (www.market-art.se), the leading Nordic/Scandinavian art event in February/March. Some of the top galleries in Scandinavia and the Nordic countries exhibit at this exciting contemporary art show at the Royal Swedish Academy of Fine Arts. It's followed by the all-important **Stockholm Spring Exhibition,** when Liljevalchs Konsthall (p 33, ❷) on Djurgården showcases new artists.

On April 30, the bonfires on **Walpurgis** night traditionally gave the Swedes protection from wicked witches. Today it's seen as a celebration of winter giving way to spring. Two places where you can ensure you're also under the spell are on Evert Taubes Terrass (p 61, ⓬) on Riddarholmen or Skansen (p 102), where the sky is lit up with bonfires.

Första Maj (May Day) is a day for the workers to protest, as it is throughout the world. Horse trotting is a huge sport in Sweden, so everyone turns out for **Elitloppet** (☎ 08-635 90 00, www.elitloppet. se), the major European Elite Race at Solvalla, Sweden's biggest harness race track, northwest of Stockholm. At the end of the month, the largest women-only bicycle race, **Tjejtrampet** (www.tjejtrampet. com), takes place when the 48km (30-mile) course sees thousands of women cyclists pedaling away from Gärdet.

The **Archipelago Fair** (www. skargardsmassen.se) takes place at the end of May in Djurgården. Classic boats gather at the harbor; there are stalls selling traditional crafts, entertainment, and food from all around the Baltic. Allied to this is **Skärgårdsbatens Dag** (Archipelago Boat Day;

Previous Page: The Swedish flag.

www.skargardstrafikanten.se) when classic steamboats assemble at Strömkajen for a trip to Vaxholm. Here they're greeted with bands and a market before returning.

SUMMER. The **Parkteatern** (Park Theater; ☎ 08-506 20 284, www. stadsteatern.stockholm.se) is a wide-ranging free festival in outdoor venues from workshops on folk dancing to serious plays. Daily at parks throughout the city June to August.

Stockholm Early Music Festival (Tyska Brinken 13, Gamla Stan; ☎ 070-460 03 90, www.semf.se), one of the top European baroque, Renaissance, and early music festivals, is held in the first week of June in the old buildings of Gamla Stan, such as the German Church and the Royal Armory. Wonderful surroundings to hear a European assortment of medieval lutes, madrigals, and baroque ensembles.

Smaka På Stockholm (A Taste of Stockholm; www.smakapastockholm.se) runs for a week in early June. Taking place in Kungsträdgården (appropriately as this was originally the King's Garden), it showcases around 25 chefs. It's the chance to taste dishes from restaurants you might not be able to get to.

Stockholm's **Marathon** (www. marathon.se) takes place in early June on a Saturday.

Sweden's **National Day** on June 6 celebrates the election of Gustav Vasa as King of Sweden in 1523. Since 1916, the Royal Family, dressed in traditional blue and yellow costumes, has gathered at Skansen to present flags to various organizations. The other great public summer celebration is **Midsommarafton** (Midsummer Eve) on the first Friday after June 21.

The **Stockholm Jazz Festival** (☎ 08-505 331 70, tickets: www. stockholmjazz.com) in July is one of Europe's biggest. It takes place at Skansen with some jam sessions at other venues.

Stockholm is a particularly gay-friendly city, and so its **Pride** (www. stockholmpride.org) celebration is the biggest in Scandinavia. For one week in July/August, parades, parties, entertainment, exhibitions, films, and more take place in Tantolunden Park on Södermalm and around the city.

In a country farther south, the idea of the **Midnattsloppet** (Midnight Race; ☎ 08-649 71 71, www. midnattsloppet.com) would be impossible, but in mid-August in the land of the midnight sun this huge event sees 16,000 people run 10km (6.2 miles) around Södermalm. The many spectators turn it into an all-night party.

Stockholms Kulturfestival (Stockholm's Culture Festival; www. kulturfestivalen.stockholm.se) in August has the city buzzing with events for a week. You'll see everything here from circus acts to concerts, theater, and dance. And most of it is free.

In the last week in August, the Swedes celebrate the **Crayfish Season** in restaurants, which serve overflowing plates of crayfish and aquavit.

FALL. The **Beer and Whisky Festival** (www.stockholmbeer.se) in Nacka Strand at the end of September/beginning of October is a huge event stretched over a couple of weekends.

Lidingöloppet (☎ 08-765 26 15, www.lidingoloppet.se) is the world's largest cross-country race with categories for amateurs and professionals. It's held on the last weekend in September around Lidingö.

Tennis fans congregate at Norra Djurgården in October for the

Stockholm Open Tennis tournament (☎ 08-450 26 25, www.stockholmopen.se).

In mid-November, the 10-day **Stockholm International Film Festival** (☎ 08-677 50 00, www.filmfestivalen.se) shows a range of films. More than 170 films from 40 countries, including those by experimental and young filmmakers, are shown in cinemas around Stockholm.

WINTER. The end of November/beginning of December sees the enormously popular **Stockholm International Horse Show** at Globen (☎ 077-131 00 00, www.stockholmhorseshow.com). **Christmas Markets** run from the end of November/early December to the end of December. Skansen is particularly popular (see p 102); also Gamla Stan and Sigtuna (p 58 and 156).

On **Nobeldagen** (Nobel Day, December 10; Nobel Foundation ☎ 08-663 09 20, www.nobel.se), the year's Nobel Prize laureates attend a ceremony in their honor at Konserthuset followed by a banquet at Stadshuset (p 10, **7**), along with the Royal Family and extremely distinguished guests.

Mid-December is relieved by **Luciadagen** (Lucia Day, December 13), one of Sweden's best-known festivals. The 'Queen of Light' and her attendants process through the streets before going to Skansen for fireworks.

Christmas is celebrated on Christmas Eve. It's a private, family time with a huge smorgasbord followed by present-giving from someone dressed up as Santa Claus. Many restaurants offer Christmas smorgasbords during the month. The official holiday lasts from December 24 to 26.

Nyarsafton (New Year's Eve) is a public occasion when, since 1895, crowds have gathered at Skansen. Throughout the city, the streets are full; the restaurants are booked, and the clubs keep going till dawn.

In February, skate off any festive excess in the annual 77km (48-mile) **Viking Run** (☎ 08-556 312 45, www.vikingarannet.com) from Uppsala via Sigtuna to Stockholm. But it depends on the weather and the ice. The route and date are decided only about 2 weeks before the event.

The Weather

Stockholm has real seasons and all have their attractions, although with its proximity to the sea, the city is not as cold as you might expect. May to September is when Stockholm really comes alive, with summer events and outdoor living encouraged by the long daylight hours. Around Midsummer it hardly gets dark at all. At this time Stockholm empties as its inhabitants go on holiday. Winter lasts from November to March with very short days and temperatures that can vary from just above freezing to well below zero. Snow is not predictable but when it does snow there is a glorious lightness to the city. Days are often crisp and sunny and the city takes on a fairytale quality. Rainfall also varies, with the heaviest falls in the summer.

Useful Websites

www.visitstockholm.com: The official tourism site for Stockholm with comprehensive information on events, hotels, restaurants, shops, attractions, and more. Also offers a useful online hotel booking service.

www.sweden.se: Sweden's official website administered by different organizations, including Visit Sweden, with information, blogs, and news.

www.stockholm.se: the City of Stockholm's official website with news, services, and history.

www.sl.se: The official site for Stockholm's transport system.

TEMPERATURE AND RAINFALL IN STOCKHOLM

	JAN	FEB	MAR	APR	MAY	JUNE
Daily Temp. (°C)	-1	-2	2	7	12	16
Daily Temp. (°F)	30	28	36	45	54	61
Rainfall in mm	38	27	26	30	30	3
(inches)	1.5	1.06	1.02	1.18	1.18	1.7

	JULY	AUG	SEPT	OCT	NOV	DEC
Daily Temp. (°C)	19	18	14	8	3	0
Daily Temp. (°F)	66	64	57	46	37	32
Rainfall in mm	71	66	66	48	53	30
(inches)	2.8	2.6	2.6	1.9	2.08	1.18

www.cityguide.se: Commercial site with all attractions and hotel booking service.

www.nobelprize.org: Official site of the Nobel Prizes, with full information.

www.raileurope.com: Good international booking service for all European and Swedish trains.

www.scandinaviandesign.com: Nordic products and designers, information on museums, events, etc.

Cellphones

World phones—or GSM (Global System for Mobiles)—work in Sweden (and most of the world). If your cellphone is on a GSM system, and you have a world-capable multiband phone, you can make and receive calls from Sweden. Call your wireless operator and ask for 'international roaming' to be activated. For calls within the Stockholm area, dial the area code ☎ 08 before the local number. You can buy a Swedish SIM card at Pressbyrån kiosks and at Arlanda Airport.

Car Rentals

Driving in Stockholm isn't necessary because the public transport system is good and taxis, if expensive, are plentiful. Hiring a car is relatively expensive; all the major chains have desks at Stockholm Arlanda Airport and offices in the city. It is advisable to book your car before you leave home. **Auto Europe** U.K. (☎ 0800-89 9893/00 800 223-5555-5, www.auto-europe.com), **Auto Europe** U.S.A. (☎ 1-888-223-5555, www.autoeurope.com), **Avis** (☎ 797 99 70, www.avis.com), **Budget** (☎ 0844-544 3439, www.budget.co.uk), **Europcar** U.K. (☎ 08713-849 847, www.europcar.co.uk), U.S.A. www.europcar.com), **Hertz** (☎ 08708-44 88 44, www.hertz.com). A big reasonable Swedish company is **Mabi Hyrbilar** (☎ 08-591 144 99, www.mabirent.se).

Getting **There**

By Plane

The major airport is **Arlanda** Airport (information ☎ 08-797 60 00, flight information ☎ 08-797 61 00, www.arlanda.se) 35km (22 miles) from the city center. As Sweden is the center of the Baltic region, the airport is an important transit destination, well served from all over the world with direct daily flights to and from most major European and American cities.

The major airline flying into Sweden is **SAS** (Scandinavian Airlines System) which offers the most routes and competitive prices. In the US ☎ 1-800-221 2350. In the UK ☎ 0871-226 7767. Or: www.flysas.com.

From the airport the quickest way into the center is by the **Arlanda Express** Train (☎ 771-720 200, www.arlandaexpress.com). Trains run regularly (4–6 times an hour at peak times) leaving Arlanda from 5am to 1:05am, taking 20 minutes to Central Station. A single fare is 240 SEK. Special fares: weekends two adults traveling together, single 280 SEK, return 325 SEK, unaccompanied child and students 8–25 years single 120 SEK, return 240 SEK, up to 17 years free if accompanied by an adult.

A return is 460 SEK (adult). Same conditions for children apply. Buy tickets from the Information Center, the ticket machine, or on-board (50 SEK extra).

Flygbussarna airport buses (☎ 08-588 228 28, www.flygbussarna. se) leave every 15 minutes from bus stop 11 at Arlanda and from Cityterminalen from 4am to 10pm daily. The journey takes 50 to 55 minutes; a single fare is 119 SEK for adults (99 SEK Internet price), up to four children aged 0–16 years old free with fare-paying passenger, 219 SEK return (198 Internet price). Buy your ticket from the Tourist Center, airport, online, or on the bus.

Swebus (☎ 0771-218 218, www. swebus.se) operates between Arlanda and Stockholm Cityterminalen but runs much less frequently except in rush hour when they go every 15 minutes. Prices from 74 SEK. Buy your ticket at the airport or online.

Taxis operate from Arlanda; the fixed fare is from 395 to 599 SEK depending on destination. It's marked on the side, but check first as some companies operate their own rates. The best company is Flygtaxi (☎ 08-120 920 00, www. flygtaxi.se).

Bromma Airport (☎ 08-797 68 00, www.brommaairport.se) is 8km (5 miles) west of the city center and used by some airlines from London via cities like Malmö.

Get into the city center on **Flyg-bussarna** airport buses (☎ 08-588 228 28, www.flygbussarna.se). From Bromma Monday–Friday 7:30am–10:10pm, Saturday 10:15am–4:10pm, Sunday 11:30am–7:45pm. The journey takes about 20 minutes to Cityterminalen; a single fare is 74 SEK, a return is 148 SEK for adults; unaccompanied youths 16–25 years 54 SEK single, 108 SEK return, up to four children aged 15 and under travel free with fare-paying adult.

By Car

From Denmark you can use the stunning Öresund toll bridge (www. oresundsbron.com) between Copenhagen and Malmö, from 40€ one way. The bridge connects with the **E4,** the 550km (342-mile) motorway to Stockholm.

There are car ferries from Denmark (Frederikshavn) and Germany (Kiel) to Gothenburg connecting with the **E3** to Stockholm (450 km/280 miles).

By Ferry

You can get to Stockholm easily by ferry from Helsinki (Finland) on **Silja Line** (☎ 08-330 59 90, www. tallinksilja.se) and **Viking Line** (☎ 08-452 40 00, www.vikingline.se).

Silja Line ferries dock at Värtahamnen, northeast of the city center. Take a taxi or the Silja Line bus connection to Cityterminalen; or it's a 5-minute walk to T-bana Gärdet.

Viking Line docks at the Viking terminal on Södermalm. Take a taxi from here, or it's a 10-minute walk to Slussen. Viking Line buses run from Slussen to Cityterminalen.

Tallink from Tallinn (Estonia) (☎ 08-440 59 90, www.tallinksilja. se) operates from the Frihamnen terminal, northeast of the city center near the Silja Line Terminal. Taxis and its own bus service operate between the terminal and Cityterminalen.

By Train
National (**SJ,** ☎ 0771-75 75 75, www. sj.se) and International trains arrive at **Central Station,** Vasagatan, Norrmalm.

Getting **Around**

By Tunnelbana (T-bana Subway)
The **T-bana** (run by Statens Lokaltrafik (SL), ☎ 08-600 10 00, www. sl.se) is the easiest, cheapest, and best way around the city. Three metro lines are marked by color: red, green, and blue. All run through T-Centralen. They operate between 5am and 1am Sunday to Thursday and 5am to 3am Friday and Saturday. Buying a single ticket doesn't make sense (they cost 20–60 SEK). Instead buy travelcards. 24 hours costs 100 SEK, 72 hours is 200 SEK, 7 days is 260 SEK. You will also pay an extra 20 SEK for the card itself which you can reuse. Travelcards are valid on buses, trams, and the Djurgården ferries between Slussen and Djurgården operated by Waxholmsbolaget. The **Stockholm Card** includes unlimited travel on public transport as well as other advantages (p 11). For travel information and all timetables, visit the main SL Information Center inside T-Centralen.

By Bus
Running from 5am to midnight, buses are operated by **Statens Lokaltrafik** (**SL**) (☎ 08-600 10 00, www.sl.se) with the T-bana. Same ticket prices and areas apply as the T-bana. Pre-paid tickets are stamped by the driver or pass your travelcard over the ticket machine by the driver.

By Taxi
Order by telephone, online, or hail taxis in the street. Taxi ranks are found near railway and bus stations. The initial charge is 45 SEK, with charges at around 8 SEK per km plus 5 SEK per minute. Fares increase in the evenings and at weekends. 'Black taxis' are unauthorized, so beware of using them. Use **TaxiKurir** (☎ 0771-86 00 00, www.taxikurir. se); **Taxi Stockholm** (☎ 15-00 00; www.taxistockholm.se); **Taxi 020** (☎ 020-20 20 20, www.taxi020.se).

By Tram
In the summer, tourists take the **no. 7**, which goes past many of the main sights and runs from Norrmalmstorg to Djurgården.

By Car
It really is not worth driving in Stockholm, but if you do it is relatively straightforward. Rush hours are busy 7:30 to 9:30am, noon to 1pm, and 3:30 to 6pm. The speed limit is 50kmph (31mph), reduced in some areas (near schools and hospitals) to 30kmph (19mph). On roads in and out of the city the limit is 70 kmph (43 mph); on motorways it is 90kmph (55mph). Police use hand-held radar equipment on highways and can impose on-the-spot fines. The blood-alcohol limit is so low it, in effect, means no alcohol at all. The penalties of being caught drink-driving are extremely high. There is a

congestion charge in central Stockholm. All vehicles entering the zone between 6:30am and 6:29pm have to pay between 10 and 20 SEK depending on the time of day.

By Ferry

Many ferry companies operate around Stockholm and into the archipelago.

Cinderella Båtarna ☎ 12-00 40 00, www.cinderellabatarna.com. Boats go from Nybrokajen or Strandvägen to the inner archipelago islands such as Grinda, Moja, Vaxholm and others.

Strömma Kanalbolaget ☎ 12-00 40 00, www.strommakanalbolaget. com. Boats leave from Stadshusbron to Birka and Drottningholm (p 40), and from Strandvägen to Fjäderholmarna (p 158), Vaxholm (p 160), and Sandhamn.

Waxholmsbolaget ☎ 679-58 30, www.waxholmsbolaget.com. Operates most of the traffic in the archipelago. Boats go from Stromkajen. It also operates the year-round ferry service Slussen–Skeppsholm–Allmänna grand. From May to August the boat stops at the Vasamuseet on Djurgården.

By Local Train

You can go into the suburbs and nearby towns by the SL commuter trains, using the same tickets as on the T-bana. The main commuter station is Central Station.

By Bicycle

The city runs **Stockholm City Bikes** (www.stockholmcitybikes.se) with specially designed city-friendly bikes. With over 70 stands all over the city, you get and return one with a card bought from the Tourist Information Center or from the website. A 3-day card is 125 SEK; a season ticket is 250 SEK. The season runs from April to October. Or hire a bike from **Djurgårdsbrons Sjöcafé** (p 63).

On Foot

The best way around Stockholm is by foot. But there are pedestrian traffic rules: Do not cross a road at a red light, although you do have the right of way on pedestrian crossings without traffic lights and therefore you are encouraged to use zebra crossings if there is one near by; do not walk in the lanes that are for cyclists (they normally run beside the pavement walking lanes and are marked with the sign of a bicycle) or you may get run into by an irate local.

Fast **Facts**

ACCOMMODATIONS Most of Stockholm's hotels are expensive, but there are bargains, particularly in the hostels—most of which have high standards. The Swedish capital is a big conference city, and so occupancy is high between May and November and lower in July. Rates vary according to time of year and are generally cheaper at the weekends. Book through **SVB**'s excellent booking service, in person at the Tourist Office (small fee, p 173), by

telephone ☎ 08-508 28 508, or online www.visitstockholm.com. **Destination Stockholm** (☎ 08-663 00 80, www.destination-stockholm.com) offers good rates and packages at the upper end of the scale. For rentals, short and long term, try www.chekin.se.

Bed and Breakfast Agencies offer a wide choice at good prices. **Stockholm Guesthouse,** www.stockholmguesthouse.com; **Bed and Breakfast Service**

Stockholm, www.bedbreakfast. a.se; and **Gästrummet** (The Guestroom), www.gastr ummet.com.

ATMS/CASHPOINTS Maestro, MasterCard, Cirrus, and Visa cards are readily accepted at all ATMs, which are all over the city from department stores to banks. There are two kinds: Bankomat (the joint system of the business banks) and Uttag (belonging to Swedbank).

Exchange currency either at banks or bureaux de change. **Forex** (www.forex.se) and **X-change** (www.x-change.se) are throughout the city.

BUSINESS HOURS Banks are open Monday to Friday 9am to 3pm; some open until 6pm one night a week. Most offices are open Monday to Friday 8:30am to 5pm but can close at 3pm in the summer. Most shops open 10am to 6pm or 7pm on weekdays, 10am to 4pm on Saturdays, and noon to 4pm on Sundays. Smaller shops usually open from 11am to 2pm on Saturdays and may have even more restricted Saturday hours during the summer. Department stores usually open 10am to 7pm on weekdays and 10am or 11am to 5pm or 6pm at weekends. Restaurants operate odd times. They are usually open by 11am if they serve lunch; otherwise they open around 5pm. Closing time is around midnight, though they often stay open later, particularly if they have a bar. Some restaurants close in July.

DENTAL EMERGENCIES For severe toothache and other emergency dental problems, go to **St. Eriks Hospital,** Polhemsgatan 48, Kungsholmen ☎ 08-545 512 20, open 7:45am to 8:30pm or after 8:30pm call for referrals on ☎ 08-32 01 00.

DOCTORS Dial ☎ 112 for an ambulance. For healthcare information (24-hr) ☎ 08-32 01 00.

ELECTRICITY Along with most of Europe, Sweden has 220-volt AC, 50Hz current and uses two-pin continental plugs. U.S. 110V equipment requires a current transformer.

EMBASSIES **U.S. Embassy,** Dag Hammarskjöldsväg 31, Östermalm (☎ 08-783 53 00, http://stockholm. usembassy.gov); **Canadian Embassy,** Tegelbacken 4, Norrmalm (☎ 08-453 30 00, www.canadaemb. se); **U.K. Embassy,** Skarpögatan 6–8, Östermalm (☎ 08-671 90 00, www. britishembassy.se); **Australian Embassy,** Klaraabergsviadukten 63, 8th Floor, Norrmalm (☎ 08-613 2900, www.sweden.embassy.gov.au); **New Zealand Embassy,** Nybrogatan 34, Norrmalm, (☎ 08-459 6940, www.nzembassy.com/sweden); **Irish Embassy,** Hovslagargatan 5, Norrmalm (☎ 08-545 04040, www. embassyofireland.se).

EMERGENCIES For ambulance or medical emergencies, fire and police, dial ☎ 112. Central 24-hr emergency services at: **St. Görans Hospital,** St. Görans Plan 1, Kungsholmen ☎ 08 58/ 010 00 (privately owned); **Karolinska Hospital (University Hospital),** Karolinska Vägen, Haga (off E18 North) ☎ 08-517 700 00.

GAY & LESBIAN TRAVELERS Sweden is known as one of Europe's most liberal countries. The Stockholm Tourist Board site is excellent for all information: www.stockholm-gaylesbian-network.com.

RFSL—The Swedish Federation for Lesbian, Gay, Bisexual, and Transgender Rights, Sveavägen 59 (☎ 08-501 629 50, www. rfsl.se/stockholm), the national organization for gay and lesbian rights in Stockholm, has a bookshop, restaurant, and club and gives good advice about bars, etc. The free monthly magazine **QX** (www.qx.se/english/) gives useful information on gay venues and produces a map in May.

HOLIDAYS Include January 1 (New Year's Day), January 6 (Feast of the Epiphany), March/April (Good Friday and Easter Monday), sixth Thurs after Easter (Ascension Day), May 1 (Labor Day), May/June (Whit Monday), Midsummer Eve (first Thurs after June 21st), December 25 (Christmas Day), and December 26 (Boxing Day).

INSURANCE Check your existing insurance policies before you buy travel insurance to cover trip cancellation, lost luggage, medical expenses, or car rental insurance. For travel overseas, most U.S. health plans (including Medicare and Medicaid) do not provide coverage, and the ones that do often require payment for services upfront. E.U. citizens pay a fee for all medical treatment, but must show an EHIC card (U.K.: www.ehic.org. uk; Ireland: www.ehic.ie).

INTERNET Internet access is plentiful and most hotels and hostels offer free Wi-Fi in your room and in the public areas and also have a computer you can use. Otherwise many 7-Elevens, newspaper stands, and grocery stores have Internet access. Try **Sidewalk Express** (www.sidewalk express.se) for its many terminals, including at Cityterminalen. You buy a surfing ticket for 7 days at 7-Elevens and their outlets. The main city library, **Stadsbiblioteket,** Sveagen 73 ☎ 08-508 311 00, www. biblioteket.stockholm.se offers limited, timed Internet access.

LIQUOR LAWS Most restaurants, pubs, and bars in Sweden are licensed for wine, spirits, and beer. Purchases of wine, liquor, and imported beer are available only through the government-controlled monopoly *Systembolaget*. Branch stores, spread throughout the country, are usually open Monday through Friday from 9am to 6pm. The minimum age for buying alcohol beverages in Swedish restaurants is 18, from Systembolaget you must be 18 to buy beer, but 20 to buy any other alcohol.

LOST PROPERTY For objects lost on public transport, contact **SL** (Klara Östra Kyrkogata 4, Norrmalm ☎ 08-412 69 60). For objects lost on long-distance trains, contact **SJ** (Central Station, Vasagatan, Norrmalm ☎ 08-501 255 90).

Call credit card companies the minute you discover your wallet has been lost or stolen and file a report at the nearest police station. **American Express** cardholders and traveler's check holders ☎ 020-11 04 53; **Diners Club** holders ☎ 08-14 68 78; **MasterCard** holders ☎ 020-79 13 24; **Visa** holders ☎ 020-79 56 75.

MAIL & POSTAGE The main post office is **Posten,** Central Station, Vasagatan, Norrmalm ☎ 020-23 22 20, www.posten.se. For stamps and main services, use the postal kiosks in grocery stores, and **Pressbyrån** kiosks and tourist information offices.

MONEY Sweden voted against joining the European Monetary Union, so the currency is the Swedish krona (SEK or kr). Coins are in denominations of 50 öre,100 öre, 1 SEK, 5 SEK, and 10 SEK; notes are in denominations of 20 SEK, 50 SEK, 100 SEK, 500 SEK, and 1,000 SEK. At the time of going to press, the exchange was approximately 10 SEK = $1.61, £0.98, and €1.10. For up-to-the minute exchange rates between the SEK and other currencies, check the currency converter website **www.xe.com/ ucc**.

PASSPORTS No visas are required for U.S., Canadian, Australian, New Zealand, U.K. and Irish visitors to Sweden providing your stay does not exceed 90 days. If your passport is lost or stolen, contact your country's embassy or consulate immediately. See 'Embassies' above. Make a copy of your passport's critical pages and keep it separate from your passport.

PHARMACIES Pharmacies *(apotek)* are identified by a green and white J-shaped sign. They can dispense medicines for minor ailments without a prescription and normally open Monday to Friday 8:30am to 6pm. Some open on Saturday. For a 24-hr pharmacy, go to **Apoteket CW Scheele,** Klarabergsgatan 64, Norrmalm, ☎ 08-458 81 30.

POLICE The national police emergency number is ☎ 112.

SAFETY Stockholm is a very safe city, but, as everywhere, tourists should beware of petty crime in tourist areas and major attractions such as museums, restaurants, hotels, trains, train stations, airports, subways, and ATMs.

SENIOR TRAVELERS Travelers over 65 years can get discounts on travel and admission to attractions. Carry your ID or passport for verification of your age.

SMOKING A law banning smoking in public places where food and drink is served was passed in 2005. Smoking is forbidden in most public places, including all T-bana stations and bus-stop shelters.

TAXES The sales tax ('moms' in Swedish) for most items is 25%; but it's 12% on food and hotel bills, and 6% tax on books, movie and concert tickets, and all transport. Non-E.U. residents are entitled to a reimbursement of the sales tax they have paid. Look for shops offering 'Tax Free' or 'Global Refund' shopping. Forms, obtained from the store where you made your purchase, must be stamped at Customs upon departure. For more information see www.globalrefund.com.

TELEPHONES For national telephone information, ☎ 118 118. For international telephone information, ☎ 118 119. For the national and international operator ☎ 90 200. There are few public telephone

kiosks as most people have mobiles. Kiosks are operated by card only, which you buy at newspaper kiosks and in shops. To make a call within Stockholm, dial ☎ 08 before the local number. To make an international call, dial ☎ 00, the country code, the area code (without the initial 0), and then the local number.

TIPPING This is a difficult subject which even Swedes are confused about. The general wisdom is that staff is well paid. The bill, however, will leave blank the section for adding the tip. It is becoming increasingly common to tip, and to tip up to 10% if you have good service, though many will leave 5%. Beware, however, the section left blank for the cloakroom; only pay if you have left your coat there. Round up the bill at bars and to taxi drivers.

TOILETS Public toilets are abundant and kept scrupulously clean. The TOALETT (small green booths) cost 5 SEK.

TOURIST INFORMATION **Stockholm Tourist Center,** Vasagatan 14 (opposite Central Station), Norrmalm, ☎ 08-508 28 508 , www.visit stockholm.com, is the main tourist office. It is large, well stocked, and very busy. Get the free monthly magazine *What's On Stockholm* here. You can also book hotels, buy the Stockholm Card, theater and concert tickets, and change money at the Forex exchange bureau. It is open Monday to Friday 9am to 7pm, Saturday 10am to 5pm, Sunday 10am to 4pm. T-bana: T-Centralen.

TRAVELERS WITH DISABILITIES Stockholm is a very good city for disabled travelers, with wide pavements and ramps at curbs for wheelchairs. By Swedish law all public areas must be accessible for both visually and physically disabled people, putting Stockholm way ahead of most other cities. The Tunnelbana has lifts and most buses 'kneel' at bus stops.

Find more information at **De Handikappades Riksförbund**, Katrinebergsvägen 6, Liljeholmen ☎ 08-685 80 00, www.dhr.se.

Access-Able Travel Source, www.access-able.com, is a good resource for information on disabled travel abroad.

Stockholm: **A Brief History**

A.D. 550–MID-11TH CENTURY The Vikings dominate Sweden.

1008 King Olof Skötkonung converts to Christianity.

1229 Birger Jarl becomes king after deposing Erik Erikssen.

1252 Birger Jarl founds Stockholm with his Tre Kronor fortress on Gamla Stan. The town becomes an important trading center, part of the German Hanseatic League that traded in the Baltic.

1397 Sweden, Norway, and Denmark sign the Kalmar Union, forming a Nordic alliance to challenge the Hanseatic League. It eventually includes Finland, Iceland, and Greenland, becoming the largest kingdom in Europe.

1471 Sten Sture the Elder defeats the Danish King Kristian at the battle of Brunkeberg in Stockholm.

1520 Sten Sture the Younger is killed by the Danish King Christian II who then kills 80 Swedish noblemen in the 'Stockholm Bloodbath.'

1520 Gustav Vasa, who had escaped the Bloodbath, ousts the Danish king from Sweden.

1523 Gustav Vasa is named King on 6th June (Sweden's National Day). Sweden enters a period of greater prosperity under a hereditary monarchy.

1633–54 Queen Kristina comes to the throne at the age of 6. Her reign is marked by an emphasis on science and philosophy.

17TH CENTURY The major European Thirty Years War results in the Swedes getting land in northern Germany, parts of Norway, and Danish provinces. Sweden then becomes the most powerful nation in northern Europe.

1697 The Tre Kronor fortress is destroyed by fire.

1709 A devastating defeat at Poltava in Russia marks the end of Sweden as a European great power.

MID-18TH CENTURY Stockholm's population grows to 70,000. Key figures in Sweden's cultural life include Carl von Linné (aka Linnaeus 1707–78), the philosopher Emanuel Swedenborg (1688–1772), Anders Celsius (1701–44) inventor of the centigrade temperature scale, and the poet Carl Michael Bellman (1740–95).

1771–92 Reign of Gustav III, who makes the monarchy absolute after a *coup d'état* in 1772. But in 1792, opposition from the nobles to his absolute power leads to his assassination at a masked ball at the Kungliga Operan.

1805 His successor, Gustav IV Adolf (1792–1809), is drawn into the Napoleonic Wars on the British side.

1809 Sweden loses Finland in the war against Russia (1808–9) and the king abdicates.

1810 Parliament chooses one of Napoleon's marshalls, Jean-Baptiste Bernadotte, to become King Karl XIV Johan even though he speaks no Swedish and his wife prefers Paris.

1813 Victory against Napoleon leads to Denmark handing over Norway to Sweden, forming a union which lasts from 1814 to 1905.

1850–1900 Sweden's farmers and rural workers suffer, but the country's Industrial Revolution brings railways between Stockholm and the rest of the country. Stockholm booms with the steel and safety match industry, and the establishment of large industries producing steam engines, cast-iron stoves, and shoes. Lars Magnus Ericsson opens his telephone company in Stockholm in 1876, giving the Swedes the greatest number of phones per capita in Europe.

1860S–1880s Stockholm is transformed by Paris-style town planning. August Strindberg (1849–1912) is an international figure; Artur Hazelius founds the Nordiska Museet and Skansen. The Academy of Stockholm (now the university) is founded in 1878, and in 1896 Alfred Nobel donates his fortune to fund the Nobel Awards.

1900 Despite mass emigration to America (1.5 million leave between the 1850s and 1930s), Sweden's population reaches 5 million, with Stockholm at 300,000.

1921 Universal Suffrage for men and women is introduced.

1930s From 1932 to 1972 the Social Democrats rule the country and with the Farmers' Union set about making the welfare state the main plank of Sweden's government.

1939–45 Sweden declares its neutrality in World War II as it had done in World War I. In 1942–3 Raoul Wallenberg, among others, stops the SS deportation of 100,000 Hungarian Jews. Wallenberg is arrested as a spy and disappears, probably dying in a Moscow prison.

1960s Sweden develops its famous Third Way, which combines corporate capitalism with a full-blown welfare state, from cradle to grave.

1970–1990 A booming economy leads to immigration, at its peak in 1969–70 with over 75,000 people entering Sweden annually. By the mid-1990s, 11% of the population is foreign born. In 1974 the monarch loses all political power.

1982–6 Prime Minister Olof Palme suffers from international economic pressures that begin to attack the Third Way ideal. His assassination in 1986 is a national trauma.

1990s A center-right coalition coincides with a severe recession and a devaluation of the krona. Unemployment is 14% and in 1994 the Social Democrats return to power.

1995 On 1st January Sweden joins the European Union.

2000 The Öresund bridge between Denmark and Sweden opens.

2003 Sweden votes to stay outside the single currency zone.

2006 The Social Democrats are defeated by the Alliance—four center-right parties.

2010 Stockholm is awarded the European Green Capital Award by the E.U., and is celebrated as Europe's first Green Capital.

2010 In the General Election the Alliance loses ground but continues to rule as a minority government.

Stockholm's **Architecture**

Drattninghalm Palace.

Medieval 12th Century

The city started on Gamla Stan, but there is very little left of the original buildings except the 12th-century defensive wall and later 16th- and 17th-century brick vaults of **Kungliga Slottet** (p 9, **4**). The 13th-century Royal church and Birger Jarl's Tower remain on Riddarholmen. The renovated Medeltidsmuseet (Museum of Medieval Stockholm) on Norrbro, tells more about this period (p 84, **5**), and also the Renaissance, baroque, and rococo 16th–18th century.

The golden age of Stockholm's architecture was largely due to one family. Nicodemus Tessin the Elder (1615–81) designed **Drottningholm Palace** (p 41) in a wonderfully ornate baroque style; his son Nicodemus Tessin the Younger (1654–1728) designed the **Royal Palace** and other buildings on Gamla Stan (p 9, **5**). Gracious buildings such as the Dutch baroque **Riddarhuset** (p 61, **9**) and the magnificent, baroque, 17th-century **churches** illustrate Sweden's power as a great nation.

Swedish Romanticism & Functionalism (1900s–1930)

Using elements of the late 19th-century Jugendstil (best seen in the flamboyant **Kungliga Dramatiska Teatern** (p 81, **12**) of 1908), a Swedish Romantic style appeared, boosted by a rise in nationalist feeling, producing the extraordinary red brick **Stadshuset** (p 10, **7**) of 1923 by Ragnar Östberg (p 10). Buildings such as the **Nordiska Museet** (p 13, **1**) were a Swedish version of Renaissance style (1907).

The most famous proponent of the Functionalist style was Gunnar Asplund (p 98) whose great work, the neoclassical **Stadsbiblioteket** (City Library) marked the transition. Functionalism as a part of town planning is seen at **Tessinparken** in Gärdet.

Modern Architecture: Late 20th & Early 21st Century

The post-war period and the 1960s saw the destruction of a large part of the city center, replaced by concrete buildings such as the **Kulturhuset** (p 85, **10**) in **Sergels Torg** (p 85, **9**). They were luckily stopped before major damage was done to the rest of

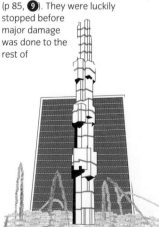

Sergels Torg.

Stockholm. The building of the **Tunnelbana** in the 1950s led to the development of the suburbs. The most ambitious area is at **Hammarby Sjöstad,** where ecology has taken center stage, resulting in a suburb using recycling and sustainable energy sources.

Stadshuset.

Useful Phrases

ENGLISH	SWEDISH	PRONUNCIATION
Hello	Hej	hay
How are you?	Hur mår du?	Hewr mawr dew
Very well	Mycket bra	mewkay brah
Thank you	Tak	tak
Pleased to meet you	Trevligt att träffas	treavlil att traiffas
Goodbye	Hej då/adjö	ah-haydaw/ahyour
Please	Varsågod	varshawgood
Yes	Ja	yah
No	Nej	nay
Excuse me	Ursakta	ewrshekta
I would like	Jag skulle vilja	Yah skewleh vilya
Do you have . . . ?	Har du/ni . . . ?	Hahr dew/nee
What?	Vad?	Vah
How much is this?	Hur mycket kostar den har?	Hewr mewkay kostar dehn hair
Do you take credit cards?	Tar du/ni kreditkort?	Tahr dew/nee kredeetkoort
Yesterday	Igår	ee gawr
Today	Idag	ee dahg
Tomorrow	I morgon	moron
Good	Bra	brah
Bad	Dålig	dawleeg
Enough	Tillråcklig	tillraikleeg
Do you speak English?	Talar du/ni engelska?	Tahlar dew/nee engelska
Could you speak more slowly please?	Kan du/ni tala långsammare, tack	kan dew/nee tahla lawngsamareh, tack
I don't understand	Jag förstår inte	yah furshtawr inteh
What time do you open?	Nar öppnar ni?	Nair urpnar nee
Call a doctor!	Ring efter en doctor!	Ring efter ehn doktor
Do you have any vacancies?	Har ni några lediga rum?	Hahr nee negra leadiga rewm
I have a reservation	Jag har beställt rum	yah hahr bestelt rewm

Index

See also Accommodations and Restaurant indexes, below.

Photo **Credits**